UnSpun

UnSpun

Community Lists... Ranked!

A Compendium of the Best Lists from unspun.com.

Editor:

Jonathan Leblang

Cover Design and Illustrations:

Michael Geminder

ISBN: 1440465037
ISBN-13: 978-1440465031

Printed in the United States of America.

To everyone who has ever—
1. *made*
2. *debated*
3. *organized*
4. *reordered*
5. *added to*
6. *complained about*
                    a list.

Contents

Introduction &
Acknowledgments

What is this, and just who is responsible?

It was the classic Chicken and Egg problem. Amazon had come up with an idea for great new system called Mechanical Turk. It would allow programmers to give tasks to people—tasks that were easy for humans, but difficult for computers. So it was built. And no one came.

"No one is working."

"Well, no one's put any work into the system."

"Why not?"

"There aren't any workers."

"Get some workers."

"There isn't any work for them to do. ..."

So great minds thought. And thought. And thought some more. Until—

"We'll make some work for folks to do. Then we'll have workers, then more work will come, and more workers, and more work, and..."

"We got it—but what kind of work?"

More thinking.

"We'll just ask questions."

"What questions?"

"Doesn't matter. Favorite movie. Best date restaurant. Worst '80s song."

So questions were asked. Workers came. Work arrived. More workers, more work. And then a Mechanical Turk developer noticed that a disk was filling up with the answers to all those questions. And the answers were interesting. Lists of restaurants, movies, bad songs.

"Hey, these lists are really cool."

"Yeah, what should we do with them?"

"Lets build a website. Anyone can create a list, and anyone (including all those Mechanical Turk workers) can add items. Folks can vote items up and down, and we'll show what the whole community thinks..."

"Cool! Not just one person's opinion, *everyone's* opinion. The lists won't have any spin put on them by someone pushing their own agenda."

"So everyone can put their own spin on their own list, but the community list won't be spun at all."

"Yes! Community lists with no spin. We'll call it..."

"TopN"

And so it was built. And it was renamed UnSpun (though TopN lives on in perforce). And a few people visited the UnSpun site. And features were added. And a few people visited the UnSpun site. And the site was cleaned up and made easier to use. And a few people visited the UnSpun site. And a widget was created to allow lists to be put on any site. And a few people visited the UnSpun site and clicked on the widget. And a Facebook application was written to encourage sharing and comparing. And a few people visited the UnSpun site and the Facebook app and clicked on the widget. And a blog was created and music previews were added. And *still* a few people visited the site and the Facebook app and clicked on the widget.

But a few people, not being many people, were not enough to sustain the UnSpun site. So it was shut down. But because we still think that the lists are fun, we wrote a book. And here it is.

People Who Built UnSpun
Our only unordered list

1. Andy Harbick
1. Matt Garman
1. Josh Lasser
1. Andy Jassy
1. Jonathan Leblang
1. Mark Veerman
1. Adam Selipsky
1. Michael Geminder
1. Jeff Bezos
1. Peter Cohen
1. Rebecca Jones
1. Vidal Graupera
1. Ian Freed

Frequently Asked Questions

What is UnSpun? How does it work? How are lists ranked?
These and other questions were answered on our website.
Here is an extract from that online FAQ.

What is the point of UnSpun?

Existing methods for community collaboration on the Web aren't good at developing consensus rankings. If you do a web search for "sexiest movies," you might find websites that have lists of "sexiest movies," but each will be the opinion of the individual who authored that website.

Wikis (as prominently and beautifully exemplified by Wikipedia) are an excellent mechanism for community collaboration, but they don't support consensus rankings. Imagine a large group of people editing and re-editing a wiki page that purported to have a ranked list of "sexiest movies." It wouldn't work—they'd step on each other.

So that's the niche that UnSpun endeavors to fill.

If you want to see the community consensus on what's the best or the worst, the scariest or the funniest, the tastiest or the dumbest, UnSpun provides the right amount of structure to make that possible.

Give it a whirl.

Is UnSpun supposed to be fun or useful?

Yes. We designed UnSpun to be useful, but as we've played with it and have seen some of the lists people submit for creation, we've found that it turns out to be both.

Can I create my own lists?

There are lots of lists that might not exist yet on UnSpun, so it is up to you to create them! Simply enter the list you are looking for in the search box on the homepage. If you can't find the list you are looking for, simply click the orange button on the page and follow the instructions to log in and create your list. Please be sure your title appears exactly how you want it to be on the site and that the list you are creating doesn't already exist. Once the list is created, UnSpun will immediately start gathering results from Amazon Mechanical Turk and from the UnSpun community. Usually you should see results start to show up within several minutes.

How does UnSpun use Mechanical Turk?

UnSpun leverages the Amazon Mechanical Turk web service to access a network of human intelligence, whereby people help populate a list created on UnSpun and then help identify the most relevant web links for each item.

What is "Amazon Mechanical Turk?"

Each new list created on UnSpun is immediately sent to Amazon Mechanical Turk, where people vote their top 3 items to populate the list and get it started. Those results appear on UnSpun by Amazon within minutes, where the UnSpun community can expand and personalize the rankings. For more information on Amazon Mechanical Turk, visit mturk.amazon.com.

Why is it called UnSpun?

We liked the name because community consensus rankings aren't subject to "spin" (and it rhymes with itself).

Won't UnSpun rankings be subject to vote spam?

UnSpun provides a number of mechanisms to eliminate bad votes. The first is that people must first log in with a valid Amazon account before they can vote, submit new items, or create new lists. Each user can only vote one time per item so one user is not able to "stuff the ballot box" with votes. Additionally, merges of duplicate items and deletions of inappropriate items (items that don't belong in that particular list) are corroborated by a combination of the community and an editorial team. The combination of these features will help us to maintain the integrity of the rankings.

How do I vote or add my own rankings?

Once you have logged in, you will be able to vote for items on the public list or create your own set of rankings. UnSpun will only record your vote one time per item while it is in the same position, but if an item moves up or down in the rankings you can vote again. If you want to create your own rankings or add an item to the list, click on the "Your Rankings" link just below the list title and arrange the items in your rankings to show what you think the rankings should be. Your personal rankings will automatically be incorporated in the public rankings as well.

Will my rankings be viewable to the public?

Yes, UnSpun is a community site and any rankings you submit, new lists you create, and individual rankings that you give to any lists, will be visible to the rest of the community. The "Lists You Recently Viewed" information on the "Your Spin" are only visible to you.

How long does it typically take for a new list to be populated once it has been created?

Results will be automatically updated as they come in. Typically, you can expect results to start appearing within several minutes of creating your list.

How do you ensure the quality of the rankings?

UnSpun requires users to log in before they are able to add rankings to the lists. If we find any users that have been abusing the site, we can roll back any changes or additions that user has made to the site. Because you have to have an account to contribute to UnSpun, we can be sure that the rankings are not done by automated bots and can limit the spam added to the site. Also, every list page contains edit links that encourage the UnSpun community to merge duplicates, edit misspellings, identify misplaced items, and tag offensive content. In this way, inappropriate entries can be quickly eliminated.

Most Popular Lists

Here are the 250 most popular lists on UnSpun. Popularity was determined by the number of items on the list, the number of rankings, and the number of different people who voted on the list. We've shown just the top 40 items from each list.

Top Albums
12578 votes by 2201 people

1. Pink Floyd – The Dark Side of the Moon
2. The Beatles – The Beatles ("The White Album")
3. The Beatles – Abbey Road
4. The Beatles – Sgt. Pepper's Lonely Hearts Club Band
5. Pink Floyd – The Wall
6. Nirvana – Nevermind
7. Led Zeppelin – IV (Zoso)
8. U2 – The Joshua Tree
9. Radiohead – OK Computer
10. The Beatles – Revolver
11. Metallica – Metallica (The Black Album)
12. Guns N' Roses – Appetite For Destruction
13. AC/DC – Back In Black
14. Pearl Jam – Ten
15. Green Day – American Idiot
16. Fleetwood Mac – Rumours
17. Pink Floyd – Wish You Were Here
18. Metallica – Master of Puppets
19. The Smashing Pumpkins – Siamese Dream
20. Queen – A Night at the Opera
21. Radiohead – Kid A
22. U2 – Achtung Baby
23. Bruce Springsteen – Born To Run
24. Nine Inch Nails – The Downward Spiral
25. Depeche Mode – Violator
26. Led Zeppelin – Led Zeppelin II
27. Eagles – Greatest Hits
28. Eagles – Hotel California
29. Prince – Purple Rain
30. Weezer – Weezer (Blue Album)
31. Metallica – ...And Justice for All
32. Tool – Lateralus
33. Linkin Park – Meteora
34. The Who – Who's Next
35. Alanis Morissette – Jagged Little Pill
36. Led Zeppelin – Houses of the Holy
37. Tool – Aenima
38. Pink Floyd – Animals
39. Bob Dylan – Blonde On Blonde
40. The Jimi Hendrix Experience – Are You Experienced?

Best Programming Language
6107 votes by 1399 people

1. Ruby
2. Python
3. Java
4. Lisp
5. C
6. PHP
7. C++
8. Perl
9. APL
10. C#
11. JavaScript
12. Objective-C
13. Smalltalk
14. Scheme
15. Haskell
16. J
17. SQL
18. Erlang
19. Pascal
20. Basic
21. Fortran
22. Delphi
23. Assembler
24. K
25. Ada
26. Forth
27. D
28. R
29. Cold Fusion
30. O'Caml
31. Standard ML
32. Cobol
33. Icon
34. Toontalk
35. Io
36. Prolog
37. Abap
38. Groovy
39. Logo
40. CSS

Top Beers
7445 votes by 1416 people

1. Guinness
2. Sam Adams Boston Lager
3. Heineken
4. Corona
5. Miller
6. Budweiser
7. Newcastle Brown Ale
8. Stella Artois
9. Bud Light
10. Coors
11. Bass Ale
12. Becks
13. Blue Moon
14. Rolling Rock
15. Chimay
16. Hoegaarden
17. Sierra Nevada
18. Coors Light
19. Fat Tire
20. Red Stripe
21. Killians
22. Boddington's
23. Yuengling
24. Anchor Steam
25. Pabst
26. Carlsberg
27. Grolsch
28. Fosters
29. Shiner Bock
30. Amstel Light
31. Harp
32. San Miguel
33. Duvel
34. Dos Equis Lager
35. Molson Canadian
36. Negra Modelo
37. Pilsner Urquell
38. Mac & Jack's African Amber
39. Alexander Keith's
40. Samuel Smith's Oatmeal Stout

Best Movies of All Time

6329 votes by 629 people

1. Casablanca (1942)
2. Gone with the Wind (1939)
3. The Wizard of Oz (1939)
4. Lawrence of Arabia
5. Arthur
6. The Maltese Falcon
7. Singin' in the Rain
8. Monty Python and the Holy Grail
9. The Matrix
10. Annie Hall
11. Sunset Boulevard
12. The Deer Hunter
13. It's a Wonderful Life
14. One Flew Over the Cuckoo's Nest
15. True Romance
16. Murder On the Orient Express
17. 8 1/2
18. Rear Window
19. Pretty Woman
20. 12 Angry Men
21. Rain Man
22. Empire of the Sun
23. Mutiny On The Bounty (1962)
24. Clockwork Orange
25. Harvey
26. From The Terrace (1960)
27. Camille (1936)
28. The Philadelphia Story
29. Fatal Attraction
30. Paths of Glory
31. Brazil
32. Before Sunset
33. Harry Potter
34. Earthlings
35. Tom Jones (1963)
36. Say Anything
37. Fanny and Alexander
38. 1984
39. Dawn of the Dead (1978)
40. The Color Purple

Top Women You Would Leave Your Partner for
7355 votes by 1415 people

1. Jessica Alba
2. Jennifer Aniston
3. Natalie Portman
4. Keira Knightley
5. Scarlett Johansson
6. Jessica Simpson
7. Charlize Theron
8. Nicole Kidman
9. Pamela Anderson
10. Lindsay Lohan
11. Halle Berry
12. Salma Hayek
13. Jennifer Lopez
14. Catherine Zeta Jones
15. Britney Spears
16. Monica Bellucci
17. Elisha Cuthbert
18. Paris Hilton
19. Carmen Electra
20. Heidi Klum
21. Jennifer Garner
22. Cameron Diaz
23. Julia Roberts
24. Jennifer Connelly
25. Drew Barrymore
26. Katie Holmes
27. Sandra Bullock
28. Eva Longoria
29. Rachel McAdams
30. Adriana Lima
31. Anna Kournikova
32. Kirsten Dunst
33. Shakira
34. Madonna
35. Kate Winslet
36. Beyonce
37. Hilary Duff
38. Jennifer Love Hewitt
39. Milla Jovovich
40. Demi Moore

Worst Single Moments in US History
1864 votes by 333 people

1. George W. Bush Re-Election
2. 9/11
3. Pearl Harbor
4. The Civil War
5. JFK Assassination
6. Assassination of President Abraham Lincoln
7. GW Bush declaring war on Iraq
8. Stock Market Crash of 1929
9. Trail of Tears
10. My Lai Massacre
11. Vietnam
12. Hiroshima
13. Martin Luther King Assassination
14. Oklahoma City Bombing
15. Americans freely giving up Civil Rights due to the "War on Terror"
16. Internment camps for the Japanese living in the US during WWII
17. Richard Nixon -Watergate
18. Space Shuttle Challenger exploding
19. George W. Bush's Birth
20. Richard Nixon Resignation
21. Hurricane Katrina
22. Founding fathers accept 3/5 compromise, declaring that a slave is 3/5 of a man.
23. 1916 Implementation of temporary federal income tax
24. South Carolina Succession
25. Great Depression
26. Congress' acceptance of War Powers Act, abdicating the need for declarations of war before Presidents can start wars
27. World War 1
28. New Deal
29. Nixon's pardon
30. Bombing of abortion clinic in Atlanta
31. The burning of the White House in the 1800's
32. Invasion of Panama by George Bush in 1989
33. 1961: the Bay of Pigs Invasion
34. The Alien and Sedition Acts
35. Bush Administration
36. Roe Vs Wade make abortion legal
37. Iran-Contra Affair
38. Civil War, Gettysburg
39. 1804: Aaron Burr kills Alexander Hamilton in a duel.
40. Galveston Hurricane of 1900

Top Comedy TV Shows of All-Time
4678 votes by 1228 people

1. Seinfeld
2. The Simpsons
3. I Love Lucy
4. Cheers
5. Saturday Night Live
6. All in the Family
7. Everybody Loves Raymond
8. Monty Python's Flying Circus
9. The Office (BBC)
10. Futurama
11. Frasier
12. Whose Line Is It Anyway?
13. Fawlty Towers
14. The Honeymooners
15. Home Improvement
16. Mr. Show
17. My Name is Earl
18. King of Queens
19. Blackadder
20. The Andy Griffith Show
21. The Carol Burnett Show
22. Sex and the City
23. Three Stooges
24. The Dick Van Dyke Show
25. The Mary Tyler Moore Show
26. Soap
27. The Muppet Show
28. News Radio
29. The Drew Carey Show
30. Taxi
31. Night Court
32. Late Night with Conan O'Brien
33. Laugh-In
34. The Tonight Show
35. Red Skelton Show
36. The Golden Girls
37. Two and a Half Men
38. Mystery Science Theater 3000
39. America's Funniest Home Videos
40. Hogan's Heroes

Most Attractive Female Celebrity
1809 votes by 265 people

1. Jessica Alba
2. Scarlett Johansson
3. Halle Berry
4. Keira Knightley
5. Charlize Theron
6. Salma Hayek
7. Eva Longoria
8. Jennifer Lopez
9. Beyonce
10. Elisha Cuthbert
11. Jennifer Love Hewitt
12. Jennifer Garner
13. Aishwarya Rai
14. Gina Gershon
15. Kate Winslet
16. Sarah Silverman
17. Jorja Fox
18. Julia Roberts
19. Stacy Keibler
20. Denise Richards
21. Drew Barrymore
22. Tina Fey
23. Mischa Barton
24. Sharon Stone
25. Charisma Carpenter
26. Sienna Miller
27. Michelle Pfeiffer
28. Uma Thurman
29. Holly Marie Combs
30. Cicciolina
31. Sheryl Crow
32. Lexa Doig
33. Kirsten Dunst
34. Alyssa Milano
35. Brooke Burke
36. Reese Witherspoon
37. Katie Couric
38. Alyson Hannigan
39. Tera Patrick
40. Cameron Diaz

Best Movie Characters
1656 votes by 307 people

1. Indiana Jones
2. Darth Vader
3. James Bond AKA 007
4. Han Solo
5. Captain Jack Sparrow
6. The Terminator
7. Vito Corleone
8. Yoda
9. Neo
10. Forrest Gump
11. Jeff "The Dude" Lebowski (The Big Lebowski)
12. Tyler Durden
13. Wolverine
14. Scarlett O'Hara
15. Batman
16. Keyser Soze
17. Napoleon Dynamite
18. Willy Wonka
19. William Wallace (Braveheart)
20. Sam Spade
21. Harry Potter
22. Inspector "Dirty" Harry Callahan
23. Austin Powers
24. Rhett Butler
25. Jeff Spicoli
26. Gandalf
27. John Rambo
28. Luke Skywalker
29. Rocky Balboa
30. Michael Corleone
31. Jules Winnfield (Pulp Fiction)
32. Spiderman
33. Gumby
34. Ash
35. Shrek
36. Hannibal Lecter
37. Trinity
38. Superman
39. Freddy Kruger
40. Rick Blaine (Casablanca)

Dumbest Celebrities
4116 votes by 1152 people

1. Paris Hilton
2. Jessica Simpson
3. Britney Spears
4. Tom Cruise
5. Ashlee Simpson
6. George W. Bush
7. Nicole Richie
8. Lindsay Lohan
9. Tara Reid
10. Michael Jackson
11. Pamela Anderson
12. Kevin Federline
13. Courtney Love
14. Hilary Duff
15. Ashton Kutcher
16. 50 Cent
17. Jim Carrey
18. Brad Pitt
19. Katie Holmes
20. Madonna
21. Mariah Carey
22. Cameron Diaz
23. Nick Lachey
24. Michael Moore
25. Ben Affleck
26. Jennifer Lopez
27. Jade Goody
28. Oprah Winfrey
29. Howard Stern
30. Andy Dick
31. Keanu Reeves
32. Rush Limbaugh
33. Angelina Jolie
34. Matt Damon
35. Sean Penn
36. Bill O'Reilly
37. Bono
38. Carrot Top
39. Johnny Knoxville
40. Arnold Schwarzenegger

Top "Hip" Neighborhoods to Live in Seattle, WA
1674 votes by 411 people

1. Capitol Hill
2. Fremont
3. Ballard
4. Belltown
5. Queen Anne
6. Wallingford
7. University District
8. Green Lake
9. Georgetown
10. Beacon Hill
11. Pioneer Square
12. Columbia City
13. West Seattle
14. Downtown
15. Greenwood
16. First Hill
17. Madrona
18. The CD
19. Eastlake
20. Sodo
21. Madison Park
22. Cascade
23. International District
24. Snoqualmie
25. Mercer Island
26. Bellevue
27. Judkins Park
28. Bainbridge Island
29. Leschi
30. Kirkland
31. Roosevelt
32. Montlake
33. Maple Leaf
34. Alki
35. Burien
36. Lower Queen Anne
37. Bryant
38. Hillman City
39. North Admiral
40. Laurelhurst

Top Guitar Players Ever
3060 votes by 1147 people

1. Jimi Hendrix
2. Eric Clapton
3. Duane Allman
4. Jimmy Page
5. Eddie Van Halen
6. Carlos Santana
7. Steve Vai
8. Slash
9. Joe Satriani
10. Stevie Ray Vaughn
11. David Gilmour
12. John Petrucci
13. B.B. King
14. Yngwie Malmsteen
15. Kurt Cobain
16. George Harrison
17. Randy Rhodes
18. Pete Townsend
19. Kirk Hammett
20. Brian May
21. Leo Kottke
22. Tom Morello
23. Frank Zappa
24. Chet Atkins
25. Keith Richards
26. John Frusciante
27. Buckethead
28. Bob Dylan
29. The Edge
30. Joe Perry
31. Andres Segovia
32. Jerry Garcia
33. Django Reinhardt
34. James Hetfield
35. Neil Young
36. Randy Rhoads
37. Elliott Smith
38. Johnny Marr
39. Paul McCartney
40. Chuck Berry

Best Comic Strips of All Time
1221 votes by 282 people

1. Calvin & Hobbes
2. peanuts
3. The Far Side
4. Dilbert
5. Bloom County
6. Doonesbury
7. Garfield
8. Foxtrot
9. Get Fuzzy
10. For Better or for Worse
11. Family Circus
12. The Boondocks
13. Zits
14. Non Sequitur
15. Beetle Bailey
16. Pearls before Swine
17. Dick Tracy
18. Prince Valiant
19. Haggar
20. Krazy Kat
21. Blondie
22. Cathy
23. pogo
24. This Modern World
25. Superman
26. Sherman's Lagoon
27. X-Men
28. Opus
29. Archie
30. Mutts
31. The Lockhorns
32. Lio
33. Fusco Brothers
34. Marmaduke
35. Chacha Chowdhary
36. Amazing Spider Man
37. Little Nemo
38. Beano
39. Konan
40. Batman

Best Songs Ever
2651 votes by 685 people

1. Imagine – John Lennon
2. Stairway to Heaven – Led Zeppelin
3. Yesterday – The Beatles
4. Hey Jude – The Beatles
5. Freebird – Lynyrd Skynyrd
6. Kashmir – Led Zeppelin
7. Just like Heaven – The Cure
8. Grace – Jeff Buckley
9. Let It Be – The Beatles
10. Enjoy the Silence – Depeche Mode
11. I Can't Get No Satisfaction – The Rolling Stones
12. American Pie – Don McLean
13. Revolution – The Beatles
14. Love Will Tear Us Apart – Joy Division
15. The End – The Doors
16. Losing My Religion – R.E.M.
17. Like a Rolling Stone – Bob Dylan
18. November Rain – Guns N' Roses
19. Johnny B Goode – Chuck Berry
20. Black – Pearl Jam
21. Blue Monday – New Order
22. A Day In The Life – The Beatles
23. All Along the Watch Tower – Jimmie Hendrix
24. God Only Knows – The Beach Boys
25. While My Guitar Gently Weeps – George Harrison
26. Scar Tissue – Red Hot Chili Peppers
27. Guns N' Roses – Don't Cry
28. Layla by Eric Clapton/Derek and the Dominos
29. Rock and Roll – Led Zeppelin
30. Born to Run – Bruce Springsteen
31. Summer Rain – Johnny Rivers
32. The Logical Song – Supertramp
33. Bridge Over Troubled Water – Simon and Garfunkel
34. Somewhere Over the Rainbow – Judy Garland
35. Led Zeppelin – Achilles Last Stand
36. Unchained Melody – The Righteous Brothers
37. One – U2
38. Walk Away Renee – the Left Banke
39. I'll Stand by You – the Pretenders
40. Mack the Knife – Bobby Darin

Top Brands of Vodka
4656 votes by 1433 people

1. Grey Goose
2. Absolut
3. Smirnoff
4. Stolichnaya
5. Skyy
6. Ketel One
7. Finlandia
8. Belvedere
9. Chopin
10. Pravda
11. level
12. Boru
13. Svedka
14. Three Olives
15. Popov
16. Rain
17. Vox
18. Armadale
19. Ciroc
20. White Diamond
21. Zubrowka
22. Russian Standart (Russkiy Standart)
23. Nemiroff
24. 42 below
25. Luksusowa
26. Hangar One
27. Silent Sam
28. Turi
29. Polar Ice
30. Moskovskaya
31. Jewel of Russia Classic
32. Wyborowa
33. Barton Vodka
34. Pearl
35. Monopolowa
36. Van Gogh
37. Iceberg
38. Fris
39. Vladivar
40. Fleischmann's

Top Funniest Comedians
3776 votes by 1075 people

1. Richard Pryor
2. Jerry Seinfeld
3. George Carlin
4. Chris Rock
5. Robin Williams
6. Dave Chappelle
7. Dane Cook
8. Mitch Hedberg
9. Eddie Murphy
10. Bill Cosby
11. Jim Carrey
12. Bill Hicks
13. Adam Sandler
14. Lewis Black
15. Chris Farley
16. Eddie Izzard
17. Steve Martin
18. Ellen Degeneres
19. Will Ferrell
20. Rodney Dangerfield
21. David Cross
22. Jon Stewart
23. Jeff Foxworthy
24. Conan O'Brien
25. Margaret Cho
26. Denis Leary
27. Jay Leno
28. John Cleese
29. George Lopez
30. Bob Hope
31. Ron White
32. Carlos Mencia
33. Johnny Carson
34. Peter Sellers
35. John Belushi
36. Mike Myers
37. David Letterman
38. Steven Wright
39. Ray Romano
40. Bill Murray

Top Drama TV Shows of All-Time
4779 votes by 1294 people

1. Dallas
2. The OC
3. Desperate Housewives
4. Beverly Hills 90210
5. LA Law
6. Dynasty
7. Days of Our Lives
8. Buffy the Vampire Slayer
9. Gilmore Girls
10. Dawson's Creek
11. Little House on the Prairie
12. Star Trek
13. Melrose Place
14. Dragnet
15. 7th Heaven
16. Falcon Crest
17. Knots Landing
18. Party of Five
19. Charmed
20. Miami Vice
21. Deadwood
22. China Beach
23. The Prisoner
24. Perry Mason
25. As The World Turns
26. Matlock
27. Judging Amy
28. Walker Texas Ranger
29. Gunsmoke
30. Murder She Wrote
31. The Fugitive
32. MacGyver
33. The Pretender
34. Sisters
35. Columbo
36. Angel
37. Touched by an Angel
38. Bonanza
39. Everwood
40. The Wonder Years

Best Movies That Have Come Out in 2006
809 votes by 154 people

1. Casino Royale
2. The Departed
3. Little Miss Sunshine
4. V for Vendetta
5. Inside Man
6. Borat
7. Thank You for Smoking
8. An Inconvenient Truth
9. Brick
10. The Prestige
11. Lucky Number Slevin
12. Mission: Impossible III
13. Clerks II
14. Talladega Nights
15. The Illusionist
16. X-Men: the Last Stand
17. Ice Age 2: The Meltdown
18. Silent Hill
19. Children of Men
20. We Are Marshall
21. Jesus Camp
22. Little Children
23. Night Watch (Nochnoy Dozor)
24. The Hills Have Eyes
25. The Devil & Daniel Johnston
26. When a Stranger Calls
27. An American Haunting
28. United 93
29. Cars
30. Da Vinci Code
31. Tristram Shandy: a C*ck and Bull Story
32. The Descent
33. Blood Diamond
34. The Science of Sleep
35. The Pursuit of Happyness
36. A Scanner Darkly
37. Scary Movie 4
38. Slither
39. Half Nelson
40. Superman Returns

Top Female Musical Artists

2074 votes by 520 people

1. Madonna
2. Gwen Stefani
3. Britney Spears
4. Sheryl Crow
5. Mariah Carey
6. Kelly Clarkson
7. Tori Amos
8. Jessica Simpson
9. Sarah McLachlan
10. Celine Dion
11. Beyonce
12. Alanis Morissette
13. Shakira
14. Fiona Apple
15. Alicia Keys
16. Shania Twain
17. Faith Hill
18. Bjork
19. Janis Joplin
20. Avril Lavigne
21. Cher
22. Norah Jones
23. Jewel
24. Michelle Branch
25. Christina Aguilera
26. Aretha Franklin
27. Tina Turner
28. Dido
29. Enya
30. Hilary Duff
31. Ani DiFranco
32. Liz Phair
33. Jennifer Lopez
34. Janet Jackson
35. Melissa Etheridge
36. Ella Fitzgerald
37. Martina McBride
38. Ashlee Simpson
39. Barbra Streisand
40. Whitney Houston

Top US MBA Schools
830 votes by 249 people

1. Harvard
2. Wharton
3. Stanford
4. Northwestern University (Kellogg) (IL)
5. Massachusetts Institute of Technology (Sloan)
6. Columbia
7. The University of Michigan- Ross School of Business
8. Yale
9. University of Chicago
10. University of Washington
11. University of California Berkeley – Haas School of Business
12. Cornell Johnson Graduate School of Business
13. NYU Stern
14. Dartmouth
15. Kenan-Flagler UNC
16. Duke
17. Carnegie Mellon
18. UCLA
19. Boston University
20. Urbana University
21. Louisiana State University
22. University of Florida
23. Wake Forest University
24. Michigan State University – Eli Broad College of Business
25. University of MN
26. University of Maryland
27. Rice University
28. Purdue
29. University of Texas
30. USC Marshall School of Business
31. Lehigh University
32. College of William and Mary
33. American Graduate School of International Mgmt.
34. University of Hawaii at Manoa
35. Baylor University
36. Indiana
37. Babson College
38. Brigham Young University
39. University of Virginia – Darden
40. Rutgers

Top Music Genres to Disappear
3518 votes by 1062 people

1. rap
2. Country
3. Hip Hop
4. Pop
5. emo
6. R&B
7. Disco
8. metal
9. Heavy Metal
10. punk
11. techno
12. Gangsta Rap
13. Jazz
14. Ska
15. Death Metal
16. Opera
17. bluegrass
18. Polka
19. Folk
20. reggae
21. New Age
22. Rock
23. Classical
24. Trance
25. Christian Rock
26. Boy Bands
27. Grunge
28. Punk Rock
29. Easy Listening
30. blues
31. Screamo
32. Rnb
33. Country & Western
34. Electronica
35. Gospel
36. House
37. Hardcore
38. Bubblegum Pop
39. Teen Pop
40. dance

Top Country Artists
2729 votes by 842 people

1. Johnny Cash
2. Garth Brooks
3. Hank Williams
4. Dolly Parton
5. Willie Nelson
6. Shania Twain
7. Faith Hill
8. Tim McGraw
9. Patsy Cline
10. George Strait
11. Toby Keith
12. Reba McEntire
13. Kenny Chesney
14. Kenny Rogers
15. Alan Jackson
16. Loretta Lynn
17. George Jones
18. Keith Urban
19. Dixie Chicks
20. Trisha Yearwood
21. Merle Haggard
22. Clint Black
23. LeAnn Rimes
24. Randy Travis
25. Alabama
26. Brooks and Dunn
27. John Denver
28. Waylon Jennings
29. Martina McBride
30. Tammy Wynette
31. Gretchen Wilson
32. Billy Ray Cyrus
33. Glen Campbell
34. Rascal Flatts
35. Brad Paisley
36. Emmylou Harris
37. Carrie Underwood
38. Conway Twitty
39. Neko Case
40. Charlie Daniels

Best Euphemisms for Sex

1585 votes by 526 people

1. Bumping Uglies
2. Making Love
3. Doing It
4. Getting It on
5. Knocking Boots
6. Making the Beast with Two Backs
7. Horizontal Mambo
8. Banging
9. Boinking
10. Shag
11. F*ck*ng
12. Whoopie
13. Horizontal Tango
14. Nookie
15. Doing the Nasty
16. Humping
17. Laying Pipe
18. Porking
19. Hiding the Salami
20. Screwing
21. It
22. Slurping the Avocado Juice
23. Playing Hide the Sausage
24. Doing the Deed
25. Hooking up
26. Love
27. Roll in the Hay
28. The Nasty
29. The Thing
30. Making Whoopee
31. A Bit of the Old In-Out
32. Carnal Gymnastics
33. Squeezing the Cheese
34. Riding the Pony
35. Do It
36. Making Babies
37. Filing an Extension
38. Hanky Panky
39. Getting Enronned
40. Backseat Mambo

Top Pizza Parlors in Seattle, WA
979 votes by 289 people

1. Pagliacci
2. Tutta Bella Neapolitan Pizzeria
3. Piecora's New York Pizza
4. Zeek's Pizza
5. Belltown Pizza
6. Pegasus Pizza
7. Romio's Pizza & Pasta
8. Madame K's Pizza Bistro
9. Northlake Tavern & Pizza House
10. Olympia Pizza
11. Pizza Hut
12. Cloverleaf Tavern
13. Abbondanza Pizzeria
14. Domino's
15. Papa Johns
16. Fremont Classic Pizzeria & Trattoria
17. Mad Pizza
18. Hot Mama's Pizza
19. Stellar Pizza & Ale
20. Shakey's Pizza Parlor
21. Jet City Pizza
22. Atlantic Street Pizza
23. Spud's Pizza Parlor
24. Pete's Pizza The Calzone King
25. Post Alley Pizza
26. Via Tribunali
27. New York Pizza Place
28. Zagi's
29. Delfino
30. Michael's Pizza
31. Spiro'S
32. A New York Pizza Place
33. All Purpose Pizza
34. Pudge Bros
35. Wallingford Pizza House
36. California Pizza Kitchen
37. Palermo
38. Papa Murphy's
39. Pizza Ragazzi
40. Cafe Lago

Top Beatles Songs

1945 votes by 518 people

1. Hey Jude
2. Yesterday
3. Let It Be
4. Help
5. I Want to Hold Your Hand
6. Eleanor Rigby
7. Strawberry Fields Forever
8. A Hard Day's Night
9. All You Need Is Love
10. Come Together
11. Here Comes the Sun
12. She Loves You
13. A Day in the Life
14. Can't Buy Me Love
15. Twist and Shout
16. Blackbird
17. Penny Lane
18. Sgt. Pepper's Lonely Hearts Club Band
19. I Saw Her Standing There
20. Eight Days A Week
21. Love Me Do
22. Across the Universe
23. Michelle
24. Norwegian Wood
25. Maxwell's Silver Hammer
26. Ticket to Ride
27. Something
28. The Long and Winding Road
29. Paperback Writer
30. When I'm 64
31. Day Tripper
32. Got to Get You into My Life
33. Back in the USSR
34. Fool On the Hill
35. Golden Slumbers
36. Dear Prudence
37. Nowhere Man
38. Octopus' Garden
39. All My Loving
40. Get Back

Worst Hit Songs

2464 votes by 739 people

1. Hit Me Baby One More Time – Britney Spears
2. Macarena – Los Del Rio
3. My Humps – Black Eyed Peas
4. Achy Breaky Heart – Billy Ray Cyrus
5. Ice Ice Baby – Vanilla Ice
6. Oops I Did It Again – Britney Spears
7. Mmm Bop – Hanson
8. Who Let the Dogs Out – Baha Men
9. We Built This City – Starship
10. I'm Too Sexy – Right Said Fred
11. Barbie Girl – Aqua
12. Hollaback Girl – Gwen Stefani
13. Bye Bye Bye – *N Sync
14. Don't Worry, Be Happy – Bobby McFerrin
15. Axel F – Crazy Frog
16. Tubthumping – Chumbawumba
17. Milkshake – Kelis
18. My Heart Will Go On – Celine Dion
19. Wang Chung – Everybody Have Fun Tonight
20. Mambo #5 – Lou Bega
21. Toxic – Britney Spears
22. Living La Vida Loca – Ricky Martin
23. Like a Virgin – Madonna
24. I Will Always Love You – Whitney Houston
25. I'm a Slave 4 U – Britney Spears
26. Wannabe – Spice Girls
27. She Bangs – Ricky Martin
28. Genie in a Bottle – Christina Aguilera
29. In Da Club – 50 Cent
30. Laffy Taffy – D4L
31. Don't Cha – Pussycat Dolls
32. Rollin' – Limp Bizkit
33. Blue (Da BA De) – Eiffel 65
34. Ebony and Ivory – Paul McCartney and Stevie Wonder
35. Blame It on the Rain – Milli Vanilli
36. Candy Shop – 50 Cent
37. The Thong Song – Sisqo
38. Party All the Time
39. Thriller – Michael Jackson
40. I Want It That Way – Backstreet Boys

Best Pickup Lines
624 votes by 130 people

1. I was wondering if you had a moment to spare for me to hit on you
2. Is that 2%? Cuz you could be drinking whole milk
3. So what haven't you been told tonight?
4. How ya doin'?
5. Hi
6. Heaven must be missing an angel because your here with me!
7. Did the fall from heaven hurt?
8. Hello, what's your name?
9. You are the most beautiful person I've ever seen.
10. Do you come here often?
11. What's a nice girl like you doing in a dirty mind like mine?
12. Are you tired, because you have been running through my mind
13. I've lost my number ... can I borrow yours?
14. If I told you you had a great body, would you hold it against me?
15. Hey good looking whats cooking
16. Nice shoes, wanna f*ck?
17. Do I know you from somewhere?
18. I Love Your Laugh
19. That dress is becoming on you, if I were that dress I would be...
20. What's your sign?
21. You are a 9.999. Well, You'd be a perfect 10 if you were with me.
22. "See my friend over there? He wants to know if you think I'm cute."
23. Apart from being sexy, what do you do for a living?
24. Where have you been all my life?
25. Your place or my place?
26. Can I buy you a drink?
27. Do I know you?
28. You must be a parking ticket, you have fine written all over you
29. How much does a polar bear weigh?
30. If I flip a coin, what are the chances that I get head?
31. That outfit looks good on you, but it would look better on the floor next to my bed
32. Your name is "Susan"? My mother's name is "Susan" TOO!
33. Is that a gun in your pocket, or are you just happy to see me?
34. Can you say Constantinople backwards? Me neither, but I just wanted to ask.
35. What did you have for breakfast?
36. You must use windex on your pants cause I can see me in them
37. I wish I could rearrange the alphabet, so U and I could be together.
38. Do you come here every day?
39. Hey babe
40. You are so interesting

Top Science Fiction Books
1337 votes by 317 people

1. The Hitchhiker's Guide to the Galaxy by Douglas Adams
2. Ender's Game by Orson Scott Card
3. Dune by Frank Herbert
4. Foundation by Isaac Asimov
5. I, Robot by Isaac Asimov
6. 1984 by George Orwell
7. 2001: a Space Odyssey by Arthur C. Clarke
8. Stranger in a Strange Land by Robert A. Heinlein
9. War of the Worlds by H. G. Wells
10. The Martian Chronicles by Ray Bradbury
11. Neuromancer by William Gibson
12. Snow Crash by Neil Stephenson
13. The Time Machine by H. G. Wells
14. Fahrenheit 451 by Ray Bradbury
15. Ringworld by Larry Niven
16. Lord of the Rings by J. R. R. Tolkien
17. Star Wars
18. The Time Traveler's Wife by Audrey Niffenegger
19. Brave New World by Aldous Huxley
20. The Moon Is a Harsh Mistress by Robert A. Heinlein
21. Do Androids Dream of Electric Sheep? by Philip K. Dick
22. Starship Troopers by Robert A. Heinlein
23. Jurassic Park by Michael Crichton
24. Ender's Shadow by Orson Scott Card
25. Slaughterhouse-Five by Kurt Vonnegut, Jr
26. 20,000 Leagues under the Sea by Jules Verne
27. Solaris by Stanislaw Lem
28. Rendezous with Rama by Arthur C. Clarke
29. Journey to the Center of the Earth by Jules Vernes
30. The Mote in God's Eye by Larry Niven and Jerry Pournelle
31. Star Trek
32. A Deepness in the Sky by Vernor Vinge
33. Contact by Carl Sagan
34. Battlefield Earth by L. Ron Hubbard
35. Cryptonomicon by Neal Stephenson
36. The Left Hand of Darkness by Ursula K. Le Guin
37. Cat's Cradle by Kurt Vonnegut, Jr
38. Dragonflight by Anne McCaffrey
39. Earth Abides by George R. Stewart
40. The Man in the High Castle by Philip K. Dick

Top Sushi Restaurants in Seattle, WA
925 votes by 329 people

1. Shiro's Sushi
2. Nishino
3. I Love Sushi
4. Chiso
5. Blue C Sushi
6. Mashiko Japanese Restaurant & Sushi Bar
7. Saito Japanese Cafe & Bar
8. Ototo Sushi
9. Toyoda Sushi
10. Kisaku
11. Yamashiro Sushi Bistro
12. Benihana
13. Flo Japanese Restaurant & Sake Bar
14. Sushi Zen
15. Sanmi Sushi
16. Wasabi Bistro
17. Nijo Sushi
18. Maneki
19. Osaka Sushi
20. Fuji Sushi
21. Aoki Japanese Grill & Sushi Bar
22. Izumi
23. Sakura Japanese Bistro
24. Hana Restuarant
25. Shiki Japanese Restaurant
26. Sushi Land
27. Musashi's
28. Todai Restaurant Japanese Sushi & Seafood Buffet
29. Rain
30. Bush Garden
31. Koji Osakaya Japanese Restaurant
32. Max Hotel's Red Fin
33. Sam's Sushi
34. Aoki
35. Sushi Kyo
36. Sushi Taro
37. Bento Sushi (Ballard)
38. Kaizuka Teppanyaki and Sushi Bar
39. Chinoise
40. Blue C Sushi – Fremont

Top Live Bands
3294 votes by 1018 people

1. U2
2. Rolling Stones
3. Green Day
4. Coldplay
5. Dave Matthews Band
6. Nine Inch Nails
7. Radiohead
8. Metallica
9. Aerosmith
10. System of a Down
11. Tool
12. The White Stripes
13. Foo Fighters
14. Pearl Jam
15. Linkin Park
16. They Might Be Giants
17. Dream Theater
18. Eagles
19. Barenaked Ladies
20. Depeche Mode
21. Nickelback
22. Red Hot Chili Peppers
23. Phish
24. Franz Ferdinand
25. The Killers
26. Death Cab for Cutie
27. Oasis
28. The Mars Volta
29. Iron Maiden
30. Weezer
31. The Arcade Fire
32. Korn
33. Black Eyed Peas
34. Kiss
35. Rush
36. Muse
37. Maroon 5
38. REM
39. Bon Jovi
40. Coheed & Cambria

Top Music Albums of All-Time
706 votes by 118 people

1. Dark Side of the Moon – Pink Floyd
2. The Beatles ("The White Album"), the Beatles
3. Thriller – Micheal Jackson
4. Revolver – the Beatles
5. Beatles – Sgt. Peppers Lonely Heart Club Band
6. Metallica – Black
7. Pink Floyd:The Wall
8. Eagles:Their Greatest Hits
9. Beatles – Abbey Road
10. The Joshua Tree, U2
11. Slippery When Wet – Bon Jovi
12. Nirvana – Nevermind
13. Led Zeppelin Houses of the Holy
14. The Eagles – Hotel California
15. The Beach Boys – Pet Sounds
16. The Beatles – Rubber Soul
17. Rumours – Fleetwood Mac
18. Gorillaz – Demon Days
19. Moving Pictures by Rush
20. Led Zeppelin – 4
21. Prince – Purple Rain
22. 50 Cent – Get Rich or Die Trying
23. OK Computer – Radiohead
24. Tool – Lateralus
25. Pearl Jam: 10
26. Counting Crows – This Desert Life
27. Raising Hell – Run DMC
28. Elton John: Goodbye Yellow Brick Road
29. Supernatural -Santana
30. Are You Experienced – Jimi Hendrix Experience
31. The Smiths – Meat Is Murder
32. Simon and Garfunkel Greatest Hits
33. The Posies – Failure
34. Death Cab for Cutie- Transatlanticism
35. Counting Crows- August and Everything after
36. Devo – Q: Are We Not Men? a: We Are Devo!
37. Insyders 'Greates and Rarest'
38. Third Eye Blind – Red Album
39. Pink Floyd – Echoes
40. Goldfrapp- Felt Mountain

Top Soda Drinks
2919 votes by 931 people

1. Coca Cola
2. Pepsi
3. Dr. Pepper
4. Mountain Dew
5. Sprite
6. Root Beer
7. Diet Coke
8. 7-Up
9. Cherry Coke
10. Fanta
11. Vanilla Coke
12. Cream Soda
13. Ginger Ale
14. Orange Crush
15. Surge
16. Sierra Mist
17. Wild Cherry Pepsi
18. Fresca
19. Canada Dry Ginger Ale
20. Mello Yello
21. Coke Zero
22. Tab
23. Squirt
24. orange soda
25. Mr. Pibb
26. Jolt
27. Bacardi Rum and Coke
28. Moxie
29. Ginger Beer
30. Fanta Orange
31. Barqs
32. Welch's Grape Soda
33. Sunkist
34. RC Cola
35. Cheerwine
36. Orangina
37. Crystal Pepsi
38. Schweppes
39. Diet Coke with Lime
40. Tonic Water

Favorite Ice Cream Flavors
621 votes by 177 people

1. Chocolate
2. Vanilla
3. Strawberry
4. Chocolate Chip Cookie Dough
5. Coffee
6. Cookies and Cream
7. rocky road
8. Butter Pecan
9. pistachio
10. Mint Chocolate Chip
11. Chocolate Peanut Butter
12. Banana
13. French Vanilla
14. Toffee and Caramel
15. black raspberry
16. Pralines & Cream
17. Ben and Jerry's Cherry Garcia
18. Moose Tracks
19. green tea
20. neopolitan
21. mint
22. Chunky Monkey
23. butterscotch
24. World Class Chocolate
25. Rum and Raisin
26. Cherry Jubilee
27. Pumpkin Pie
28. Caramel
29. fudge brownie
30. Stracciatella
31. Mango
32. Peppermint
33. Mint Cookies and Cream
34. Red Bean
35. Dulce de Leche
36. Phish Food
37. Pralines
38. bubble gum
39. Heavenly Hash
40. Party Cake

Top Reasons to Marry a Woman
483 votes by 108 people

1. Because You Love Her
2. Companionship
3. Having Babies
4. To have sex for free
5. Sense of Humor
6. money
7. looks
8. Compatibility
9. Her Heart
10. Can't live without her
11. Because you knocked her up
12. She is Trustworthy
13. Women are beautiful and romantic
14. She's an excellent homemaker
15. You want to spend the rest of your life with her.
16. Enjoy being with her
17. brain
18. Your parents, close family and you agree that she would be the best match for you.
19. She's the only one that said yes
20. Sex with a woman is better than with a man
21. Trust+Admiration+Respect=Love=Bingo
22. Her Father's Shotgun
23. Not being able to see yourself without her.
24. Her daddy gots a gun n taint afeared a usin it
25. She's Your Soul Mate
26. She's Single
27. Because she makes you happy
28. Security
29. She's your best friend
30. So you don't wake up when you're 55 and see yourself alone
31. She's Perfect for You
32. She would make a perfect mom
33. Strong Moral Values
34. Kiss
35. Lust
36. Men wanted to settle down
37. She is your ideal partner.
38. So someone is there to responds when you tell a joke or b*tch about the lousy TV program.
39. She's a good lover.
40. Beats Jacking off

Top Authors

3027 votes by 713 people

1. Stephen King
2. J.K. Rowling
3. William Shakespeare
4. J.R.R. Tolkien
5. John Grisham
6. Dan Brown
7. Tom Clancy
8. Ernest Hemingway
9. Charles Dickens
10. Kurt Vonnegut
11. Anne Rice
12. Terry Pratchett
13. Michael Crichton
14. Douglas Adams
15. Dean Koontz
16. Edgar Allen Poe
17. George Orwell
18. Mark Twain
19. Chuck Palahniuk
20. Neil Gaiman
21. Isaac Asimov
22. J.D. Salinger
23. C.S. Lewis
24. Jane Austen
25. Orson Scott Card
26. John Steinbeck
27. Ray Bradbury
28. John Irving
29. James Patterson
30. Robert Jordan
31. Danielle Steel
32. Agatha Christie
33. Neal Stephenson
34. George R. R. Martin
35. Ayn Rand
36. James Joyce
37. Maya Angelou
38. David Sedaris
39. Patricia Cornwell
40. R.L. Stine

Underpaid Jobs
2005 votes by 657 people

1. Teacher
2. Nurse
3. Social Worker
4. Police
5. police officer
6. janitor
7. waitress
8. garbage man
9. firefighter
10. fireman
11. Secretary
12. teaching
13. firemen
14. Doctor
15. Day Care Workers
16. computer programmer
17. waiter
18. cleaner
19. construction
20. retail
21. cashier
22. Librarian
23. Child Care Provider
24. McDonalds
25. cook
26. maid
27. fast food
28. Cops
29. Childcare Worker
30. EMT
31. college professor
32. farmer
33. Engineers
34. Mine
35. Truck Driver
36. Housekeeping
37. Nursing
38. customer service
39. accountant
40. Armed Forces

Top Female Voices
2434 votes by 716 people

1. Aretha Franklin
2. Mariah Carey
3. Whitney Houston
4. Celine Dion
5. Madonna
6. Billie Holiday
7. Kelly Clarkson
8. Ella Fitzgerald
9. Barbra Streisand
10. Tori Amos
11. Bjork
12. Christina Aguilera
13. Faith Hill
14. Enya
15. Patsy Cline
16. Shania Twain
17. Sarah Brightman
18. Karen Carpenter
19. Sarah McLachlan
20. Stevie Nicks
21. Fiona Apple
22. Tina Turner
23. Gwen Stefani
24. Britney Spears
25. Norah Jones
26. Diana Ross
27. Cher
28. Sinead O'Connor
29. Sheryl Crow
30. Nina Simone
31. Alanis Morissette
32. Maria Callas
33. Jessica Simpson
34. Alicia Keys
35. Annie Lennox
36. Etta James
37. Amy Lee
38. Dido
39. Martina McBride
40. Joni Mitchell

Favorite Beers

1821 votes by 562 people

1. Guinness
2. Budweiser
3. Bud Light
4. Miller Lite
5. Corona
6. Heineken
7. Coors Light
8. Samuel Adams
9. Coors
10. Newcastle
11. Miller Genuine Draft
12. Killian's Irish Red
13. Labatt Blue
14. Fat Tire
15. Molson Canadian
16. Yuengling Lager
17. Rolling Rock
18. Stella Artois
19. Fosters
20. Red Stripe
21. Grolsch
22. Hoegaarden, Blonde
23. Carlsberg
24. Amstel Light
25. Molson
26. Beck's
27. Sierra Nevada
28. Duvel (Belgian Ale)
29. Pabst Blue Ribbon
30. Michelob Light
31. bass
32. Leinenkugel's
33. Blue Moon
34. Romanian Beer
35. Asahi
36. Boddingtons
37. Busch
38. Stone Imperial Russian Stout
39. Moosehead
40. Leffe Blond

Top Metal Bands
2405 votes by 748 people

1. Metallica
2. Iron Maiden
3. Black Sabbath
4. AC/DC
5. Guns N Roses
6. Megadeth
7. Pantera
8. Slayer
9. Led Zeppelin
10. Judas Priest
11. Mötley Crüe
12. Kiss
13. Tool
14. Slipknot
15. Def Leppard
16. Poison
17. Korn
18. Anthrax
19. System of a Down
20. Van Halen
21. Nine Inch Nails
22. Motorhead
23. Whitesnake
24. Dream Theater
25. Aerosmith
26. Ozzy Osbourne
27. Opeth
28. Bon Jovi
29. Rammstein
30. Cradle of Filth
31. Deep Purple
32. Rage against the Machine
33. Twisted Sister
34. Manowar
35. Quiet Riot
36. GWAR
37. Cannibal Corpse
38. Alice Cooper
39. Disturbed
40. In Flames

Best Sexual Positions
627 votes by 228 people

1. "Doggy Style"
2. Missionary
3. Woman on Top
4. "69"
5. Reverse Cowgirl
6. Spooning
7. standing up
8. Missionary/Legs over Shoulders
9. Sitting
10. Her frogtied and gagged, riding on top
11. Side by Side
12. Second Posture of the Perfumed Garden
13. Two Women Tribbing (Grinding P*ssies Together)
14. The Italian Chandelier Position
15. You on Top
16. All of them
17. Her bound and gagged, spreadeagled on a bed
18. In a Sex Swing
19. Rickshaw
20. YOU under HIM: chicken soup of the sack
21. Upside down
22. Flamingo
23. The Coil
24. Towering
25. Crazy Sparrow
26. face to face
27. Sitting Position, from behind
28. Her on Top, Backwards
29. Sideways
30. On Bottom
31. Face to Crotch
32. You Sitting, Him Standing
33. Side with Leg Extended up (Female)
34. One person behind the other both standing up
35. Jackhammer
36. Turkish
37. Cat position: the Soft Rock
38. From behind
39. Rhino
40. Filling the Well

Top Soccer Players
1503 votes by 422 people

1. Pelé said "George Best was the best football player of all time"
2. Diego Maradona
3. David Beckham
4. Ronaldo
5. Ronaldinho
6. George Best
7. Zinedine Zidane
8. Mia Hamm
9. Franz Beckenbauer
10. Wayne Rooney
11. Roberto Baggio
12. Johan Cruyff
13. Gabriel Batistuta
14. Thierry Henry
15. Freddy Adu
16. Lev Yashin
17. Michael Owen
18. Marco Van Basten
19. Frank Lampard
20. Oliver Kahn
21. Eric Cantona
22. Ruud Van Nistelrooy
23. Michel Platini
24. Zbigniew Boniek
25. Youri Djorkaeff
26. Alfredo Di Stefano
27. Eusebio
28. Pavel Nedved
29. Figo
30. Bobby Charlton
31. Michelle Akers
32. Landon Donovan
33. Carlos Valderrama
34. Ferenc Puskas
35. Ruud Gullit
36. Kasey Keller
37. Cristiano Ronaldo
38. Jari Litmanen
39. Lothar Matthaus
40. Alan Shearer

Top Date Movies

1835 votes by 555 people

1. Sleepless in Seattle
2. The Notebook
3. When Harry Met Sally
4. 50 First Dates
5. Notting Hill
6. Titanic
7. Love Actually
8. Casablanca
9. The Princess Bride
10. You've Got Mail
11. Ghost
12. While You Were Sleeping
13. Shakespeare in Love
14. Pretty Woman
15. Dirty Dancing
16. Eternal Sunshine of the Spotless Mind
17. The Wedding Singer
18. Say Anything
19. Garden State
20. Ever After
21. How to Lose a Guy in 10 Days
22. Four Weddings and a Funeral
23. Scary Movie
24. Love Story
25. Wedding Crashers
26. Failure to Launch
27. Serendipity
28. Date Movie
29. Brokeback Mountain
30. Lost in Translation
31. American Pie
32. A Walk to Remember
33. French Kiss
34. Jerry Maguire
35. Walk the Line
36. Amelie
37. Gone with the Wind
38. Wedding Date
39. King Kong
40. The Matrix

Top Brands of Scotch

2827 votes by 845 people

1. Johnnie Walker
2. Glenfiddich
3. Glenlivet
4. Chivas Regal
5. Glenmorangie
6. Dewars
7. Macallan
8. Cutty Sark
9. Laphroaig
10. J&B
11. Lagavulin
12. Ballantines
13. Highland Park
14. Aberlour
15. Famous Grouse
16. Talisker
17. Oban
18. Bowmore
19. Balvenie
20. Ardbeg
21. Bells
22. Teachers
23. White Horse
24. McMaster's
25. Dalwhinnie
26. Grant's
27. Balblair
28. Passport
29. Cragganmore
30. Glenkinchie
31. Banff
32. Abbot's Choice
33. Dalmore
34. Aberfeldy
35. Edradour
36. Jura
37. Caol Ila
38. Dimple
39. Springbank
40. Hart Brothers

Top Mexican Restaurants in Seattle, WA
786 votes by 264 people

1. El Camino
2. Mama's Mexican Kitchen
3. Agua Verde
4. Cactus
5. Gordito's
6. Tacqueria Guaymas
7. La Carta de Oaxaca
8. Torero's Mexican Restaurant
9. Azteca
10. Malena's Taco Shop
11. Rosita's
12. Jalisco's
13. El Puerco Lloron
14. Bimbo's B*tch*n' Burrito Kitchen
15. Peso's Kitchen & Lounge
16. Taco Del Mar
17. Baja Fresh Mexican Grill
18. Blue Water Taco Grill
19. Ooba's Mexican Grill
20. El Gallito
21. Burrito Loco University Village
22. Las Margaritas
23. Luisa's Mexican Grill
24. Muy Macho
25. Galerias
26. Diego's Mexican Restaurant
27. La Cocina & Cantina
28. El Tapatio
29. El Quetzal
30. Mazatlan
31. Tia Lou's
32. Qdoba
33. La Palma
34. Quarter Lounge
35. La Tarascas
36. Baja Bistro
37. La Vaca
38. Taco Bell
39. Litas Tacos
40. Mariachis

Top Independent Coffee Houses in Seattle, WA

754 votes by 236 people

1. Espresso Vivace Roasteria Cafe
2. Bauhaus
3. Victrola Coffee & Art
4. Cafe Ladro
5. Zeitgeist
6. Trabant Chai Lounge
7. Uptown Espresso
8. B & O Espresso
9. Cherry St Coffee House Central
10. Diva Espresso
11. Top Pot
12. Cafe Allegro
13. Martin Henry Coffee Roasters
14. Flava Coffee House
15. Zoka's
16. Blue Dog Coffeehouse
17. Fremont Coffee Company
18. Counter Culture Cafe
19. Aurafice Internet and Coffee Bar
20. Speakeasy Cafe
21. Cafe Paradiso
22. Mr Spot's Chai House
23. Lighthouse Roasters Fine Coffees
24. Sureshot
25. Brooklyn Grinder
26. Caffe Vita
27. Wayward Coffee House
28. Ancient Grounds
29. Cafe Europa Hideout
30. Java Jazz
31. Aurafice
32. Louisa's Cafe Bakery
33. All City Coffee
34. Espresso Roma
35. Procopio
36. Black Cat Cafe
37. Jet Fuel Espresso
38. Espresso Vivace Sidewalk Bar
39. Bigfoot Java
40. Java Love

Best Cities to Live in If You're Married
2365 votes by 711 people

1. New York
2. Chicago
3. Seattle
4. San Francisco
5. Boston
6. Los Angeles
7. Portland, OR
8. San Diego
9. Miami
10. Dallas
11. Atlanta
12. Paris
13. Denver
14. Salt Lake City
15. Houston
16. London
17. Washington, DC
18. Austin, TX
19. Minneapolis
20. Indianapolis
21. Philadelphia
22. Nashville, TN
23. Kansas City
24. Las Vegas
25. Orlando
26. Detroit
27. Raleigh, NC
28. St. Louis
29. Tulsa
30. Charlotte
31. Toronto
32. Omaha, NE
33. San Jose
34. Phoenix
35. Pittsburgh, PA
36. Madison, WI
37. Rome
38. Vancouver
39. Sacramento, CA
40. Cleveland, OH

Top TV Shows

3212 votes by 991 people

1. The Simpsons
2. Desperate Housewives
3. Arrested Development
4. The Daily Show
5. Survivor
6. Law and Order
7. Grey's Anatomy
8. South Park
9. The OC
10. The Office
11. Prison Break
12. Battlestar Galactica
13. My Name is Earl
14. Aqua Teen Hunger Force
15. Seinfeld
16. ER
17. The Apprentice
18. West Wing
19. Scrubs
20. Nip/Tuck
21. Gilmore Girls
22. Futurama
23. American Dad
24. Amazing Race
25. Stargate SG-1
26. Mythbusters
27. Curb Your Enthusiasm
28. Veronica Mars
29. Smallville
30. Friends
31. The Sopranos
32. CSI: Miami
33. Las Vegas
34. NCIS
35. That 70's Show
36. Alias
37. Boston Legal
38. The Boondocks
39. The Colbert Report
40. Late Night with Conan O'Brien

Top "Hip" Neighborhoods to Live in Chicago, IL
749 votes by 195 people

1. Wicker Park
2. Lincoln Park
3. Wrigleyville
4. Bucktown
5. Logan Square
6. Gold Coast
7. Andersonville
8. Old Town
9. Lakeview
10. River North
11. The Loop
12. Hyde Park
13. Chinatown
14. Belmont
15. South Loop
16. Lincoln Square
17. Greektown
18. Rogers Park
19. Ukrainian Village
20. Edgewater
21. Downtown
22. West Loop
23. Evanston
24. North Center
25. Streeterville
26. Bridgeport
27. Uptown/Ravenswood
28. Boystown
29. Downers Grove
30. Ukranian Village
31. Lake Forest
32. Ravenswood
33. Neighborhoods: the South Side: Printers Row
34. Gapers Block
35. Pilsen
36. New Eastside
37. Albany Park
38. North Side
39. The Ukrainian Village
40. Loyola

Top Ski Resorts in North America
3078 votes by 955 people

1. Vail
2. Aspen
3. Whistler/Blackcomb
4. Breckenridge
5. Killington
6. Heavenly
7. Jackson Hole
8. Stowe
9. Steamboat
10. Beaver Creek
11. Mammoth Mountain
12. Mont Tremblant
13. Snowbird
14. Park City
15. Squaw Valley
16. Banff
17. Copper Mountain
18. Winter Park
19. Sun Valley
20. Alta
21. Taos
22. Snowmass
23. Deer Valley
24. Keystone
25. big bear
26. Sugar Mountain
27. Sugarloaf
28. Snowshoe
29. Kirkwood
30. Big Mountain
31. Northstar at Tahoe
32. Camelback
33. Big Sky
34. Hunter Mountain
35. Okemo
36. Lake Placid
37. Mt. Bachelor
38. Aspen Highlands
39. Lake Louise
40. Sugarbush

Most Overrated Movies
2076 votes by 601 people

1. Titanic
2. Brokeback Mountain
3. Star Wars
4. The Matrix
5. Lord of the Rings
6. Crash
7. King Kong
8. Citizen Kane
9. Pulp Fiction
10. The English Patient
11. Harry Potter
12. Kill Bill
13. War of the Worlds
14. The Godfather
15. Donnie Darko
16. American Pie
17. Top Gun
18. American Beauty
19. Spiderman
20. Fight Club
21. Moulin Rouge
22. Mission Impossible
23. Gladiator
24. Forrest Gump
25. Scarface
26. Blair Witch Project
27. Jurassic Park
28. Independence Day
29. The Passion of the Christ
30. Pearl Harbor
31. ET
32. Million Dollar Baby
33. Chicago
34. Dances with Wolves
35. Scary Movie
36. The Lord of the Rings: the Fellowship of the Ring
37. Troy
38. Rocky
39. Rambo
40. Silence of the Lambs

Best Inventions

3181 votes by 985 people

1. computer
2. Internet
3. Lightbulb
4. Wheel
5. Automobile
6. Telephone
7. Electricity
8. Television
9. Printing Press
10. Cell Phone
11. Toilet
12. Antibiotics
13. Airplane
14. Microwave
15. Microchip
16. Radio
17. Sliced Bread
18. Condoms
19. Refrigerator
20. Internal Combustion Engine
21. iPod
22. Indoor Plumbing
23. TiVo
24. Transistor
25. Written Language
26. Air Conditioning
27. Toaster
28. Bicycle
29. Soap
30. Integrated Circuit
31. video games
32. camera
33. Beer
34. Language
35. MP3 Players
36. Velcro
37. Birth Control
38. The Remote Control
39. Paper
40. Steam Engine

Top NCAA College Basketball Games
421 votes by 118 people

1. Duke Kentucky 1982
2. Kentucky Vs. Duke (1992)
3. Kentucky-Duke 1992
4. Univ. of Kentucky, Univ. of Louisville, 2005
5. Kentucky Michigan State 2005
6. Villanova Georgetown 1985
7. Wildcats – Duke 1978
8. Duke Vs. Kentucky 1992
9. Kentucky U. Vs Kansas U., 1991
10. Duke Vs Kentucky ('91)
11. Duke- Kentucky 1992
12. Texas Western/Kentucky 1966
13. Indiana State, Michigan State, 1979
14. UCLA Houston 1968
15. 1983 NC State Vs Houston
16. Michigan Vs. Michigan State (2004)
17. UNC Vs NC State 1982
18. Duke/UNC 2000
19. North Carolina – Georgetown 1982
20. Michigan – Seton Hall 1989
21. Indiana Vs. UCLA 1976
22. North Carolina, Georgetown 1982
23. Notre Dame, Ohio University, 1970
24. Illinois Arizona 2005
25. Connecticut and Georgia Tech 2004
26. NCAA College Basketball 2k3
27. Romeo Crennel
28. Avalon
29. Sonics Vs. Blazers
30. Duke
31. NC State – Maryland 1974
32. Duke Vs Northwestern 2004
33. Manhattan at Seton Hall
34. Duke Arizona 2001
35. Duke – VT 2005
36. Indian Vs. Syracuse, 1986
37. Indiana Vs. Syracuse, 1987

Top Console/PC Video Games of All-Time

3169 votes by 1053 people

1. Super Mario Brothers
2. Halo
3. Half-Life
4. Doom
5. The Legend of Zelda
6. Final Fantasy VII
7. Pac Man
8. The Sims
9. Grand Theft Auto
10. Tetris
11. Civilization
12. Starcraft
13. Quake
14. Diablo
15. Counter Strike
16. Donkey Kong
17. Pong
18. World of Warcraft
19. Sim City
20. Myst
21. Resident Evil 4
22. Frogger
23. Metal Gear Solid
24. Battlefield 1942
25. Nintendo
26. Tomb Raider
27. Kingdom Hearts
28. Call of Duty
29. Age of Empires
30. Goldeneye
31. Gran Turismo
32. Chrono Trigger
33. Super Mario World
34. Mortal Kombat
35. Madden
36. Asteroids
37. Star Wars: Knights of the Old Republic
38. Space Invaders
39. Deus Ex
40. Sonic the Hedgehog

Most Corrupt Politicians
1668 votes by 507 people

1. George W. Bush
2. Richard Nixon
3. Dick Cheney
4. Bill Clinton
5. Tom Delay
6. Adolf Hitler
7. Ted Kennedy
8. Joseph Stalin
9. Saddam Hussein
10. Ronald Reagan
11. Ferdinand Marcos
12. William "Boss" Tweed
13. John Kerry
14. Karl Rove
15. Fidel Castro
16. Donald Rumsfeld
17. Tony Blair
18. Ulysses S. Grant
19. Bill Frist
20. Huey Long
21. Conrad Burns
22. Andrew Jackson
23. Silvio Berlusconi
24. Randy Cunningham
25. Lyndon Johnson
26. Robert Mugabe
27. Richard Daley
28. Marion Barry
29. Joseph McCarthy
30. Warren G. Harding
31. Vladimir Putin
32. Ariel Sharon
33. Jeb Bush
34. Jacques Chirac
35. Huey P Long
36. Spiro Agnew
37. Mohamed Suharto
38. William Taft
39. Kwame Kilpatrick
40. Kim Jong Il

Greatest American Presidents

1711 votes by 518 people

1. Abraham Lincoln
2. George Washington
3. Bill Clinton
4. John F. Kennedy
5. Franklin Roosevelt
6. Ronald Reagan
7. Thomas Jefferson
8. George W. Bush
9. Theodore Roosevelt
10. Jimmy Carter
11. Harry Truman
12. Richard Nixon
13. Lyndon B. Johnson
14. Andrew Jackson
15. Thomas Woodrow Wilson
16. Dwight Eisenhower
17. John Adams
18. Gerald Ford
19. James K. Polk
20. Grover Cleveland
21. Calvin Coolidge
22. James Garfield
23. George H W Bush
24. Warren Harding
25. William McKinley
26. James Madison
27. Zachary Taylor
28. William Howard Taft
29. Ulysses S. Grant
30. Martin Van Buren
31. John Quincy Adams
32. James Monroe
33. Andrew Johnson
34. Chester Alan Arthur
35. Rutherford B. Hayes

Favorite Movies
2290 votes by 711 people

1. Lord of the Rings
2. Pulp Fiction
3. The Princess Bride
4. Gone with the Wind
5. Casablanca
6. The Big Lebowski
7. Scarface
8. Serenity
9. Citizen Kane
10. Goonies
11. Monty Python and the Holy Grail
12. V for Vendetta
13. Magnolia
14. The Wizard of Oz
15. Grease
16. Garden State
17. The Sound of Music
18. Moulin Rouge
19. Love Actually
20. Jaws
21. Lawrence of Arabia
22. The Usual Suspects
23. Goodfellas
24. Secretary
25. Fried Green Tomatoes
26. The Incredibles
27. Being John Malkovich
28. A Clockwork Orange
29. Die Hard
30. Napoleon Dynamite
31. Pirates of the Caribbean
32. Batman Begins
33. Trainspotting
34. Pretty Woman
35. It's a Wonderful Life
36. The Right Stuff
37. American Beauty
38. Dances with Wolves
39. Ever After
40. Vanilla Sky

Top Cable TV Channels

3195 votes by 1010 people

1. Comedy Central
2. HBO
3. Discovery
4. ESPN
5. MTV
6. Cartoon Network
7. CNN
8. Food Network
9. Sci-Fi
10. History Channel
11. Fox
12. HGTV
13. TLC
14. FX
15. Spike
16. VH1
17. TNT
18. TBS
19. USA
20. Bravo
21. A&E
22. Showtime
23. Nickelodeon
24. Lifetime
25. Disney
26. Fox News
27. Cinemax
28. BBC America
29. G4
30. Animal Planet
31. MSNBC
32. Turner Classic Movies
33. TV Land
34. Weather Channel
35. C-Span
36. National Geographic
37. E!
38. Travel Channel
39. BET
40. Court TV

Best Lines in Pulp Fiction

501 votes by 151 people

1. A royale with cheese. What do they call a Big Mac?
2. No, let me ask you a question. When you came pulling in here, did you see a sign out in front of my house that said dead nigger storage?
3. Butch: Zed's Dead, Baby. Zed's Dead.
4. That's Thirty Minutes Away. I'll Be There in Ten.
5. The path of the righteous man is beset on all sides by the iniquities of the selfish and the tyranny of evil men. Blessed is he, who in the name of charity and good will, shepherds the weak through the valley of darkness, for he is truly his brother'
6. "What aint no country I ever heard of. do they speak English in 'What'?"
7. English, M*th*rf*ck*r! Do You Speak It?!
8. I'm a get medieval on your *ss.
9. Jules: It's the one that says bad M*th*rf*ck*r.
10. Jules: Oh, I'm sorry, did I break your concentration?
11. I'm a Mushroom Cloud Layin' M*th*rf*ck*r, M*th*rf*ck*r
12. The wolf: well, let's not start sucking each other's dicks Just yet.
13. Alright, everybody be cool, this is a robbery!
14. Any One of You F*ck*ng Pricks Move, I'll Execute Every M*th*rf*ck*ng Last One of Ya
15. "That's a pretty f*ck*ng good milkshake. I don't know if it's worth five dollars but it's pretty f*ck*ng good."
16. Hamburgers, the cornerstone of any nutritious breakfast
17. The Wolf: If I'm curt with you, it's because time is a factor here. I think fast, I talk fast, and I need you guys to act fast if you want to get out of this. so, pretty please, with sugar on top, clean the f*ck*ng car
18. You see, this profession is filled to the brim with unrealistic m*th*rf*ck*rs. m*th*rf*ck*rs who thought their *ss would age like wine. if you mean it turns to vinegar, it does. if you mean it gets better with age, it don't.
19. I'm prepared to scour the the earth for that m*th*rf*ck*r. If Butch goes to Indochina, I want a nigger waiting in a bowl of rice ready to pop a cap in his *ss.
20. I do believe Marsellus Wallace, my husband, your boss, told you to take me out and do WHATEVER I WANTED. Now I wanna dance, I wanna win. I want that trophy, so dance good.
21. I'm Pretty F*ck*n' Far from Okay.
22. Normally, both your asses would be dead as f*ck*ng fried chicken, but you happen to pull this sh*t while I'm in a transitional period so I don't wanna kill you, I wanna help you. but I can't give you this case, it don't belong to me.
23. Bring out the Gimp
24. I don't remember askin you a GOD DAMN THING
25. Eatin' a b*tch out, and givin' a b*tch a foot massage ain't even the same f*ck*n' thing.

26. "Oh man, I shot Marvin in the face"

27. Whether or not what we experienced was an according to Hoyle miracle is insignificant. What is significant is that I felt the touch of God. God got involved.

28. This is america, Honey. Our names don't mean sh*t.

29. Jules: say what again. SAY WHAT AGAIN. I dare you, I double dare you, m*th*rf*ck*r. Say what one more goddamn time.

30. Maynard: nobody kills anyone in my store except me and Zed.

31. Do I nobody kills anyone in my store except me?!

32. what?

33. You know what they call a Quarter Pounder with Cheese in France? ... a Royale with Cheese.

34. And you will know my name is the Lord when I lay my vengeance upon thee!

35. Mia: I'll lay my vengeance upon thee.

36. Vincent: [To Marvin] Why the f*ck didn't you tell us somebody was in the bathroom? Slipped your mind? Did you forget that somebody was in there with a goddamn hand cannon?

37. Sorry Baby, I had to crash that honda.

38. Paul: Hey, my name's Paul and this sh*t's between y'all.

39. Personality goes a long way

40. That's when you know you've found somebody special. When you can just shut the f*ck up for a minute and comfortably enjoy the silence.

Top Mixed Drinks
3158 votes by 994 people

1. Martini
2. Long Island Iced Tea
3. screwdriver
4. Margarita
5. Rum and Coke
6. Gin and Tonic
7. White Russian
8. Cosmopolitan
9. Bloody Mary
10. Sex on the Beach
11. Pina Colada
12. Jack and Coke
13. Whiskey Sour
14. Mojito
15. Tequila Sunrise
16. Manhattan
17. Fuzzy Navel
18. Strawberry Daiquiri
19. Tom Collins
20. Vodka Tonic
21. Mudslide
22. Amaretto Sour
23. 7 and 7
24. Midori Sour
25. Black Russian
26. Mai Tai
27. Vodka Cranberry
28. Daiquiri
29. Kamikaze
30. Vodka Redbull
31. Cuba Libre
32. Sludge
33. Captain and Coke
34. Hurricane
35. Scotch and Water
36. Sea Breeze
37. Cape Codder
38. Zombie
39. Whiskey and Coke
40. Shirley Temple

Best Cyclist of All Time

477 votes by 152 people

1. Lance Armstrong
2. Eddy Merckx
3. Miguel Indurain
4. Greg Lemond
5. Bernard Hinault
6. Fausto Coppi
7. Jacques Anquetil
8. Jan Ullrich
9. Major Taylor
10. George Langford
11. Marco Pantani
12. Jeannie Longo
13. Mario Cipollini
14. Sheldon Brown
15. Antonio Cruz
16. Sean Kelly
17. Joop Zoetemelk
18. Lucho Herrera
19. Mat Hoffman
20. Geoff Kabush
21. Floyd Landis
22. Chris Boardman
23. Stuart O'Grady
24. Raymond Poulidor
25. Joseba Beloki
26. Tyler Hamilton
27. Klaus Meingast
28. Gary Fisher
29. Phil Anderson
30. Charly Gaul
31. Gianni Bugno
32. Sante Gaiardoni
33. Mark McCormack
34. Alex Merckx
35. Aaron Chase
36. Gary Niewand
37. Fred Rodriguez
38. Seiichi Nishiji
39. Chris Horner
40. Levi Leipheimer

Top Coolest Companies
3081 votes by 964 people

1. Google
2. Apple
3. Amazon
4. Microsoft
5. Sony
6. Nintendo
7. eBay
8. Yahoo
9. Dell
10. Nike
11. Coca Cola
12. Pepsi
13. IBM
14. Starbucks
15. Pixar
16. Target
17. Walmart
18. Intel
19. AMD
20. Disney
21. Adidas
22. Mozilla
23. Ben & Jerry's
24. Costco
25. Best Buy
26. Virgin
27. Ferrari
28. Tivo
29. Newegg.com
30. American Apparel
31. General Electric
32. Old Navy
33. McDonalds
34. Ikea
35. Geico
36. Verizon
37. Netflix
38. 3M
39. Bungie
40. Coke

Worst Things about Austin, TX
438 votes by 100 people

1. Traffic
2. Heat
3. allergies
4. Californians
5. It's in Texas
6. Pollution
7. Long stop lights
8. Needs more late night public transportation
9. Rednecks
10. republicans
11. Slow/Bad Drivers
12. Not Being There
13. Religious Zealots
14. too crowded
15. College Students.
16. Women
17. Many Homeless People
18. Traffic caused by city counsel with no new roads policy.
19. housing
20. Public Restrooms
21. Austin Drivers
22. Highways
23. Housing and Rental Costs
24. Yuppies.
25. Too Expensive to Live in
26. Revolves around UT
27. Temperatures can quickly drop due to the "blue norther" phenomenon.
28. heart disease
29. Crime
30. Unsafe City to Drive in
31. Hippies
32. UT Football
33. Residents Are Prejudice
34. Housing Costs
35. politics
36. Public Transportation
37. smog
38. I-35
39. Freeways designed to accomodate traffic levels from the 1970's
40. Roads

Most Likely People to Be US President in 2008
2574 votes by 821 people

1. Hillary Clinton
2. John McCain
3. Condoleezza Rice
4. John Kerry
5. Al Gore
6. Barack Obama
7. Rudy Giuliani
8. Jeb Bush
9. Dick Cheney
10. John Edwards
11. Colin Powell
12. Arnold Schwarzenegger
13. Howard Dean
14. Joe Biden
15. Oprah Winfrey
16. Russ Feingold
17. Mark Warner
18. Mitt Romney
19. Ralph Nader
20. Bill Frist
21. Evan Bayh
22. Christopher Walken
23. George Pataki
24. George Allen
25. Wesley Clark
26. Al Sharpton
27. Joe Lieberman
28. Ross Perot
29. Bob Dole
30. Newt Gingrich
31. Jon Stewart
32. Laura Bush
33. Donald Trump
34. Pat Buchanan
35. Bill Gates
36. Michael Bloomberg
37. Chuck Norris
38. Gary Colemen
39. John Carrey
40. Trent Lott

Most Physically Challenging Sports

1511 votes by 467 people

1. Soccer
2. Hockey
3. Rugby
4. Marathon
5. basketball
6. wrestling
7. boxing
8. Triathlon
9. swimming
10. cross country skiing
11. mountain climbing
12. weight lifting
13. Decathlon
14. baseball
15. gymnastics
16. Tennis
17. rock climbing
18. Iron Man Triathlon
19. Cycling
20. Lacrosse
21. Long Distance Running
22. Rowing
23. American Football
24. Water Polo
25. Mixed Martial Arts / Ultimate Fighting
26. Ultra marathoning
27. snowboarding
28. Figure Skating
29. track
30. Golf
31. downhill skiing
32. Curling
33. Skateboarding
34. Track & Field
35. Luge
36. Jousting
37. World's Strongest Man
38. ice skating
39. Surfing
40. Pentathlon

Worst Movies
1923 votes by 588 people

1. Gigli
2. Battlefield Earth
3. Glitter
4. Titanic
5. Attack of the Killer Tomatoes
6. From Justin to Kelly
7. Plan 9 from Outer Space
8. Crossroads
9. Waterworld
10. Spice World
11. Catwoman
12. Batman and Robin
13. Ishtar
14. Brokeback Mountain
15. Manos: Hands of Fate
16. Armageddon
17. Freddy Got Fingered
18. Anaconda
19. House of the Dead
20. Dukes of Hazzard
21. The Blair Witch Project
22. Scary Movie
23. Son of the Mask
24. Scream
25. War of the Worlds
26. The Avengers
27. The Cell
28. Vanilla Sky
29. White Chicks
30. Sleepless in Seattle
31. Terminator 3
32. Ultraviolet
33. Open Water
34. Zoolander
35. Cabin Fever
36. The Postman
37. Date Movie
38. Basic Instinct 2
39. Howard the Duck
40. The Hills Have Eyes

Top Men You Would Leave Your Partner for

3150 votes by 947 people

1. Brad Pitt
2. Johnny Depp
3. George Clooney
4. Tom Cruise
5. Orlando Bloom
6. Jude Law
7. Harrison Ford
8. Matt Damon
9. Mel Gibson
10. Sean Connery
11. Bill Gates
12. none
13. Vin Diesel
14. Heath Ledger
15. Matthew McConaughey
16. George Bush
17. Tom Hanks
18. Bruce Willis
19. Ben Affleck
20. Keanu Reeves
21. Hugh Jackman
22. Ewan McGregor
23. Colin Farrell
24. Pierce Brosnan
25. Denzel Washington
26. Edward Norton
27. Jake Gyllenhaal
28. Bill Clinton
29. Ashton Kutcher
30. Leonardo DiCaprio
31. Jon Bon Jovi
32. Will Smith
33. John Cusack
34. Adam Sandler
35. Chuck Norris
36. Richard Gere
37. Jim Carrey
38. Colin Firth
39. Viggo Mortenson
40. Russell Crowe

Best Dressed Cities (Worldwide)
1668 votes by 552 people

1. Paris, France
2. New York, New York
3. London, England
4. Milan, Italy
5. Tokyo, Japan
6. Los Angeles, California
7. Rome
8. San Francisco, California
9. Chicago
10. Toronto
11. Boston
12. Miami
13. Atlanta
14. Hollywood
15. Las Vegas
16. Amsterdam
17. Montreal
18. Washington D.C.
19. Hong Kong
20. Berlin
21. Houston
22. Madrid
23. Venice, Italy
24. Barcelona
25. Melbourne
26. Sydney
27. Seattle
28. Beverly Hills
29. San Diego
30. Florence, Italy
31. Vancouver, Canada
32. Dublin
33. Prague
34. Rio de Janeiro
35. Zurich
36. Sydney, Australia
37. Moscow
38. Philadelphia
39. Buenos Aires, Argentina
40. Sault Ste Marie

Best Songs of All Time

498 votes by 121 people

1. Stairway to Heaven
2. Yesterday – The Beatles
3. Let It Be
4. Imagine – John Lennon
5. Like a Rolling Stone – Bob Dylan
6. Bohemian Rhapsody
7. With or Without You
8. Hotel California
9. Smells like Teen Spirit
10. Thriller
11. Happy Birthday
12. Strawberry Fields Forever
13. My Heart Will Go On
14. Hey Jude
15. Enter Sandman – Metallica
16. Friends in Low Places
17. Pink Floyd – Money
18. The Star Spangled Banner
19. One – Metallica
20. I Will Always Love You
21. Billie Jean – Michael Jackson
22. I Want You to Want Me
23. Eleanor Rigby
24. Piano Man – Billy Joel
25. Dust in the Wind – Kansas
26. Bridge over Troubled Water
27. Help!
28. Over the Rainbow – Judy Garland
29. Unchained Melody
30. You Can't Always Get What You Want – Rolling Stones
31. Only Happy When It Rains – Garbage
32. Sympathy for the Devil
33. Fall on Me – R.E.M, 1986
34. Like a Virgin
35. Alice in Chains – Don't Follow
36. Take Five
37. Wonderwall – Oasis
38. A Day in the Life – The Beatles
39. (I Can't Get No) Satisfaction – Rolling Stones
40. Achilles' Last Stand – Led Zeppelin

Top Male Voices
2114 votes by 661 people

1. Frank Sinatra
2. Freddie Mercury
3. Elvis Presley
4. Michael Jackson
5. John Lennon
6. Luciano Pavarotti
7. Barry White
8. Robert Plant
9. Johnny Cash
10. Bono
11. Paul McCartney
12. Jeff Buckley
13. Nat King Cole
14. Clay Aiken
15. Usher
16. Sting
17. Roger Daltry
18. Jim Morrison
19. Garth Brooks
20. Kurt Cobain
21. Elton John
22. Robbie Williams
23. David Bowie
24. Placido Domingo
25. Andrea Bocelli
26. Chris Cornell
27. Eddie Vedder
28. Luther Vandross
29. Tom Waits
30. Ray Charles
31. Thom Yorke
32. Axel Rose
33. Morrissey
34. Prince
35. Steve Perry
36. Justin Timberlake
37. Billy Joel
38. Bruce Dickinson
39. Tom Jones
40. Steven Tyler

Top Movie Directors
1969 votes by 612 people

1. Steven Spielberg
2. Peter Jackson
3. Quentin Tarantino
4. George Lucas
5. Ron Howard
6. Martin Scorsese
7. Alfred Hitchcock
8. Stanley Kubrick
9. Ang Lee
10. Francis Ford Coppola
11. Tim Burton
12. Woody Allen
13. James Cameron
14. Kevin Smith
15. Clint Eastwood
16. Akira Kurosawa
17. M. Night Shyamalan
18. David Lynch
19. Ridley Scott
20. Orson Welles
21. David Fincher
22. Michael Moore
23. Frank Capra
24. Spike Lee
25. Michael Mann
26. Federico Fellini
27. Robert Altman
28. Oliver Stone
29. Steven Soderbergh
30. Sam Raimi
31. Roman Polanski
32. Mel Gibson
33. Rob Reiner
34. Bryan Singer
35. Wes Anderson
36. Paul Thomas Anderson
37. Joss Whedon
38. Robert Rodriguez
39. George Clooney
40. Darren Aronofsky

Top Italian Restaurants in Seattle, WA
399 votes by 125 people

1. Mamma Melina Ristorante
2. Assaggio Ristorante
3. Serafina
4. Tulio Ristorante
5. Buca di Beppo
6. Salumi
7. Il Terrazzo Carmine
8. Pink Door
9. Cafe Juanita
10. Fremont Classic Pizzeria & Trattoria
11. Mama Stortini's
12. Perche'No
13. Brad's Swingside Cafe
14. Il Bistro
15. Osteria La Spiga
16. Asteroid Cafe
17. Tutta Bella Neapolitan Pizzeria
18. Bizzarro Italian Cafe
19. Olive Garden
20. Vince's
21. Romios
22. Lombardi's Italian Restaurant
23. Piatti
24. Machiavelli Ristorante
25. Palomino Euro Bistro
26. La Panzanella
27. Poulsbo Pasta Co
28. Angelina's Trattoria
29. La Rustica
30. Salvatores Ristorante Italiano
31. Pasta Bella (In Queen Anne District)
32. Ciao Bella
33. Il Fornio
34. Pomodoro
35. Santorini Pizza and Pasta
36. Pasta Bella (Ballard)
37. Trattoria Mitchelli Restaurant
38. That's Amore
39. Denunzio
40. Gaspare Ristorante and Bar

Worst Baby Names for Girls

1816 votes by 510 people

1. Apple
2. Bertha
3. Gertrude
4. Britney
5. Ashley
6. Jennifer
7. Mary
8. Shaniqua
9. Madison
10. Jessica
11. Ethel
12. Gretchen
13. Mildred
14. Beatrice
15. Paris
16. Tiffany
17. Dakota
18. Amber
19. Brittany
20. Helga
21. Amanda
22. Martha
23. Agnes
24. Linda
25. Jane
26. Crystal
27. Sarah
28. Sally
29. Morgan
30. Matilda
31. Summer
32. Susan
33. Anna
34. hazel
35. Melissa
36. Myrtle
37. Maria
38. Destiny
39. Taylor
40. candy

Best ORM Layer
273 votes by 117 people

1. ActiveRecord
2. Hibernate
3. Toplink
4. Carbonado
5. cayenne
6. NHibernate
7. iBATIS
8. Barracuda
9. Neo
10. Genome
11. RMI
12. Raptier
13. PHP
14. .NET Persistence
15. ORM.NET
16. Llblgen Pro
17. Django
18. Ezpdo
19. Active Record Factory (ARF)
20. Uniqueext Constraints
21. Pragmatier Data Tier Builder
22. Torque
23. SQL
24. Coldfusion
25. Object Layer
26. Norma
27. Bazaar
28. Objectz.Net
29. Enterprise Objects Framework
30. Common Lisp
31. Perl
32. The Code
33. Force4
34. Joram
35. Nolics.NET
36. Casetalk
37. Propel
38. Expdo
39. Norpheme
40. Gentle.NET

Best Cities to Live in If You're Single
3141 votes by 1060 people

1. New York
2. Los Angeles
3. San Francisco
4. Miami
5. Chicago
6. Boston
7. Las Vegas
8. Seattle
9. London
10. Austin
11. Paris
12. Washington, DC
13. Dallas
14. San Diego
15. Atlanta
16. Denver
17. Philadelphia
18. Orlando
19. Toronto
20. Amsterdam
21. Houston
22. New Orleans
23. Portland
24. Minneapolis
25. Montreal
26. Sydney
27. Rome
28. Berlin
29. Salt Lake City
30. Tampa
31. Honolulu
32. Vancouver
33. Hollywood
34. St Louis
35. Tokyo
36. San Diego, California
37. Baltimore
38. Boulder, Colorado
39. Tel Aviv
40. Sacramento

Best Active NBA Basketball Players

571 votes by 117 people

1. Lebron James
2. Kobe Bryant
3. O'Neal, Shaquille
4. Steve Nash
5. Dwayne Wade
6. Tim Duncan
7. Allen Iverson
8. Dirk Nowitzki
9. Tracy McGrady
10. Kevin Garnett
11. Vince Carter
12. Yao Ming
13. Carmelo Anthony
14. Jason Kidd
15. Gilbert Arenas
16. Ben Wallace
17. Ron Artest
18. Tony Parker
19. Ray Allen
20. Chauncey Billups
21. John Edwards
22. Raja Bell
23. Paul Gasol
24. Darren Williams
25. Jamal Crawford
26. Nate Robinson
27. Pat Burke Phnx Suns
28. Brian Cook
29. Carlos Boozer
30. Elton Brand
31. Mike Bibby
32. Manu Ginobli
33. Jermaine O'Neal
34. Jason Richardson
35. Brent Barry
36. Josh Smith
37. Anderson Varejao
38. Adonal Foyle
39. Eddie House Phnx Suns
40. Allan Houston

Top Restaurants in Seattle
299 votes by 68 people

1. Rover's
2. Cafe Juanita
3. El Gaucho
4. Wild Ginger
5. Dahlia Lounge
6. Robertiello's
7. Metropolitan Grill
8. Seven Stars Pepper
9. Crush
10. Matt's in the Market
11. Canlis
12. Harvest Vine
13. The Oceanaire
14. Boat Street Cafe
15. Le Pichet
16. Husky Deli
17. Salumi
18. Campagne
19. Mistral
20. The Asteroid Cafe
21. Earth and Ocean
22. Palace Kitchen
23. Ipanema
24. Barolo
25. Brasserie Margaux
26. Torero's Mexican Restaurant
27. Icon Grill
28. Mama's Kitchen
29. Costas
30. Coldwater Bar and Grill
31. Cassis
32. Kiku
33. May
34. Hurricane Cafe
35. Lodge at Eagle Ridge
36. Med Kitchen Seattle
37. Ray's Boathouse
38. Chez Shea
39. The Herbfarm
40. Waterfront Seafood Grill

Best Casinos in Las Vegas
451 votes by 146 people

1. Bellagio
2. Caesar's Palace
3. MGM Grand
4. The Venetian
5. Mandalay Bay
6. Luxor
7. New York, New York
8. The Mirage
9. Paris Casino Las Vegas
10. Wynn Las Vegas
11. Treasure Island
12. Circus Circus
13. Hard Rock
14. Palms
15. Sahara
16. Excalibur
17. Las Vegas Hilton
18. Flamingo Las Vegas
19. The Rio
20. Alladin
21. Bally's
22. Casino Royale
23. Monte Carlo
24. Golden Nugget
25. Tropicana
26. Slots O Fun
27. Imperial Palace
28. Orleans
29. Stardust
30. Green Valley Ranch
31. El Cortez
32. Stratosphere Las Vegas Hotel & Casino
33. Gold Coast
34. Four Queens
35. Barbary Coast
36. Binion's
37. Fitzgerald's
38. South Coast
39. Frontier
40. Westin Casuarina Hotel & Spa

Top Names You Would Never Name Your Child
2220 votes by 708 people

1. Dick
2. Adolf
3. Apple
4. John
5. Bertha
6. Gertrude
7. George
8. Jesus
9. Bob
10. Gaylord
11. Harry
12. Richard
13. Shaniqua
14. Britney
15. Fred
16. Bill
17. Candy
18. Peter
19. Helga
20. Madison
21. Eugene
22. Ashley
23. Orangello
24. Paris
25. Ethel
26. Osama
27. Eunice
28. Mortimer
29. Jessica
30. Jennifer
31. Agnes
32. Brutus
33. Chastity
34. Saddam
35. Wayne
36. Albert
37. Boris
38. Robert
39. Mark
40. Hortense

Top Thai Restaurants in Seattle, WA

618 votes by 212 people

1. Mae Phim Thai Restaurant
2. Sea-Thai
3. Chantanee Family Thai Restaurant
4. Jai Thai
5. Thai Tom
6. Little Thai Express
7. Thai Ginger
8. Thai Kitchen
9. Siam on Broadway
10. Bahn Thai Restaurant
11. Typhoon!
12. Thaiku
13. Thai Star
14. May Restaurant and Lounge
15. Tup Tim Thai
16. Djan's Dining
17. Thai Siam
18. Jamjuree
19. Toi
20. Bangkok Thai Restaurant
21. Thai Ku
22. Ayutthaya Thai Restaurant
23. Bada Lounge
24. Racha
25. Thai-Ger Room
26. Mae Phim
27. Orrapin Thai Cuisine
28. Krittika's Noodles & Thai Cuisine
29. Malay Satay Hut
30. Araya's
31. Kaosamai Thai Restaurant
32. Royal Palm
33. Chantanee
34. Lotus Thai Cuisine
35. Treasure Thai
36. Typhoon! Redmond
37. Araya's Vegetarian Place
38. Kwanjai
39. Noodle Ranch
40. Thai Ocean (in Greenlake)

Best Indian Restaurant in Seattle
292 votes by 76 people

1. Preet's
2. Taste of India
3. Bombay Grill
4. India Bistro
5. Pabla Indian Cuisine
6. Roti
7. Chutneys Bistro – Wallingford Center
8. Udupi Palace
9. Kababhouse
10. Jewel of India
11. Tandoor
12. Chutney's Grille on the Hill
13. Bengal Tiger
14. Moghul Palace
15. Tandoor Indian Restaurant
16. Chutneys Bistro
17. Nan and Curry
18. Cedar's
19. Cedars Restaurant on Brooklyn
20. India Express
21. Pabla
22. Punjab Sweets
23. Sahib
24. Spice Route
25. Marsala
26. Shangrila
27. Apna Bazar
28. Massa Palace
29. India Palace – Ballard
30. Banjara Cuisine of India
31. Spice Rack
32. Namasthe Cuisine of India
33. Malay Satay Hut
34. Anapurna
35. Chutney
36. Beba's -N- Cinnamons
37. India Bistro
38. Shamiana in Kirkland
39. India Express Restaurant

Top Albums You Would Never Admit to Owning
1674 votes by 541 people

1. Britney Spears
2. Backstreet Boys
3. Michael Jackson
4. Spice Girls
5. Britney Spears – Baby One More Time
6. Ace of Base
7. New Kids on the Block
8. nSync
9. Milli Vanilli
10. Hanson – Middle of Nowhere
11. Bee Gees Greatest Hits
12. Barry Manilow
13. Hanson
14. Barry Manilow's Greatest Hits
15. Vanilla Ice
16. Kelly Clarkson – Breakaway
17. Purple Rain
18. Saturday Night Fever Soundtrack
19. Air Supply
20. Thriller
21. Aqua – Aquarium
22. Bee Gees
23. Celine Dion
24. Aqua
25. Jessica Simpson
26. Yanni
27. Hillary Duff
28. Spice Girls – Spice World
29. Gary Glitter – Greatest Hits
30. Green Day – American Idiot
31. Abba
32. Nirvana – Nevermind
33. Elton John
34. John Tesh – Live at Red Rocks
35. Abba Gold
36. The Black Album
37. Ashlee Simpson
38. Grease
39. Alvin and the Chipmunks
40. Tiffany

Top Classical Music Composers
2121 votes by 666 people

1. Wolfgang Amadeus Mozart
2. Ludwig van Beethoven
3. Johann Sebastian Bach
4. Frédéric Chopin
5. Antonio Vivaldi
6. Pyotr Ilyich Tchaikovsky
7. Richard Wagner
8. Johannes Brahms
9. Georg Friedrich Handel
10. Franz Joseph Haydn
11. Claude Debussy
12. Antonín Dvořák
13. Sergei Rachmaninoff
14. Dmitri Shostakovich
15. Gustav Holst
16. Gustav Mahler
17. Richard Strauss
18. Giuseppe Verdi
19. Vangelis
20. Igor Stravinsky
21. Franz Schubert
22. John Williams
23. Carl Orff
24. Johann Pachelbel
25. Maurice Ravel
26. Georges Bizet
27. Franz Liszt
28. Hector Berlioz
29. Erik Satie
30. Sergei Prokofiev
31. Modest Mussorgsky
32. Robert Schumann
33. Aaron Copland
34. Niccolò Paganini
35. Giacomo Puccini
36. William Byrd
37. Samuel Barber
38. Jean Sibelius
39. Camille Saint-Saëns
40. Jonathan FeBland

Top Movie Comedies of All-Time
459 votes by 117 people

1. Monty Python and the Holy Grail
2. Caddyshack
3. Airplane!
4. Blazing Saddles
5. Some Like It Hot
6. Something About Mary
7. This is Spinal Tap
8. The Naked Gun
9. Young Frankenstein
10. Dumb and Dumber
11. Animal House
12. Spaceballs
13. Zoolander
14. Blues Brothers
15. Dr. Strangelove
16. Dodgeball
17. Duck Soup
18. The Other Sister
19. Office Space
20. Monty Python's Life of Brian
21. Ferris Bueler's Day off
22. National Lampoon's Christmas Vacation
23. American Pie
24. Groundhog Day
25. 40 Year Old Virgin
26. His Girl Friday
27. Up in Smoke
28. The Pink Panther
29. Big
30. A Fish Called Wanda
31. Beetlejuice
32. The Princess Bride
33. Ace Ventura
34. The Jerk
35. stripes
36. Austin Powers: International Man of Mystery
37. The Mask
38. Meet the Parents
39. Half Baked
40. Old School

Loudest Bands
2056 votes by 660 people

1. Metallica
2. The Who
3. AC/DC
4. Kiss
5. Rolling Stones
6. Motorhead
7. Slipknot
8. Led Zeppelin
9. Black Sabbath
10. Pantera
11. Iron Maiden
12. Manowar
13. Aerosmith
14. Megadeth
15. The Ramones
16. Slayer
17. Korn
18. System of a Down
19. Nirvana
20. Mötley Crüe
21. Spinal Tap
22. Van Halen
23. Guns N' Roses
24. Deep Purple
25. Linkin Park
26. Green Day
27. GWAR
28. U2
29. Rammstein
30. Nine Inch Nails
31. Judas Priest
32. Anthrax
33. Poison
34. Def Leppard
35. Rage Against the Machine
36. Queen
37. Sex Pistols
38. Tool
39. Sepultura
40. Limp Bizkit

Most Beautiful View Spots in Seattle, WA
586 votes by 204 people

1. Space Needle
2. Alki Beach
3. Kerry Park
4. Gas Works Park
5. Queen Anne Hill
6. Golden Gardens
7. Discovery Park
8. Green Lake
9. Chittenden Locks & Carl English Botanical Gardens
10. Belvedere Viewpoint
11. Smith Tower
12. Magnolia Bluff
13. Snoqualmie Falls
14. Elliot Bay
15. The Arboretum
16. Pike Place Market
17. Bainbridge Island
18. Salty's on Alki
19. Fisherman's Terminal
20. Puget Sound
21. Columbia Tower Club
22. Seattle Waterfront
23. Washington Park Arboretum
24. Carkeek Park
25. Lake Washington
26. Safeco Field
27. Lincoln Park
28. 1st Avenue overlooking Puget Sound
29. Hamilton Viewpoint
30. Pike Market
31. 34th Ave S looking east over the I-90 Floating Bridge
32. Volunteer Park
33. Queen Anne Hill – Walkway on the southside on top of the hill
34. Olympic Peninsula
35. Waterfront Park
36. Pioneer Square
37. I-5 Southbound Bridge just before downtown exits.
38. South Lake Union from the water
39. Skinlogic – Skin Care Center
40. Warwick Hotel

Top Girl Names

2308 votes by 746 people

1. Jennifer
2. Sarah
3. Mary
4. Jessica
5. Hannah
6. Emily
7. Elizabeth
8. Ashley
9. Michelle
10. Rachel
11. Emma
12. Amanda
13. Katherine
14. Julia
15. Christina
16. Laura
17. Samantha
18. Amy
19. Maria
20. Melissa
21. Katie
22. Lauren
23. Tiffany
24. Sophia
25. Nicole
26. Stephanie
27. Jenny
28. Jane
29. Victoria
30. Heather
31. Rebecca
32. Alexis
33. Susan
34. Lisa
35. Linda
36. Angelina
37. Alice
38. Alexandra
39. Madison
40. Amber

Top Parks in Seattle, WA
604 votes by 199 people

1. Discovery Park
2. Gasworks Park
3. Washington Park Arboretum
4. Woodland Park Zoo
5. Green Lake
6. Volunteer Park
7. Alki Beach Park
8. Carkeek Park
9. Golden Gardens
10. Seward Park
11. Marymoor Park
12. Warren G. Magnuson Park
13. Lincoln Park
14. Klondike Gold Rush Natl Park
15. Myrtle Edwards Park
16. 10th Ave E-E Roanoke Park
17. Denny Park
18. Bloedel Reserve
19. Freeway Park
20. Albert Davis Park
21. Fun Forest Amusement Park
22. Ravenna Park
23. Madison Park
24. Waterfall Garden
25. Bellevue Downtown Park
26. Seattle City of: Seattle Aquarium
27. Harbor View Park
28. Cal Anderson Park
29. Hamilton Viewpoint
30. Olympic Sculpture Park
31. Kirkland Waterfront
32. Ablert Davis Park
33. Old Man House
34. Summer Nights at South Lake Union Park
35. Candlebury Park
36. Blake Island
37. Columbia Park
38. Cedar Park
39. Seattle Parks & Recreation
40. Space Age Amusement

Top Movie Lines
421 votes by 105 people

1. Frankly, my dear, I don't give a damn
2. I'll be back
3. Asta la vista, baby
4. Go ahead – make my day
5. I'll be back – Terminator
6. May the force be with you
7. Here's looking at you kid – Casablanca
8. ...You had me at hello
9. Toto, I've got a feeling we're not in Kansas anymore.
10. You Talkin' to Me?
11. Bond...James Bond
12. Show me the Money
13. I'm going to make him an offer he can't refuse. – The Godfather
14. Say ello to my little friend!
15. You complete me.
16. Get busy livin' or get busy dyin'
17. I feel the need... the need for speed.
18. I've Got a Bad Feeling about This.
19. A census taker once tried to test me. I ate his liver with some fava beans and a nice Chianti."
20. Rosebud...
21. Hail to the king, baby.
22. Just when I thought I was out, they pulled me back in"
23. E.T. phone home
24. I am serious, and don't call me Shirley.
25. What we got here is failure to communicate.
26. Gentlemen, you can't fight in here! This is the War Room.
27. That was totally wicked!
28. You're gonna need a bigger boat.
29. Who's scruffy looking?
30. There's a shortage of perfect breasts in the world. It would be a pity to damage yours
31. Help me Obi-Wan, You're my only hope
32. Alright, Mr. DeMille, I'm ready for my closeup.
33. If they can't start a meeting without you, well, that's a meeting worth going to, isn't it? And that's the only kind of meeting you should ever concern yourselves with – Swimming with Sharks
34. Mama always said life was like a box a chocolates, never know what you're gonna get.
35. I haven't been f*ck*d like that since second grade.
36. "Awww, you made me ink..."
37. This town needs an enema.
38. Trust me.

Most Underrated Movies

1583 votes by 493 people

1. Serenity
2. Office Space
3. Boondock Saints
4. Donnie Darko
5. Shawshank Redemption
6. The Iron Giant
7. Memento
8. Fight Club
9. The Princess Bride
10. The Money Pit
11. Garden State
12. Swingers
13. Dark City
14. Crash
15. Starship Troopers
16. Requiem for a Dream
17. Amelie
18. The Village
19. Fear and Loathing in Las Vegas
20. Zoolander
21. Waterworld
22. Eternal Sunshine of the Spotless Mind
23. V for Vendetta
24. American History X
25. The Butterfly Effect
26. Super Troopers
27. Dogma
28. The Game
29. High Fidelity
30. Better Off Dead
31. Being John Malkovich
32. Pi
33. Napoleon Dynamite
34. Vanilla Sky
35. Minority Report
36. Equilibrium
37. Titanic
38. Rounders
39. Jersey Girl
40. Underworld

Top Pizza Parlors in Chicago, IL
627 votes by 207 people

1. Giordano's
2. Gino's East
3. Lou Malnati's Pizzeria
4. Pizzeria Uno
5. Home Run Inn
6. Bella Bacino's
7. Pat's Pizzeria & Ristorante
8. Aurelio's Pizza
9. Bricks Chicago
10. Pizza Hut
11. Chicago Pizza & Oven Grinder
12. Piece
13. Freddie's Pizza & Pasta Parlor
14. Connie's Pizza
15. South Shore Pizza Parlor
16. Jani's Pizza Parlor
17. Pequod's Pizzeria
18. Pompei
19. Leona's
20. Pizza DOC
21. Pizzeria Due
22. My Pi
23. Bellacino's Pizza & Grinders
24. Carmen's Restaurant
25. Freddies Pizza & Pasta Parlor
26. The Godfather's Famous Pizza
27. Bacci's
28. Trattoria Pizzeria Roma
29. Zazzo Pizzeria
30. Edwardo's
31. Pizza Trio
32. Vito & Nick's
33. Uno Chicago Grill
34. Pizza Capri
35. Rosati's
36. Spacca Napoli
37. Father & Sons
38. Candlelight
39. Pizza Metro
40. Uno's

Best Baby Names for Boys

1746 votes by 509 people

1. Michael
2. John
3. David
4. Matthew
5. James
6. Andrew
7. Joshua
8. Thomas
9. Daniel
10. Jack
11. William
12. Adam
13. Jacob
14. Joseph
15. Mark
16. Jonathan
17. Alex
18. Steve
19. Jason
20. Christopher
21. Dan
22. Robert
23. Bill
24. Justin
25. Joe
26. Ryan
27. Alexander
28. Tom
29. Brian
30. Sean
31. Bob
32. Peter
33. Eric
34. Gabriel
35. Jeremy
36. Patrick
37. Nicholas
38. Samuel
39. Stephen
40. Kevin

Top Universities or Colleges

1639 votes by 530 people

1. Harvard University
2. Yale University
3. Massachusetts Institute of Technology
4. Stanford University
5. Princeton University
6. UCLA
7. Duke University
8. University of California, Berkeley
9. University of Michigan
10. Brown University
11. California Institute of Technology
12. Ohio State
13. University of Texas
14. University of Southern California
15. University of Notre Dame
16. Cornell University
17. New York University
18. University of Pennsylvania
19. University of Florida
20. Virginia Tech
21. Penn State
22. University of Chicago
23. UNC
24. Northwestern University
25. Columbia
26. University of Wisconsin
27. Boston University
28. University of Illinois
29. BYU
30. University of Georgia
31. University of California, Santa Barbara
32. Indiana University
33. Reed College
34. University of Minnesota
35. Rutgers University
36. Oxford
37. Carnegie Mellon University
38. University of Alabama
39. Purdue
40. University of Nebraska

Top Sports Cars
1612 votes by 510 people

1. Porsche 911
2. Chevrolet Corvette
3. Ford Mustang
4. Ferrari Enzo
5. Dodge Viper
6. Lamborghini Diablo
7. Jaguar E-Type
8. McLaren F1
9. Nissan 350Z
10. Lotus Elise
11. Ford GT
12. BMW M3
13. Bugatti Veyron
14. Ferrari Testarossa
15. Mazda Miata
16. Porsche Carrera GT
17. Chevy Camaro
18. Audi TT
19. Lamborghini Murcielago
20. BMW Z3
21. Mazda Rx8
22. Mitsubishi Eclipse
23. Dodge Charger
24. BMW M5
25. Toyota Celica
26. Aston Martin DB7
27. BMW Z4
28. Acura NSX
29. Porsche Boxster
30. Pontiac Firebird
31. Toyota Supra
32. Ferrari 360 Modena
33. Saleen S7
34. Honda S2000
35. Ferrari Superamerica
36. Pontiac GTO
37. Infiniti G35
38. MG Midget
39. Aston Martin Vanquish
40. 2006 Pontiac Solstice Roadster

Top Clutch Athletes

2955 votes by 946 people

1. Michael Jordan
2. Joe Montana
3. Tiger Woods
4. Larry Bird
5. Derek Jeter
6. John Elway
7. Wayne Gretzky
8. Tom Brady
9. Reggie Jackson
10. Brett Favre
11. Reggie Miller
12. Magic Johnson
13. Peyton Manning
14. David Ortiz
15. Babe Ruth
16. Kobe Bryant
17. Muhammad Ali
18. Robert Horry
19. Kirk Gibson
20. Barry Bonds
21. Adam Vinatieri
22. Jerry Rice
23. Dan Marino
24. Tracy McGrady
25. Pete Rose
26. Cassie Johnson
27. Lance Armstrong
28. Lebron James
29. Joe Namath
30. Ted Williams
31. Walter Payton
32. Mariano Rivera
33. Steve Young
34. Patrick Roy
35. Barry Sanders
36. Curt Schilling
37. Mario Lemieux
38. Pelé
39. Michael Vick
40. Sandy Koufax

Best Front-Person of a Music Band
256 votes by 54 people

1. Freddie Mercury – Queen
2. Bono – U2
3. Axl Rose
4. Dave Matthews
5. Roger Daltry – The Who
6. Mick Jagger – Rolling Stones
7. Jim Morrison
8. Robert Plant – Led Zeppelin
9. Steven Tyler – Aerosmith
10. Kurt Cobain
11. John Bon Jovi
12. Gwen Stefani
13. Eddie Vedder
14. Ozzy Osbourne
15. Gavin Rosdale – Bush
16. Thom Yorke
17. Billie Joe Armstrong
18. Chris Martin
19. Maynard James Keenan
20. Robert Plant
21. John Lennon
22. Roger Waters
23. David Lee Roth
24. James Hetfield
25. Adam Levine – Maroon 5
26. Iggy Pop.
27. Morrissey
28. Robert Smith
29. Johnny Cash
30. Sammy Hagar – Van Halen
31. Mira Aroyo – Ladytron
32. Davy Havoc – A.F.I
33. Stephen Tyler
34. Mick Jagger
35. Ginger Coyote – The White Trash Debutantes
36. Layne Staley
37. Jon Bon Jovi – Bon Jovi
38. Marty Casey
39. Michael Stipe
40. Annie Lennox –The Eurythmics

Best India Pale Ales

361 votes by 115 people

1. Anchor Liberty Ale
2. Stone IPA
3. Alexander Keith's
4. Victory Brewing Company's Hopdevil Ale
5. Diamond Knot
6. Smuttynose IPA
7. Sierra Nevada Pale Ale
8. Dogfish Head
9. Samuel Smith's India Ale
10. Ruination
11. Sam Adams Pale Ale
12. Dog Fish Head 90-Minute
13. Greene King IPA
14. Laconner India Pale Ale
15. India Pelican Ale
16. Tankhouse Ale
17. Red Hook
18. Summit India Pale Ale
19. Hodgson's Ipa
20. Long Trail Unfiltered IPA
21. Full Sail IPA
22. Lagunitas Maximus
23. Big A IPA
24. Brooklyn East Pale India Ale
25. Magic Hat HIPA
26. Bridgeport IPA
27. Sprecher India Pale Ale
28. Saranac
29. Taj
30. Berkshire Brewing Company Steel Rail Extra Pale Ale
31. C-Note Imperial IPA
32. Chinook
33. Shefford Pale Ale
34. Arcadia IPA
35. Three Floyd's Dreadnaught
36. Stoudt's Double IPA
37. Freeminer Trafalgar
38. Santa Fe Pale Ale
39. McEwan's
40. Anderson Valley Brewing Company Hop Ottin' IPA

Top after Work Bars in Seattle, WA
554 votes by 166 people

1. Contour
2. Marcus' Martini Heaven
3. Fado Irish Pub
4. Chapel
5. Linda's Tavern
6. Celtic Bayou Brewpub
7. The People's Pub
8. Zig Zag Cafe
9. Chandler's Crabhouse
10. Norm's Eatery & Ale House
11. Temple Billiards
12. Del Rey
13. The Garage
14. Nite Lite Lounge
15. Neumo's
16. Metropolitan Grill
17. Capitol Club
18. Bluwater Bistro
19. Alibi Room
20. Six Arms
21. Fox Sports Grill
22. Red Door
23. Elliott Bay Brewery & Pub
24. Fx McRory's
25. Six Arms McMenamins
26. Barca
27. Viceroy
28. El Camino
29. Fado's
30. Owl 'N Thistle Irish Pub
31. Elysian
32. Pink Door
33. The War Room
34. Columbia City Ale House
35. Pegasus Coffee Bar
36. Peoples Pub
37. Marcus'
38. Bad Juju Lounge
39. Wasabi Bistro
40. Collins Pub

Most Obnoxious Celebrities

3000 votes by 946 people

1. Paris Hilton
2. Tom Cruise
3. Britney Spears
4. Jessica Simpson
5. Lindsay Lohan
6. Nicole Richie
7. Howard Stern
8. Courtney Love
9. Carrot Top
10. Madonna
11. Donald Trump
12. Jennifer Lopez
13. Bill O'Reilly
14. Brad Pitt
15. Joan Rivers
16. George Bush
17. Michael Jackson
18. Ashton Kutcher
19. Oprah Winfrey
20. Jim Carrey
21. Angelina Jolie
22. Hilary Duff
23. Rush Limbaugh
24. Michael Moore
25. 50 Cent
26. Kanye West
27. Tara Reid
28. Roseanne Barr
29. Martha Stewart
30. Sean Penn
31. Russell Crowe
32. Rosie O'Donnell
33. Tom Green
34. Andy Dick
35. Jennifer Aniston
36. Eminem
37. Pamela Anderson
38. Jack Black
39. Mariah Carey
40. Jay Leno

Top Movies You Watch over and over

2148 votes by 693 people

1. Star Wars
2. The Matrix
3. Fight Club
4. Lord of the Rings
5. The Princess Bride
6. Pulp Fiction
7. Dirty Dancing
8. The Shawshank Redemption
9. Monty Python and the Holy Grail
10. LOTR I: The Fellowship of the Ring
11. Donnie Darko
12. The Godfather
13. The Wizard of Oz
14. The Big Lebowski
15. Office Space
16. Serenity
17. Titanic
18. The Empire Strikes Back
19. When Harry Met Sally
20. Braveheart
21. Back to the Future
22. Die Hard
23. Terminator 2
24. Forrest Gump
25. Finding Nemo
26. Shrek
27. Gone with the Wind
28. The Blues Brothers
29. Moulin Rouge
30. LOTR III: The Return of the King
31. Return of the Jedi
32. Kill Bill
33. Napoleon Dynamite
34. Casablanca
35. Dumb and Dumber
36. Boondock Saints
37. Anchorman
38. Raiders of the Lost Ark
39. Blade Runner
40. You've Got Mail

Best Stripper Names

1462 votes by 468 people

1. Candy
2. Bambi
3. Crystal
4. Tiffany
5. Brandy
6. Destiny
7. ginger
8. Lola
9. Angel
10. Star
11. Amber
12. Bubbles
13. Jenna
14. Bunny
15. Jessica
16. Chastity
17. Cherry
18. Misty
19. Cinnamon
20. diamond
21. Mercedes
22. Sugar
23. Daisy
24. Rose
25. Trixie
26. Sparkle
27. Asia
28. Britney
29. Princess
30. Jewel
31. Peaches
32. Samantha
33. Alexis
34. Sierra
35. flower
36. Lolita
37. Jade
38. Lacy
39. Tawny
40. Lulu

Top Harry Potter Books
951 votes by 297 people

1. Harry Potter and the Goblet of Fire
2. Harry Potter and the Sorcerer's Stone
3. Harry Potter and the Prisoner of Azkaban
4. Harry Potter and the Half-Blood Prince
5. Harry Potter and the Order of the Phoenix
6. Harry Potter and the Chamber of Secrets
7. Harry Potter and the Deathly Hallows
8. Irresistible Rise of Harry Potter
9. Fantastic Beasts and Where to Find Them
10. Looking for God in Harry Potter
11. Quidditch through the Ages
12. Barry Trotter and the Unauthorized Parody by Michael Gerber and Rodger Roundy
13. God, the Devil, and Harry Potter: a Christian Minister's Defense of the Beloved Novels
14. The Sorcerer's Companion

Top Arcade Video Games of All-Time

3020 votes by 1007 people

1. Pac-Man
2. Space Invaders
3. Street Fighter
4. Donkey Kong
5. Mortal Kombat
6. Galaga
7. Pong
8. Asteroids
9. Frogger
10. Centipede
11. Dance Dance Revolution
12. Tetris
13. Mario Brothers
14. Time Crisis
15. Tekken
16. Area 51
17. Defender
18. Dig Dug
19. Joust
20. Teenage Mutant Ninja Turtles
21. Gauntlet
22. Golden Axe
23. X-Men
24. Metal Slug
25. Tempest
26. Pole Position
27. Marvel Vs Capcom
28. Soul Calibur 2
29. Galaxian
30. Q-Bert
31. Doom
32. Robotron 2084
33. Rampage
34. Pinball
35. The Simpsons
36. Outrun
37. House of the Dead
38. Double Dragon
39. Missile Command
40. Arkanoid

Top Books You've Read More Than Once
1648 votes by 529 people

1. Harry Potter and the Prisoner of Azkaban
2. Lord of the Rings
3. The Bible
4. Catcher in the Rye
5. 1984
6. The Stand
7. The Hitchhiker's Guide to the Galaxy
8. The Hobbit
9. Pride and Prejudice
10. Ender's Game
11. DaVinci Code
12. To Kill a Mockingbird
13. Gone with the Wind
14. Animal Farm
15. Dune
16. Little Women
17. Snow Crash
18. Catch 22
19. The Lion, the Witch, and the Wardrobe
20. The Great Gatsby
21. The Fellowship of the Ring
22. The Runaway Jury – John Grisham
23. The Stand by Stephen King
24. Jane Eyre
25. Wuthering Heights
26. Jack & Jill – James Patterson
27. A Game of Thrones
28. Memoirs of a Geisha
29. The Jungle
30. The Shining
31. On the Road – Jack Kerouac
32. War and Peace
33. The Hobbit – JRR Tolkien
34. The Two Towers
35. Angels and Demons
36. The Outsiders
37. Brave New World by Aldous Huxley
38. She's Come Undone
39. The Thorn Birds
40. Emma by Jane Austen

Alternate Names for Mechanical Turk

1116 votes by 363 people

1. mturk
2. Mechturk
3. The Turk
4. Amazon Turk
5. Turking
6. Artificial Artificial Intelligence
7. Money Machine
8. MT
9. Easy Money
10. Amt
11. Turker
12. Cheap Labor
13. Mechanical Jerk
14. free money
15. Money Maker
16. HI (Human Intelligence)
17. Penny for Your Thoughts
18. Aai
19. Real People
20. cheap
21. Waste of Time
22. That Amazon Thing
23. Metu
24. Human Bots
25. Worker Bee
26. Borg
27. Time Killer
28. The Collective
29. Hit Parade
30. Automatic Turk
31. Pennies from Heaven
32. HAI (Humanized Artificial Intelligence)
33. Intelligent Artificial Artificial Intelligence
34. Work for Slave Wages
35. Lot of Work for Little Money
36. Addiction Central
37. Pennies from Amazon
38. Mr. T
39. Humanfactor
40. Computing for Peanuts

Best Companies to Work for

2542 votes by 836 people

1. Google
2. Microsoft
3. Apple
4. IBM
5. Amazon
6. Genentech
7. Starbucks
8. Pixar
9. Dell
10. Wegmans
11. Disney
12. Walmart
13. Yahoo
14. Intel
15. Costco
16. Whole Foods
17. Sony
18. Nintendo
19. SAS
20. Ford
21. Target
22. ebay
23. UPS
24. General Electric
25. GE
26. Best Buy
27. Nike
28. US Government
29. FedEx
30. REI
31. McDonalds
32. Boeing
33. Verizon
34. General Motors
35. Pepsi
36. Wegmans Food Markets
37. Southwest Airlines
38. Proctor and Gamble
39. Coca Cola
40. Valero Energy

Top Hip Neighborhoods to Live in San Francisco
701 votes by 226 people

1. Mission
2. Haight-Ashbury (Upper Haight)
3. North Beach
4. Nob Hill
5. Castro
6. Bernal Heights
7. Soma (South of Market)
8. Chinatown
9. Sunset
10. Hayes Valley
11. Union Square
12. Noe Valley
13. Pacific Heights
14. Berkeley
15. Fisherman's Wharf
16. Deco Ghetto (Mid-Market)
17. Marina
18. Potrero Hill
19. Russian Hill
20. Cole Valley
21. Richmond District
22. Haight & Ashbury
23. Marina District
24. Japantown
25. Alamo Square
26. Twin Peaks
27. Tenderloin
28. Telegraph Hill
29. Golden Gate Park
30. The Haight
31. South Beach
32. Sausalito
33. Fillmore
34. Presidio
35. Bay View
36. Treasure Island
37. Glen Park
38. Columbia Ave
39. Financial District
40. Embarcadero

Best Thrash Metal Bands
369 votes by 105 people

1. Slayer
2. Metallica
3. Megadeth
4. Anthrax
5. Exodus
6. Pantera
7. Overkill
8. Sepultura
9. Motorhead
10. Voivod
11. Gwar!
12. AC/DC
13. Testament
14. Death Angel
15. System of a Down
16. Venom
17. Suicidal Tendencies
18. Dark Angel
19. Rammstein
20. Skid Row
21. We Are the Dead
22. Children of Bodom
23. Snot
24. Vengence Rising
25. Rob Zombie
26. Berzerker
27. Evostic
28. Aggression
29. Mod
30. Fearless Iranians from Hell
31. heavy
32. Wrathchild
33. Chronical Diarrhoea
34. Iron Maiden
35. Cryptic Slaughter
36. S.O.D.
37. Ratt
38. Arch Enemy
39. Poison
40. Kreator

Top Funniest People on TV Today (Real Name)
2612 votes by 853 people

1. Jon Stewart
2. Conan O'Brien
3. Dave Chappelle
4. Jay Leno
5. David Letterman
6. Ellen Degeneres
7. Chris Rock
8. Steve Carell
9. Stephen Colbert
10. Jerry Seinfeld
11. Ray Romano
12. Jim Carrey
13. Jason Lee
14. Larry David
15. David Cross
16. Zach Braff
17. Robin Williams
18. George Lopez
19. Drew Carey
20. Bernie Mac
21. Dane Cook
22. Ricky Gervais
23. Will Farrell
24. Lewis Black
25. Jason Bateman
26. Carlos Mencia
27. Kevin James
28. Charlie Sheen
29. Adam Sandler
30. George Bush
31. Jeff Foxworthy
32. Matt Leblanc
33. Hugh Laurie
34. Bill Cosby
35. Tina Fey
36. Seth MacFarlane
37. George Carlin
38. Bill Maher
39. Jimmy Kimmel
40. Tony Shalhoub

Top Dog Names
2176 votes by 703 people

1. Spot
2. Rover
3. Fido
4. Rex
5. Lassie
6. Spike
7. Max
8. Buddy
9. Sparky
10. Skip
11. Lucky
12. Jake
13. Buster
14. Rocky
15. Fluffy
16. Rufus
17. Sam
18. Rusty
19. Snoopy
20. Lady
21. Princess
22. Sandy
23. Duke
24. King
25. Killer
26. Bailey
27. Shadow
28. Scruffy
29. Butch
30. Benji
31. Bowser
32. Tommy
33. Blackie
34. Bob
35. Bingo
36. Bello
37. Champ
38. Tiger
39. Toby
40. Bud

Top Small Live Music Venues in Seattle, WA

550 votes by 174 people

1. Showbox
2. Neumo's
3. Crocodile Cafe
4. Tractor Tavern
5. Chop Suey
6. Jazz Alley
7. El Corazon
8. The Triple Door
9. Howl At The Moon
10. Sunset Tavern
11. Fenix
12. Vera Project
13. Fun House
14. Studio Seven
15. The Hideaway
16. Benaroya Hall
17. Madison's Cafe Music House
18. Seattle Theater Group
19. Neighbors -Disco
20. Sky Church
21. Catwalk
22. Fenix Underground
23. Tost
24. King Theater
25. The Vogue
26. High Dive
27. The Vera Project
28. J&M Cafe
29. Monkey Pub
30. The Paragon
31. Last Supper Club
32. Celtic Swell
33. Highway 99 Blues Club
34. Hattie's Hat
35. Mural Amphitheater
36. Cafe Darclee
37. Under the Rail
38. Music Experience Project
39. Oar
40. Ladies Musical Club

Best Baseball Players on Steroids

2866 votes by 919 people

1. Barry Bonds
2. Mark McGwire
3. Sammy Sosa
4. Jason Giambi
5. Rafael Palmeiro
6. Jose Canseco
7. Ken Caminiti
8. Alex Sanchez
9. Gary Sheffield
10. Alex Rodriguez
11. Derek Jeter
12. Albert Pujols
13. Roger Clemens
14. Matt Lawton
15. Babe Ruth
16. David Ortiz
17. Jorge Piedra
18. Nomar Garciaparra
19. Jamal Strong
20. Miguel Tejada
21. Mike Piazza
22. Ryan Franklin
23. Mike Morse
24. Curt Schilling
25. Manny Ramirez
26. Jeff Bagwell
27. Frank Thomas
28. Agustin Montero
29. Jim Thome
30. Felix Heredia
31. Darrel Strawberry
32. Johnny Damon
33. Bret Boone
34. Carlos Delgado
35. Bernie Williams
36. Mickey Mantle
37. Carlos Almanzar
38. Joe Dimaggio
39. Javi Herrera
40. Luis Gonzalez

Top Comic Books of All-Time
1217 votes by 384 people

1. Superman
2. Spiderman
3. Batman
4. X-Men
5. Sandman – Neil Gaiman
6. The Watchmen – Alan Moore & Dave Gibbons
7. Sin City – Frank Miller
8. The Dark Knight Returns (Batman) – Frank Miller
9. Archie
10. Calvin and Hobbes
11. Fantastic Four
12. V for Vendetta – Alan Moore & David Lloyd
13. The Hulk
14. The Uncanny X-Men
15. Asterix / Obelix (French)
16. Richie Rich
17. Wolverine
18. Garfield
19. peanuts
20. Daredevil
21. The Punisher
22. Maus – Art Spiegelman
23. Johnny the Homicidal Maniac
24. Spawn
25. Batman – Bob Kane
26. Preacher – Garth Ennis & Steve Dillon
27. Popeye – E. Segar
28. Transmetropolitan – Warren Ellis
29. Wonder Woman
30. Fables – Bill Willingham
31. G.I. Joe
32. The Avengers
33. Saga of the Swamp Thing – Alan Moore
34. League of Extraodinary Gentlemen – Alan Moore
35. The Crow – James O'Barr
36. Hitchhiker's Guide to the Universe by Douglas Adams
37. Hellboy
38. Hellblazer (John Constantine)
39. Green Lantern
40. The Flash

Top Independent Coffee Houses in Chicago, IL

523 votes by 162 people

1. Intelligentsia Coffee
2. Metropolis
3. Savor the Flavor Coffee House
4. Filter
5. Julius Meinl Cafe
6. Bourgeois Pig
7. Sip
8. Uncommon Ground
9. Atomix
10. Kafein
11. Kristoffer's Cafe & Bakery
12. F212
13. Jinx (1928 W Division)
14. The Perfect Cup
15. Albert's Cafe & Patisserie
16. Caffe de Luca
17. Gourmand Coffee & Teas
18. Ace Coffee Bar
19. The Plush Horse
20. Earwax Cafe
21. Sweet Thang
22. Ritz Coffee House
23. Toast
24. Manny's Coffee Shop & Deli
25. Ohio House Coffee Shop
26. West Gate Coffeehouse
27. Ashbary Coffee House
28. Angelica's Coffee House
29. AL Cappacino's
30. Cafe Origin
31. The Grind
32. Pick Me up Cafe
33. Kopi – a Traveler's Cafe
34. Beans and Bagels
35. A Taste of Heaven
36. Petersen's Espresso Cafe
37. Some like It Black Coffee Club
38. Crimsoncup Coffee & Tea
39. Mojoe's Cafe Lounge
40. Bean Addiction

Top Rock Star Deaths
2969 votes by 957 people

1. Kurt Cobain
2. John Lennon
3. Elvis Presley
4. Jimi Hendrix
5. Jim Morrison
6. Buddy Holly
7. Janis Joplin
8. Freddie Mercury
9. Jerry Garcia
10. Michael Hutchence
11. Dimebag Darrell
12. John Bonham
13. Tupac Shakur
14. Cliff Burton
15. Keith Moon
16. Mama Cass
17. Johnny Cash
18. Richie Valens
19. Stevie Ray Vaughn
20. Sid Vicious
21. Ian Curtis
22. George Harrison
23. Layne Staley
24. Bon Scott
25. Elliott Smith
26. John Denver
27. Bob Marley
28. Duane Allman
29. Randy Rhoads
30. Brian Jones
31. Frank Zappa
32. Aaliyah
33. John Entwistle
34. Jeff Buckley
35. Joey Ramone
36. Bradley Nowell
37. James Dean
38. Gram Parsons
39. Karen Carpenter
40. Marvin Gaye

Worst Inventions
3037 votes by 958 people

1. Atomic Bomb
2. cell phones
3. Pet Rock
4. Chia Pet
5. The Clapper
6. Television
7. guns
8. Landmines
9. Segway
10. Flowbee
11. Cigarettes
12. Spork
13. Reality TV
14. Spray-Paint Hair
15. Internet
16. computer
17. Pay Toilet
18. Car Alarms
19. Religion
20. iPod
21. New Coke
22. Solar Powered Flashlight
23. Spam
24. the wheel
25. gunpowder
26. car
27. Electric Chair
28. Furby
29. microwave
30. Microsoft Windows
31. Electronic Voting MacHines
32. Pagers
33. Suvs
34. edible underwear
35. Sports Utility Vehicle
36. Firearms
37. Sliced Bread
38. Pocket Fisherman
39. War
40. Call Waiting

Top Movies You Secretly Loved

1989 votes by 635 people

1. Titanic
2. The Notebook
3. Princess Bride
4. Mean Girls
5. Dirty Dancing
6. Gone with the Wind
7. Brokeback Mountain
8. Beaches
9. Star Wars
10. Moulin Rouge
11. 10 Things I Hate about You
12. Bambi
13. Amelie
14. Pretty Woman
15. Dumb and Dumber
16. Steel Magnolias
17. Bring it On
18. Sleepless in Seattle
19. Grease
20. Lion King
21. A Walk to Remember
22. Legally Blonde
23. Armageddon
24. Sound of Music
25. Love Actually
26. Crash
27. Waterworld
28. The Cutting Edge
29. Casablanca
30. Notting Hill
31. Saw
32. The Goonies
33. Finding Nemo
34. Serendipity
35. Crossroads
36. Red Dawn
37. Sixteen Candles
38. Terminator 2
39. Spiceworld
40. Clueless

Top Small Live Music Venues in Chicago, IL
582 votes by 174 people

1. The Metro
2. Schubas Tavern
3. Empty Bottle
4. Double Door
5. Aragon
6. House of Blues
7. Green Mill Cocktail Lounge
8. Park West
9. Elbo Room
10. The Vic
11. Buddy Guy's Legends
12. Abbey Pub
13. Beat Kitchen
14. Martyrs'
15. Kingston Mines
16. Davenport's
17. Kaz Bar
18. Blue Chicago
19. Fireside Bowl
20. Old Town School of Folk Music
21. The Wild Hare
22. Oasis One-Sixty
23. Velvet Lounge
24. Bottom Lounge
25. Subterranean
26. Hothouse
27. Jilly's
28. Logan Square Auditorium
29. Funky Buddha Lounge
30. House of Blues Chicago
31. Andy's Jazz Club
32. The Bottom Lounge
33. Uncommon Ground
34. Riviera Theater
35. Vic
36. The Park West
37. Millenium Park
38. Galway Arms
39. Aragon Ballroom
40. Wild Hare Limited

Top Steak Houses in Seattle, WA

625 votes by 217 people

1. Metropolitan Grill
2. Ruth's Chris Steak House
3. El Gaucho
4. Daniel's Broiler
5. JaK's Grill
6. Morton's
7. Union Square Grill
8. The Keg
9. Rock Salt Steaks & Seafood
10. Outback
11. Black Angus
12. Brooklyn Seafood-Steak House
13. Melrose Grill
14. 94 Stewart Restaurant
15. The Iris Grill
16. Benihana
17. Buenos Aires Grill
18. Rimrock Steakhouse
19. F X MC Rory's Steak Chop
20. Ponti
21. Geneva
22. Stanley & Seafort's
23. Taj Cafe
24. Duke's
25. The Ale House
26. George Martin
27. Longhorn
28. DC Grill
29. Claim Jumper
30. Hanks Place
31. 94 Stewart
32. Ana Barbeque Shop
33. The Islander
34. Billys Philly Steakhouse
35. Icon Grill
36. Applebee's
37. Jack's Broiler
38. Jakes Grill
39. Chris' Steak House
40. Spencers

Top Classic Novels of All-Time
959 votes by 296 people

1. Pride and Prejudice
2. Moby Dick
3. The Adventures of Huckleberry Finn
4. Gone with the Wind
5. Jane Eyre
6. The Great Gatsby
7. To Kill a Mockingbird
8. Crime and Punishment
9. Great Expectations
10. A Tale of Two Cities
11. War and Peace
12. Wuthering Heights
13. Catcher in the Rye
14. Little Women
15. Grapes of Wrath
16. 1984
17. Tom Sawyer
18. The Count of Monte Cristo
19. Lord of the Flies
20. The Scarlet Letter
21. David Copperfield
22. A Tale of Two Cities
23. Of Mice and Men
24. Les Miserables
25. Oliver Twist
26. Catch 22
27. Frankenstein
28. Lord of the Rings
29. Emma
30. Dracula
31. Lolita
32. Tom Sawyer
33. Don Quixote
34. The Hobbit
35. The Old Man and the Sea
36. Moby Dick
37. Catch-22
38. Anna Karenina
39. War of the Worlds
40. The Grapes of Wrath

Top Rap Artists

2102 votes by 676 people

1. Eminem
2. Tupac
3. Dr. Dre
4. 50 Cent
5. Snoop Dogg
6. Run DMC
7. Notorious BIG
8. Jay-Z
9. Public Enemy
10. Kanye West
11. Beastie Boys
12. LL Cool J
13. Nelly
14. Will Smith
15. MC Hammer
16. Ice Cube
17. P Diddy
18. Ice T
19. Grandmaster Flash
20. Coolio
21. NWA
22. DMX
23. Ludacris
24. Eazy-E
25. Nas
26. Vanilla Ice
27. Busta Rhymes
28. Rakim
29. A Tribe Called Quest
30. Missy Elliot
31. Outkast
32. Mos Def
33. Aesop Rock
34. Wu Tang Clan
35. Dr. Dre (Andre Romel Young)
36. De La Soul
37. Kurtis Blow
38. Queen Latifah
39. Krs-One
40. Paul Wall

Top Musicians to Dine with
2758 votes by 898 people

1. Bono
2. Paul McCartney
3. Madonna
4. John Lennon
5. Bob Dylan
6. David Bowie
7. Sting
8. Trent Reznor
9. Ozzy Osbourne
10. Mick Jagger
11. Elton John
12. Eminem
13. Dave Matthews
14. Eric Clapton
15. Billy Joel
16. Mozart
17. Kurt Cobain
18. Michael Jackson
19. Alanis Morissette
20. Britney Spears
21. Jimi Hendrix
22. Thom Yorke
23. Bon Jovi
24. Elvis Presley
25. Tom Waits
26. Frank Sinatra
27. Jimmy Page
28. Prince
29. Marilyn Manson
30. Jim Morrison
31. Johann Sebastian Bach
32. Bruce Springsteen
33. Billy Corgan
34. Mariah Carey
35. John Mayer
36. Roger Waters
37. Michael Stipe
38. Robert Plant
39. Weird Al Yankovic
40. Freddie Mercury

Top Books That Changed Your Life
884 votes by 277 people

1. The Bible
2. Catcher in the Rye
3. 1984
4. The DaVinci Code
5. The Color Purple – Alice Walker
6. Lord of the Rings
7. Ender's Game
8. On the Road – Jack Kerouac
9. The Giver
10. The Celestine Prophecy
11. To Kill a Mockingbird
12. Women Are from Venus : How to Get What You Want in Your Relationships – John Gray
13. Lord of the Flies
14. The Great Gatsby
15. Jane Eyre
16. The Seven Habits of Highly Effective People
17. The Fountainhead
18. Roots – Alex Haley
19. Animal Farm
20. Stranger in a Strange Land
21. The Five People You Meet in Heaven
22. The Color Purple
23. Brave New World
24. The Perks of Being a Wallflower
25. The Stranger
26. In Cold Blood
27. Fear and Loathing in Las Vegas
28. Atlas Shrugged
29. Tuesdays with Morrie
30. Of Mice and Men
31. Girlfriend in a Coma
32. Go Ask Alice
33. The Monk Who Sold His Ferrari
34. A Tree Grows in Brooklyn
35. The Koran
36. One Day in the Life of Ivan Denisovich
37. The World is Flat
38. The Alchemist
39. The Stand
40. On the Road

Top Hockey Teams
889 *votes by 280 people*

1. Detroit Red Wings
2. Montreal Canadiens
3. Toronto Maple Leafs
4. New York Rangers
5. Boston Bruins
6. New Jersey Devils
7. Edmonton Oilers
8. Pittsburgh Penguins
9. Chicago Blackhawks
10. New York Islanders
11. Philadelphia Flyers
12. Dallas Stars
13. Mighty Ducks
14. San Jose Sharks
15. LA Kings
16. Colorado Avalanche
17. Los Angeles Kings
18. Ottawa Senators
19. Calgary Flames
20. Vancouver Canucks
21. Carolina Hurricanes
22. St. Louis Blues
23. Florida Panthers
24. Capitals
25. Buffalo Sabres
26. Canada
27. Russia
28. Minnesota Wild
29. Wisconsin Badgers
30. Nashville Predators
31. Tampa Bay Lightning
32. St. Louis Blues 2000-01
33. Dallas Stars 1999
34. Montreal, Montreal Canadiens, 1960
35. Germany
36. Oulun Kärpät
37. 2005 Anaheim Mighty Ducks
38. 1980 U.S.A
39. The Wild
40. Detroit Flyers

Best Interview Questions for a Programmer

392 votes by 121 people

1. Languages Known
2. What projects have you worked on?
3. Reverse a linked list
4. What languages can you program in?
5. How much experience have you had using our software?
6. Tell me about a program you wrote for your personal use.
7. Describe software development life cycle?
8. What language do you use?
9. How often do you contact the client during development?
10. Why did you make this?
11. What is the biggest time waster for commercial software developers? How do you handle that?
12. What websites do you subscribe to?
13. What did you learn in college?
14. What books have you read about development?
15. What industry sites and blogs do you read regularly?
16. Tell me about a time you missed a deadline; how did you recover?
17. Why did you choose this profession?
18. Do you prefer to work alone or on a team?
19. Why are manhole covers round?
20. What's a singleton?
21. What is your favorite programming language and why?
22. Here is a workstation, write a function to...
23. What is the toughest problem you have ever delt with?
24. What is a deterministic finite automaton?
25. What is your software process?
26. What design patterns do you find most useful?
27. If given a new problem, what is your first step in producing code?
28. What purpose does your software serve?
29. If a general procedure has no error handler enabled and an error occurs, what happens?
30. Define "race condition".
31. Here's a light bulb. determine its volume.
32. What separates your software from others in the same category?
33. What is the ratio between design, code, test and how would you modify them to optimize quality and efficiency
34. What do you consider important when improving a given piece of software, and why?
35. Given two dates, ranging from between 1 AD and today, write a function to return the number of days between the dates
36. What could have been improved in your last project?
37. What is the biggest technology of the next 10 years?

Top Web 2.0 Startup Ideas
186 votes by 50 people

1. del.icio.us
2. digg.com
3. gmail
4. Social Networking
5. ww.flickr.com
6. Facebook
7. Google Maps Mashups
8. newsvine.com
9. 30boxes
10. reddit.com
11. Pandora
12. AJAX Interface
13. Paypal
14. listafterlist.com
15. meebo.com
16. blinklist.com
17. Flukiest
18. yahoo.com
19. Desktop Publishing
20. Firefox
21. Assistant Interface for Collaborative Projects
22. Program that reads aloud blogs in TV character voice and personality
23. yelp.com
24. Crowdsourcing
25. Free Movies
26. Complete Ajax Based Office Suite
27. riya.com
28. Netvibes
29. Wikipedia
30. YouTube
31. farecast.com
32. "Wikipyramid Power" hats to capture the wisdom of the crowds
33. Free TV Shows
34. Mobile Phone Search
35. Location Based Wiki
36. Consultant
37. Interactive Charting
38. rojo.com
39. Tech News Site: Techcrunch
40. housingmaps.com

Top Jazz Musicians
1629 votes by 525 people

1. Miles Davis
2. Louis Armstrong
3. John Coltrane
4. Duke Ellington
5. Charlie Parker
6. Thelonious Monk
7. Ella Fitzgerald
8. Dizzy Gillespie
9. Count Basie
10. BB King
11. Dave Brubeck
12. Charles Mingus
13. Billie Holiday
14. Kenny G
15. Ray Charles
16. Wynton Marsalis
17. Benny Goodman
18. Norah Jones
19. Herbie Hancock
20. Bill Evans
21. Ornette Coleman
22. Chet Baker
23. Buddy Rich
24. Stan Getz
25. Cab Calloway
26. Sun Ra
27. Nina Simone
28. Jelly Roll Morton
29. George Benson
30. Sidney Bechet
31. Django Reinhardt
32. Cole Porter
33. Eric Dolphy
34. Pat Metheny
35. Tommy Dorsey
36. Jaco Pastorius
37. Lionel Hampton
38. Gene Krupa
39. Glenn Miller
40. Oscar Peterson

Top Guitar Players
1597 votes by 513 people

1. Jimi Hendrix
2. Eric Clapton
3. Jimmy Page
4. Carlos Santana
5. Eddie Van Halen
6. Stevie Ray Vaughan
7. Slash
8. Steve Vai
9. B.B. King
10. Joe Satriani
11. Kurt Cobain
12. Yngwie Malmsteen
13. John Petrucci
14. Tom Morello
15. George Harrison
16. Brian May
17. Randy Rhoads
18. Kirk Hammett
19. Jerry Garcia
20. Andres Segovia
21. Robert Johnson
22. Bob Dylan
23. David Gilmour
24. Buckethead
25. Jeff Beck
26. Chuck Berry
27. Johnny Cash
28. The Edge
29. Angus Young
30. Dave Mustaine
31. Elvis Presley
32. AL Di Meola
33. Duane Allman
34. Keith Richards
35. Mark Knopfler
36. Neil Young
37. Paul McCartney
38. John Mayer
39. Pete Townshend
40. Chet Atkins

Clever Restaurant Names
907 votes by 284 people

1. Once upon a Thai
2. Burger King
3. McDonalds
4. Hooters
5. Olive Garden
6. Dew Drop Inn
7. IHOP
8. Outback
9. Wok and Roll
10. Central Perk
11. The Stinking Rose
12. Taco Bell
13. Red Lobster
14. Seoul Food
15. Pizza Hut
16. Tequila Mockingbird
17. What the Pho?
18. Brew Ha Ha
19. Buca di Beppo
20. Chili's
21. Thai Tanic
22. Serendipity
23. Fu King Chinese
24. In-n-Out
25. Utterly Ice Cream
26. Kentucky Fried Chicken
27. Roadkill Café
28. TGI Fridays
29. Wendy's
30. Dick's Last Resort
31. Subway
32. Chipotle
33. Eat at Joes
34. T.G.I. Fridays
35. Somewhere Else Cafe
36. Baja Fresh
37. Aroma Borealis
38. Apple
39. Cheesecake Factory
40. Fuddruckers

Least Talented Stars
2079 votes by 676 people

1. Britney Spears
2. Ashlee Simpson
3. Jessica Simpson
4. Lindsay Lohan
5. 50 Cent
6. Hillary Duff
7. Madonna
8. William Hung
9. Eminem
10. Justin Timberlake
11. Christina Aguilera
12. Mariah Carey
13. Milli Vanilli
14. Paris Hilton
15. Avril Lavigne
16. Backstreet Boys
17. Kelly Clarkson
18. Jennifer Lopez
19. Vanilla Ice
20. Clay Aiken
21. Michael Jackson
22. Courtney Love
23. Scott Stapp
24. Celine Dion
25. Puff Daddy
26. Fred Durst
27. Gwen Stefani
28. P. Diddy
29. Kevin Federline
30. Yoko Ono
31. Aaron Carter
32. R. Kelly
33. Michael Bolton
34. Cher
35. William Shatner
36. Janet Jackson
37. pink
38. Kanye West
39. Good Charlotte
40. Green Day

Top Movies to Cheer You up

1641 votes by 528 people

1. Office Space
2. Shrek
3. The Princess Bride
4. The Sound of Music
5. Amelie
6. Finding Nemo
7. Dumb and Dumber
8. Happy Gilmore
9. Super Troopers
10. Ice Age
11. American Pie
12. The Shawshank Redemption
13. Monty Python and the Holy Grail
14. Napoleon Dynamite
15. Spaceballs
16. When Harry Met Sally
17. Pulp Fiction
18. Fight Club
19. Star Wars
20. The Matrix
21. It's a Wonderful Life
22. Zoolander
23. Wedding Crashers
24. Meet the Parents
25. Pretty Woman
26. Back to the Future
27. Toy Story
28. The Blues Brothers
29. There's Something about Mary
30. Garden State
31. Clerks
32. Dodgeball
33. The Wizard of Oz
34. Anchorman
35. Top Gun
36. Old School
37. Half Baked
38. Scary Movie 3
39. Love Actually
40. The Incredibles

Top Console Video Games

1548 votes by 510 people

1. Halo 2
2. Xbox 360
3. Grand Theft Auto: San Andreas
4. Playstation 2
5. Call of Duty 2
6. Madden 2006
7. Resident Evil 4
8. Final Fantasy X
9. PS2
10. Gamecube
11. Nintendo DS
12. Metal Gear Solid
13. We Love Katamari
14. Katamari Damacy
15. God of War
16. Shadow of the Colossus
17. The Sims 2
18. Project Gotham Racing 3
19. Need for Speed: Most Wanted
20. Gran Turismo 4
21. Mario Kart DS
22. Gun
23. Nintendo Gamecube
24. Super Smash Brothers
25. Perfect Dark Zero
26. PSP
27. Socom
28. Half Life 2
29. Animal Crossing
30. Dragon Quest VIII
31. Kingdom Hearts
32. NBA Live 2006
33. Guitar Hero
34. Star Wars Battlefront II
35. Prince of Persia
36. Fifa 2006
37. King Kong
38. GTA San Andreas
39. Madden Football
40. Spiderman 2

Top Romance Novels
687 votes by 218 people

1. Pride and Prejudice
2. Gone with the Wind
3. Jane Eyre
4. Wuthering Heights
5. Outlander by Diana Gabaldon
6. The Notebook
7. Devil in Winter
8. Paradise – Judith McNaught
9. Emma
10. Bridges of Madison County
11. A Walk to Remember
12. Montana Sky – Nora Roberts
13. It Had to Be You by Susan Elizabeth Phillips
14. Rebecca
15. Sense and Sensibility
16. The Villa – Nora Roberts
17. To Love Again – Danielle Steele
18. Lord of Scoundrels
19. Thorn Birds
20. On Beauty: a Novel
21. A Breath of Snow and Ashes
22. Time Traveler's Wife – Audrey Niffenegger
23. Dragonfly in Amber by Diana Gabaldon
24. Persuasion
25. The Other Boleyn Girl
26. Dream a Little Dream by Susan Elizabeth Phillips
27. This Can't Be Love
28. Love Story by Erich Segal
29. Shanna
30. Shopgirl
31. Master of Pleasure
32. A Kingdom of Dreams – Judith McNaught
33. Remember When – Judith McNaught
34. Love Story
35. Poison Study
36. Shanna by Kathleen Woodiwiss
37. Harry Potter and the Prisoner of Azkaban
38. Dark Lover by J.R. Ward
39. Romeo & Juliet
40. Lolita – Vladimir Nabokov

Best Charitable Organizations
2499 votes by 820 people

1. Red Cross
2. Salvation Army
3. United Way
4. UNICEF
5. Goodwill
6. Habitat for Humanity
7. Oxfam
8. American Cancer Society
9. Make a Wish Foundation
10. Doctors without Borders
11. Humane Society
12. ASPCA
13. Amnesty International
14. Greenpeace
15. Make a Wish
16. World Wildlife Fund
17. World Vision
18. Catholic Charities
19. March of Dimes
20. PETA
21. Feed the Children
22. Ronald McDonald House
23. Bill and Melinda Gates Foundation
24. Christian Children's Fund
25. American Heart Association
26. Heifer International
27. WWF
28. ACLU
29. Planned Parenthood
30. Toys for Tots
31. Cancer research
32. Childs Play
33. Electronic Frontier Foundation
34. CARE
35. Boys & Girls Club
36. Second Harvest
37. St. Jude's Children's Hospital
38. St. Judes
39. Friends of the Public Garden
40. Special Olympics

Top Soap Stars

862 votes by 265 people

1. Susan Lucci
2. Deidre Hall
3. Kelly Ripa
4. Kelly Monaco
5. Eric Braeden
6. Anthony Geary
7. Maurice Benard
8. Lisa Rinna
9. Alison Sweeney
10. Kristian Alfonso
11. Erika Slezak
12. Shane Richie
13. Peter Reckell
14. Martha Byrne
15. Heather Locklear
16. Jess Walton
17. Roger Howart
18. Jacob Young
19. Kim Zimmer
20. Melody Thomas Scott
21. Julia Barr
22. Jennifer Aniston
23. Thorsten Kaye
24. Eva Longoria
25. Katherine Kelly Lang
26. Lauralee Bell
27. Cameron Mathison
28. Barbara Windsor
29. Ashley Jones
30. Demi Moore
31. Rick Springfield
32. Larry Hagman
33. Rebecca Budig
34. Michael E. Knight
35. Cady McClain
36. Hunter Tylo
37. Bobbie Eakes
38. David Canary
39. Jack Wagner
40. Jon Lindstrom

Top Pizza Parlors in San Francisco, CA

889 votes by 279 people

1. Goat Hill Pizza
2. North Beach Pizza
3. Tommasso's
4. Arinell Pizza
5. Extreme Pizza
6. Little Star Pizza
7. ZA Pizza
8. Arizmendi
9. Pinky's Pizza Parlor
10. Golden Boy
11. Mr. Pizza Man
12. Pizza Hut
13. Amici's East Coast Pizzeria
14. Pauline's Pizza
15. Zachary's Chicago Pizza
16. Pizza Orgasmica
17. Pizzetta 211
18. Postrio
19. Go Getters Pizza
20. Papa Johns
21. Straw Hat Pizza
22. Escape from New York Pizza
23. Dominos
24. Vino E Cucina Trattoria
25. Marina Pizza Parlor
26. Cheese Board
27. Pomodoro Gourmet Pizza
28. Blondie's
29. A16
30. North Beach Pizza: North Beach
31. California Pizza Kitchen
32. Napoli Pizza
33. Dinos Pizza
34. Mozzarella Di Bufala Pizzeria (West Portal)
35. Zante Pizza
36. Blondies
37. Round Table Pizza
38. All Nite Pizza
39. Bamboo Pizza
40. Palio d'Asti

Political Dictators
1572 votes by 504 people

1. Adolf Hitler
2. Josif Stalin
3. Fidel Castro
4. Saddam Hussein
5. Mussolini
6. George W. Bush
7. Mao Zedong
8. Julius Caesar
9. Pol Pot
10. Napoleon Bonaparte
11. Kim Jong Il
12. Francisco Franco
13. Idi Amin
14. Augusto Pinochet
15. Lenin
16. Manuel Noriega
17. Ferdinand Marcos
18. Alexander the Great
19. Hugo Chavez
20. Muammar AL-Qaddafi
21. Osama Bin Laden
22. Vladimir Putin
23. Ho Chi Minh
24. Kim Il Sung
25. Robert Mugabe
26. Roosevelt
27. Nicolae Ceausescu
28. Ghengis Khan
29. Bill Clinton
30. Nero
31. Josip Broz Tito
32. Nelson Mandela
33. Anwar Sadat
34. Marx
35. Francois 'Papa Doc' Duvalier
36. Mahmoud Ahmadinejad
37. King Zog of Albania
38. Charles Taylor
39. Santa Anna
40. Alexander III of MacEdon

Top Chinese Restaurants in Seattle, WA

517 votes by 169 people

1. Judy Fu's Snappy Dragon
2. Black Pearl
3. Shanghai Garden
4. P F Chang's China Bistro
5. Uptown China
6. Tai Tung
7. Hunan Garden
8. Chan's Place – Issaquah
9. Chop Suey
10. Malay Satay Hut
11. Sea Garden
12. Hong's Garden
13. Bamboo Garden
14. Bamboo Garden Vegetarian Cuisine
15. Forbidden City Restaurant
16. Noble Court Restaurant
17. Yeas Wok
18. Sichuanese Cuisine Restaurant
19. Azura Asian Bistro
20. Bada Lounge
21. Shallots Asian Bistro
22. Honey Court Seafood Restaurant
23. Chan's Place
24. Tai Tung Chinese Restaurant
25. Chan's Place – Kirkland
26. House of Hong
27. China Gate
28. Chinese Deli Restaurant
29. Top Gun Seafood
30. Panda Express
31. GA GA Loc Chinese Restaurant
32. Orchid Tree Chinese Restaurant
33. Pandasia Restaurant
34. Jeem Asian Restaurant
35. Jade Garden
36. China First
37. Seven Stars Pepper Szechuan Restaurant
38. Genghis Khan Restaurant
39. John's Wok on Western
40. Moon Temple Restaurant

Top Independent Book Stores in Boston, MA

520 votes by 137 people

1. Brattle Book Shop
2. Brookline Booksmith
3. Trident Booksellers & Cafe
4. Harvard Book Store
5. Calamus Bookstore
6. Newbury Comics
7. New England Mobile Book Fair
8. Grolier Poetry Bookshop
9. Globe Corner Bookstore
10. Avenue Victor Hugo Bookshop
11. Commonwealth Books
12. Cowley & Cathedral Bookstore
13. Wentworth Bookstore
14. Raven Used Books
15. Avila's Christian Book Store
16. Village Books
17. Buddenbrooks
18. Barbara's Best Sellers
19. Sundial Bookstore Incorporated
20. Trident
21. Harvard Coop
22. Wentworth Book Store
23. Spenser's Mystery Bookshop
24. Emerson College Book Store
25. Trident Booksellers and Café
26. Brattle Bookshop
27. Globe Corner Book Stores
28. Barnes and Noble
29. Bromer Booksellers
30. Buck-A-Book
31. Barbara's Bestsellers
32. Buck a Book
33. Curious George Goes to Wordsworth
34. MIT Press Bookstore
35. Bsfbsb
36. Cowley and Cathedral Bookstore
37. Lorem Ipsum
38. Follet Book Store
39. Treesavers Book Outlet
40. Cathedral Crossing Books Resources

Most Controversial Music Artists
2009 votes by 660 people

1.   Eminem
2.   Madonna
3.   Michael Jackson
4.   Marilyn Manson
5.   Elvis Presley
6.   Prince
7.   Ozzy Osbourne
8.   Sinead O'Connor
9.   The Beatles
10. 2 Live Crew
11. Kanye West
12. 50 Cent
13. John Lennon
14. Elvis
15. Jim Morrison
16. Alice Cooper
17. Britney Spears
18. Sex Pistols
19. Courtney Love
20. Milli Vanilli
21. Boy George
22. Tupac
23. Tupac Shakur
24. Marylin Manson
25. NWA
26. Kiss
27. Bob Dylan
28. Ice T
29. The Rolling Stones
30. Janet Jackson
31. Axl Rose
32. GG Allin
33. Iggy Pop
34. Kurt Cobain
35. Elton John
36. Green Day
37. Jimi Hendrix
38. Jerry Lee Lewis
39. George Michael
40. Rage against the Machine

Top Overrated Celebrities

1562 votes by 503 people

1. Paris Hilton
2. Tom Cruise
3. Britney Spears
4. Jessica Simpson
5. Brad Pitt
6. Jennifer Aniston
7. Angelina Jolie
8. Ashlee Simpson
9. Lindsay Lohan
10. Jennifer Lopez
11. Nicole Richie
12. Madonna
13. Ben Affleck
14. Oprah Winfrey
15. Hilary Duff
16. Michael Jackson
17. Donald Trump
18. Arnold Schwarzenegger
19. 50 Cent
20. Pamela Anderson
21. Ashton Kutcher
22. George Clooney
23. William Shatner
24. Julia Roberts
25. Eminem
26. Kevin Federline
27. Keanu Reeves
28. Johnny Depp
29. Nicole Kidman
30. Jim Carrey
31. Tom Hanks
32. Justin Timberlake
33. Celine Dion
34. Orlando Bloom
35. Katie Holmes
36. Martha Stewart
37. Olsen Twins
38. Sean Penn
39. David Beckham
40. Mariah Carey

Top Airlines

3041 votes by 1009 people

1. Southwest
2. American Airlines
3. Delta
4. United
5. Jet Blue
6. British Airways
7. Continental
8. Northwest
9. US Airways
10. Virgin Atlantic
11. Singapore Airlines
12. Lufthansa
13. Alaska
14. Qantas
15. KLM
16. Air France
17. Air Canada
18. Cathay Pacific
19. Emirates
20. WestJet
21. Midwest
22. JAL
23. Ryanair
24. Frontier
25. TWA
26. Swiss Air
27. Song
28. easyjet
29. Hawaiian Airlines
30. Midwest Express
31. El AL
32. airtran
33. All Nippon Airways
34. Spirit
35. ATA
36. Alitalia
37. Aer Lingus
38. SAS
39. Pan Am
40. Air New Zealand

Best Pet Names

376 votes by 106 people

1. Spot
2. Buddy
3. Fluffy
4. Spike
5. Rover
6. Max
7. Duke
8. Fido
9. Killer
10. Puff
11. honey
12. Rocko
13. Rusty
14. pepper
15. Rex
16. Bailey
17. Frankie
18. Roscoe
19. Star
20. Robo
21. Daisy Mae
22. Sparky
23. Lassie
24. King
25. baby doll
26. Bootsie
27. Baby Boy
28. Ruffie
29. Barney
30. Bella
31. Scooby
32. Duster
33. Snark
34. Molly
35. Danger
36. Beowulf
37. Tom
38. Gizmo
39. Sweetlips
40. Patches

Best Pho Restaurants in Seattle, WA
149 votes by 74 people

1. Pho Than Brothers
2. Pho Bac
3. Pho Cyclo
4. Saigon Bistro
5. Tamarind Tree
6. Pho 99 Authentic Vietnamese
7. Pho Hoa
8. Vietnam Restaurant
9. Saigon Restaurant
10. Pho Pasteur
11. I Love Pho
12. Than Brothers, University Way
13. Pho Bac Restaurant
14. Pho GA
15. Bambuza Vietnamese Bistro
16. Pho & Banh-Mi Saigon
17. Best Pho & Thai
18. Phi
19. Cafe Hue
20. Than Brothers Restaurant & Deli
21. Pho GA 900
22. Pho Bok
23. Fai
24. Pho Ha
25. Stoneway Cafe & Pho Restaurant
26. The Green Papaya
27. Pho-White Center
28. Fum
29. Joy Palace
30. Pho Van
31. Pho Phang
32. Ballet Restaurant

Top Scary Movies
1744 votes by 571 people

1. The Ring
2. The Exorcist
3. The Shining
4. Saw
5. Psycho
6. Halloween
7. Alien
8. Scream
9. Nightmare on Elm Street
10. Silence of the Lambs
11. The Grudge
12. Jaws
13. Texas Chainsaw Massacre
14. Friday the 13th
15. Poltergeist
16. The Sixth Sense
17. The Blair Witch Project
18. Hellraiser
19. Amityville Horror
20. The Omen
21. Evil Dead
22. Night of the Living Dead
23. It
24. The Birds
25. 28 Days Later
26. Signs
27. The Others
28. Dawn of the Dead
29. The Haunting
30. The Village
31. Scary Movie
32. Event Horizon
33. The Hills Have Eyes
34. Hostel
35. What Lies Beneath
36. I Know What You Did Last Summer
37. Rosemary's Baby
38. Seven
39. House on Haunted Hill
40. White Noise

Best Cities to Live in If You Are Poor

2152 votes by 692 people

1. New York, NY
2. Los Angeles, CA
3. Miami, FL
4. Chicago, IL
5. San Francisco, CA
6. Portland, OR
7. New Orleans, LA
8. Detroit, MI
9. Atlanta, GA
10. Houston, TX
11. Seattle, WA
12. San Diego, CA
13. Washington, DC
14. Dallas, TX
15. Boston, MA
16. Phoenix, AZ
17. Las Vegas, NV
18. Austin, TX
19. San Antonio, TX
20. Birmingham, AL
21. Little Rock, AR
22. Minneapolis, MN
23. Baltimore, MD
24. St. Louis, MO
25. Philadelphia, PA
26. Nashville, TN
27. Toronto, Ontario, Canada
28. Orlando, FL
29. London, England
30. Tulsa, OK
31. Tucson, AZ
32. Salt Lake City, UT
33. Denver, CO
34. Oklahoma City, OK
35. Oakland, CA
36. Pittsburgh, PA
37. Vancouver, BC, Canada
38. Mexico City, Mexico
39. Cleveland, OH
40. Honolulu, HI

Worst Things about San Diego, CA

471 votes by 142 people

1. Traffic Congestion
2. Cost of Living/Housing
3. Pollution, Smog, Dirt
4. Types of people living here
5. Population Overcrowding
6. Weather/Climate
7. Political Corruption
8. Crime
9. Poor public transportation
10. Immigrants, Border Patrol, etc.
11. Lack of good fine dining
12. Conservative Politics
13. Tourists
14. No beautiful scenery
15. Gas Prices
16. Military Relations
17. The Airport
18. We don't have a professional basketball team
19. Marine Layer
20. Schools
21. The Rare Earthquakes
22. Brushfires
23. Parking
24. Too spread out, not good for walking
25. The Padres don't spend enough money to make them competative.
26. Pot Holes
27. Poor radio station and cell phone coverage
28. Cultural centers are few and far between
29. Overpriced and substandard housing
30. Standard of Living
31. Distance from other places
32. It doesn't rain much
33. Apartments
34. Border Issues
35. Dating Scene
36. Proximity to Los Angeles
37. Rough Areas
38. Weather can be unpredictable
39. Too far from Los Angeles
40. Dry Santa Ana winds

Worst Companies to Work for
2311 votes by 787 people

1. Walmart
2. McDonalds
3. Microsoft
4. Enron
5. Ford
6. IBM
7. General Motors
8. Burger King
9. Kmart
10. Halliburton
11. Apple
12. Electronic Arts
13. Dell
14. Taco Bell
15. Best Buy
16. Nike
17. Disney
18. Target
19. Google
20. Coca-Cola
21. Wendy's
22. GM
23. AT&T
24. Intel
25. General Electric
26. AOL
27. Worldcom
28. UPS
29. American Airlines
30. Sony
31. Home Depot
32. Lucent
33. Starbucks
34. Comcast
35. MCI
36. Fed Ex
37. Verizon
38. Exxon
39. US Government
40. Pizza Hut

Top Wineries in the World
282 votes by 74 people

1. Chateau d'Yquem
2. St. Supery Winery
3. Chateau Margaux
4. Chateau Lafite Rothschild
5. 1 Pirramimma Winery, Australia
6. Jacob's Creek
7. Shafer Vineyards
8. Dom Perignon
9. Robert Mondavi
10. Gallo
11. Oasis Winery
12. Quilceda Creek
13. Leonetti Cellar
14. Hunter Valley
15. Brotherhood Winery
16. Chateau Latour
17. Domaine Chandon
18. Chateau Haut Brion
19. Artessa
20. Cakebread Cellars
21. Flag Hill Winery
22. Dehlinger Winery
23. Magnum Collection
24. Chartreuse de Mougeres Winery, France
25. Abarbanel Wines
26. Magnotta
27. Winnie
28. Chateau Lagrange
29. Montinore
30. Bare Foot
31. Robert Craig
32. Tamarack Cellars
33. Arroyo Robles Winery, Bakersfield, CA
34. Stag's Leap
35. Grgich Hills Winery
36. Andalucía- a South-Western Spanish Province
37. A Secret Garden Winery,Pikeville, NC
38. Annie's Lane
39. Kittling Ridge Estate Wines and Spirits
40. Mission Hill

Best Corporate IT Tools
330 votes by 96 people

1. Microsoft Office
2. Microsoft Exchange Server
3. gmail
4. VNC
5. Firefox
6. Visual Studio 2005
7. Blackberry
8. McAfee Virusscan
9. Ethereal
10. Dreamweaver
11. Symantec Ghost
12. Dameware
13. Oracle Database
14. Norton Ghost
15. MS Office
16. Lotus Notes
17. Google
18. VMware Workstation
19. Sap
20. Microsoft Visio
21. Spybot
22. Apache
23. password.amazon.com
24. Nectarclean
25. System Management Server
26. Adobe
27. Symantec Antivirus
28. Microsoft Outlook Email
29. Adobe Acrobat Reader
30. Linux
31. Skype
32. Microsoft Internet Explorer
33. Microsoft Windows 2003
34. Microsoft Windows
35. Microsoft Powerpoint
36. Google Desktop Search – Enterprise Edition
37. Oracle SQL Plus
38. Windiff
39. CA Unicenter
40. Nmap

Top People You'd Like to Have a Bladder Accident
2586 *votes by 856 people*

1. George W. Bush
2. Britney Spears
3. Paris Hilton
4. Dick Cheney
5. Tom Cruise
6. Hillary Clinton
7. Oprah Winfrey
8. Jessica Simpson
9. Michael Jackson
10. Bill Gates
11. Donald Trump
12. Osama Bin Laden
13. Brad Pitt
14. Angelina Jolie
15. Bill O'Reilly
16. Saddam Hussein
17. Martha Stewart
18. Donald Rumsfeld
19. Madonna
20. Michael Moore
21. Tony Blair
22. Ted Kennedy
23. John Kerry
24. Ashlee Simpson
25. Jennifer Lopez
26. Jay Leno
27. Condoleeza Rice
28. Kevin Federline
29. Lindsay Lohan
30. 50 Cent
31. Justin Timberlake
32. Simon Cowell
33. Eminem
34. David Letterman
35. The Pope
36. Derek Jeter
37. Karl Rove
38. Tom Delay
39. Ryan Seacrest
40. Arnold Schwarzenegger

Best Death Metal Bands

367 votes by 104 people

1. Morbid Angel
2. Metallica
3. Black Sabbath
4. Cannibal Corpse
5. death
6. Carcass
7. Sepultura
8. Iron Maiden
9. Sodom
10. Slayer.
11. Napalm Death
12. Childrem of Bodom
13. Deicide
14. Obituary
15. Cradle of Filth
16. Massacra
17. At the Gates
18. Megadeth
19. Slayer
20. Entombed
21. Opeth
22. Possessed
23. Nile
24. Bolt Thrower
25. Dimmu Borgir
26. Dark Tranquility
27. Nuclear Assault
28. Amon Amarth
29. Pestilence
30. Necrophagist
31. Pantera
32. Behemoth
33. GWAR
34. Arch Enemy
35. Death Angel
36. Tool
37. Atheist
38. Meshuggah
39. Trivium
40. Burzum

Stupidest Politicians
2867 votes by 941 people

1. George W. Bush
2. Dick Cheney
3. John Kerry
4. Bill Clinton
5. Tom Delay
6. Ted Kennedy
7. Tony Blair
8. Al Gore
9. Condoleeza Rice
10. Arnold Schwarzenegger
11. Howard Dean
12. Donald Rumsfeld
13. Dan Quayle
14. Bill Frist
15. Karl Rove
16. Rick Santorum
17. Joe Lieberman
18. Ted Stevens
19. Jack Thompson
20. Nancy Pelosi
21. John McCain
22. Trent Lott
23. Paul Martin
24. Barbara Boxer
25. Richard Nixon
26. Orrin Hatch
27. John Howard
28. Stephen Harper
29. Bob Dole
30. Saddam Hussein
31. Silvio Berlusconi
32. Newt Gingrich
33. Al Sharpton
34. Ross Perot
35. Ralph Nader
36. Jacques Chirac
37. John Ashcroft
38. Harry Reid
39. Mahmoud Ahmadinejad
40. Hugo Chavez

Top Things You Do on a Sunday Morning

2823 votes by 936 people

1. sleep
2. read the paper
3. Eat Breakfast
4. go to church
5. watch TV
6. drink coffee
7. read
8. shower
9. have sex
10. work
11. Clean
12. relax
13. wake up
14. surf the internet
15. play video games
16. laundry
17. go for a walk
18. Homework
19. watch football
20. watch a movie
21. go shopping
22. drink tea
23. Watch Cartoons
24. Check My E-Mail
25. Read the Funnies
26. stay in bed
27. Attend Church
28. Read the Comics
29. walk the dog
30. Play with My Kids
31. go out to eat
32. Jogging
33. exercise
34. take a walk
35. Watch Sports
36. Get Ready for Church
37. Play computer games
38. yoga
39. Spend Time with Family
40. Brush My Teeth.

Best Things about the City in Minneapolis, MN

290 votes by 84 people

1. Lakes
2. nice people
3. Weather
4. Music scene
5. Parks
6. Diversity
7. Clean
8. Friendly people
9. Good Schools
10. Mall of America
11. Uptown
12. Walker Art Center
13. Low Crime Rate
14. University of Minnesota
15. Perfect size, not too big, not too small
16. Weather in the Summer
17. Lakes & Parks
18. The Skyway System downtown
19. Local Music Scene
20. 22 lakes exist within the city limits
21. trees
22. Art Museums
23. Local Music
24. Hard Times Cafe
25. The Electric Fetus
26. Amount of parkland and open space
27. Art & Music Venues
28. Arts/ Guthrie Theater
29. Big city amenities, with a small town feel
30. There are hundreds of activities for all ages like festivals.
31. Night Life
32. No Smog
33. Temple of the River
34. Public Parks
35. Education
36. Cultural Attractions
37. Community
38. Abundant Park Land
39. Parks System

Top Pizza Parlors in New York, NY
771 votes by 244 people

1. Lombardi's
2. Famous Joe's Pizza
3. John's Pizza
4. Grimaldi's
5. Ray's Pizza
6. Sal's & Carmine Pizza
7. Totonno's
8. John's of Bleecker Street
9. Di Fara Pizzeria
10. Two Boots
11. Joe's Pizza
12. Pizza Hut
13. Vinnalli & Lupa Pizza Parlor
14. Patsy's
15. De Marco's
16. Frank's Pizzeria Parlor
17. Angelo's Pizza
18. Famous Original Ray's Pizza
19. Denino's Pizzeria
20. Downtown Pizza
21. Giorgione
22. My Little Pizzeria
23. Nick's Pizza
24. Papa Joe's Pizza
25. Cascina Ristorante
26. Abitino's
27. Fornino
28. Sal's Pizzeria
29. Dominos
30. Famous Famiglia
31. Three of Cups
32. Sbarro
33. Otto Enoteca Pizzeria
34. Arturo's
35. Gino's
36. Pizza Cave
37. Beacon
38. Sal's and Carmine Pizza
39. Pizza Bar
40. Una Pizza Napoletana

Top Independent Book Stores in Seattle, WA
536 votes by 170 people

1. Elliott Bay Book Company
2. Twice Sold Tales
3. Bailey/Coy Books
4. University Book Store
5. Third Place Books
6. Left Bank Books
7. Secret Garden Bookshop
8. City Books
9. Seattle Mystery Bookshop
10. Cinema Books
11. Half-Price Books
12. East West Bookshop
13. Arundel Books
14. Armchair Sailor
15. Beyond the Closet Bookstore
16. Madison Park Books
17. Hullabaloo Books
18. Square One Books
19. Third Place
20. Kinokuniya Book Stores
21. Borders
22. Wessel & Lieberman Booksellers
23. Left Bank Books Collective
24. Magus Books
25. Bauhaus Books & Coffee
26. Fremont Place Book Co
27. Magus Bookstore
28. Ophelia's Books
29. Brentano's Bookstore
30. Ballard Books
31. Flora and Fauna Books
32. amazon.com Incorporated
33. Nudelman Booksellers ABAA
34. East West Books
35. University Bookstore
36. Arundel
37. Astrology ET AL Metaphysical Center
38. Quest Bookshop
39. Snowgoose Bookstore

Best Things about the City in Austin, TX
371 votes by 109 people

1. Live Music
2. the people
3. 6th Street
4. Weather
5. The University of Texas
6. food
7. Zilker Park
8. Barton Springs
9. Liberal
10. South by Southwest
11. Parks
12. Town Lake
13. The Hill Country
14. Retains some counterculture charm
15. Eclectic and Liberal
16. The Greenbelt
17. Grady
18. The Texas Longhorns football team
19. The Culture
20. Hyde Park Bar and Grill
21. Bullock Museum's IMAX Movies
22. SXSW Music Festival
23. Casino El Camino
24. beautiful women
25. Ironworks BBQ
26. Space Station
27. barbeque
28. Lakeline Mall
29. The cost of living considering it is so cool
30. The Parks
31. Dining
32. grocery stores
33. Austin Music Hall
34. barbecue
35. The Vibrancy of the City
36. Culturally Diverse
37. Green Fields
38. Parks and Outdoor Activities
39. Home at 1408 Ruth
40. Lots of parks and bike paths

Top Cities You Wish Would Disappear

2873 votes by 952 people

1. Baghdad
2. Los Angeles
3. Paris
4. New York
5. Washington DC
6. Tehran
7. Detroit
8. New Orleans
9. Houston
10. Mexico City
11. Dallas
12. Beijing
13. London
14. Tokyo
15. Pyongyang
16. Miami
17. Jerusalem
18. San Francisco
19. Las Vegas
20. Calcutta
21. Moscow
22. Newark, NJ
23. Kabul
24. Salt Lake City
25. Hong Kong
26. Atlanta
27. Boston
28. Chicago
29. Berlin
30. Hollywood
31. Birmingham
32. Gaza
33. Bombay
34. Bangkok
35. Philadelphia
36. Cleveland
37. Vatican City
38. Gary, Indiana
39. Crawford, TX
40. Buffalo

Top Dog Breeds
1564 votes by 529 people

1. Labrador Retriever
2. Golden Retriever
3. German Shepherd
4. Poodle
5. Beagle
6. Husky
7. Pug
8. Cocker Spaniel
9. Boston Terrier
10. Pit bull
11. Boxer
12. Chihuahua
13. Collie
14. Jack Russell Terrier
15. Dalmatian
16. Great Dane
17. Border Collie
18. Rottweiler
19. Dachshund
20. Pomeranian
21. Doberman
22. Greyhound
23. Bulldog
24. Shih Tzu
25. Chow Chow
26. West Highland White Terrier
27. Basset Hound
28. Puggle
29. Akita
30. Yorkshire Terrier
31. Springer Spaniel
32. Irish Setter
33. Shetland Sheepdog
34. Newfoundland
35. Corgi
36. Pembroke Welsh Corgi
37. Yorkie
38. Australian Shepherd
39. English Bulldog
40. St Bernard

Top US Cities to Party in
2947 votes by 974 people

1. New York
2. Los Angeles
3. Miami
4. Las Vegas
5. New Orleans
6. San Francisco
7. Chicago
8. Boston
9. Seattle
10. Austin, TX
11. Atlanta
12. Orlando
13. San Diego
14. Houston
15. Washington D.C.
16. Dallas
17. Hollywood
18. Madison, WI
19. Ft. Lauderdale
20. Philadelphia
21. Daytona
22. Detroit
23. San Antonio
24. Manhattan
25. Minneapolis
26. Denver
27. St. Louis
28. Honolulu
29. Key West
30. South Beach, FL
31. Santa Barbara
32. Gainesville, FL
33. Atlantic City
34. San Jose
35. Reno
36. Athens, OH
37. Phoenix
38. Tampa
39. Portland
40. Raleigh, NC

Worst Baby Names for Boys
1602 votes by 505 people

1. Dick
2. Bob
3. John
4. George
5. Bert
6. Richard
7. Michael
8. Jack
9. Peter
10. Charles
11. Frank
12. Gaylord
13. David
14. Justin
15. Joe
16. Tyler
17. Harry
18. Bill
19. Eugene
20. Jesus
21. Harold
22. Adolf
23. Fred
24. Sue
25. Wayne
26. Dakota
27. Ashley
28. Francis
29. Kyle
30. Bubba
31. Ronald
32. Joshua
33. Sam
34. Ralph
35. Percy
36. Matthew
37. Adolph
38. Mike
39. James
40. Cody

Top Names for a 51st State in the USA
1400 votes by 461 people

1. Puerto Rico
2. Canada
3. Iraq
4. Mexico
5. Guam
6. Cuba
7. South California
8. Jefferson
9. Lincoln
10. Virgin Islands
11. Freedom
12. Iran
13. East Dakota
14. Bushland
15. Kennedy
16. Clinton
17. Washington DC
18. New New York
19. Afghanistan
20. England
21. Franklin
22. Columbia
23. Israel
24. Samoa
25. Jesusland
26. Americana
27. New Texas
28. Alberta
29. United Kingdom
30. Quebec
31. Zion
32. South Texas
33. Baja
34. Hell
35. blue
36. District of Columbia
37. New York City
38. Cascadia
39. Haiti
40. Oilabama

Top "Hip" Neighborhoods to Live in Boston, MA

502 votes by 155 people

1. Back Bay
2. Beacon Hill
3. South End
4. Cambridge
5. North End
6. Allston
7. Brookline
8. Jamaica Plain
9. Chinatown
10. Mission Hill
11. Harvard Square
12. Roxbury
13. South Boston
14. Brighton
15. Charlestown
16. Davis Square
17. Somerville
18. Downtown
19. Bay Village
20. Quincy
21. Dorchester
22. Kenmore Square
23. Hyde Park
24. Southie
25. Chestnut Hill
26. Fenway
27. Hingham
28. Allston/Brighton
29. West End
30. Davis Sq
31. Waterfront
32. Beacon Street
33. Eastie
34. Dorchestor
35. Rockport
36. Fenway/Kenmore
37. Porter Square
38. Wakefield, MA
39. Shrewsbury

Worst Things about Portland, OR

426 votes by 135 people

1. Traffic
2. Rain
3. Weather
4. Crime
5. F- ing hippsters all over the place
6. Pollution
7. Homeless
8. traffic congestion
9. cost of living
10. Parking
11. Vegans
12. poverty
13. People
14. High housing prices
15. smog
16. Can't pump your own gas.
17. smell
18. Nightlife
19. drug use
20. Diversity
21. Urban Sprawl
22. Snobbery
23. The Hobos
24. Expensive housing
25. Only sport is basketball
26. Bad Streets
27. The high concentration of snobby hipsters
28. No Parking
29. Permanent high concentration of snobby hipstays
30. Housing Cost
31. Potholes
32. Lack of Pro Sports
33. Local Government
34. Sun sets too early in winter
35. PGE Park
36. Segregation
37. B.O.H
38. High Taxes
39. Liberal political orientation
40. Panhandlers

Top US Cities for Chinese Food

3044 votes by 1007 people

1. New York
2. San Francisco
3. Los Angeles
4. Chicago
5. Seattle
6. Boston
7. Washington DC
8. Philadelphia
9. Houston
10. Miami
11. LA
12. Las Vegas
13. San Diego
14. NYC
15. New York, New York
16. Portland, OR
17. Denver
18. Dallas
19. China Town
20. Atlanta
21. Los Angeles, California
22. San Jose
23. Oakland
24. Honolulu
25. Detroit
26. Orlando
27. Sacramento
28. Monterey Park, CA
29. Baltimore
30. Austin
31. New Jersey
32. NY
33. Hollywood
34. Minneapolis
35. Brooklyn
36. Bowling Green
37. New Orleans
38. Chicago, Illinois
39. Arcadia, CA
40. Phoenix

Romantic Movies
1520 votes by 489 people

1. Casablanca
2. Titanic
3. Sleepless in Seattle
4. When Harry Met Sally
5. The Notebook
6. Gone with the Wind
7. Pretty Woman
8. Ghost
9. Love Story
10. You've Got Mail
11. Love Actually
12. The Princess Bride
13. A Walk to Remember
14. Notting Hill
15. Dirty Dancing
16. Serendipity
17. Romeo and Juliet
18. Say Anything
19. Eternal Sunshine of the Spotless Mind
20. Pride and Prejudice
21. Amelie
22. City of Angels
23. Breakfast at Tiffany's
24. Shakespeare in Love
25. An Affair to Remember
26. Moulin Rouge
27. Message in a Bottle
28. 50 First Dates
29. An Officer and a Gentleman
30. Return to Me
31. While You Were Sleeping
32. Somewhere in Time
33. Garden State
34. Chocolat
35. Great Expectations
36. Dr. Zhivago
37. West Side Story
38. Ever After
39. Bridges of Madison County
40. How to Lose a Guy in 10 Days

Top Hair Bands
1732 votes by 570 people

1. Poison
2. Mötley Crüe
3. Bon Jovi
4. Whitesnake
5. Guns N Roses
6. Kiss
7. Twisted Sister
8. Def Leppard
9. Ratt
10. Van Halen
11. Cinderella
12. Metallica
13. Skid Row
14. Warrant
15. Aerosmith
16. AC/DC
17. Quiet Riot
18. Alice Cooper
19. ZZ Top
20. Europe
21. Queen
22. Winger
23. Journey
24. Dokken
25. White Lion
26. Beatles
27. Iron Maiden
28. The Darkness
29. The Scorpions
30. Nelson
31. Black Sabbath
32. Flock of Seagulls
33. Led Zeppelin
34. Extreme
35. Stryper
36. Judas Priest
37. Tesla
38. Slayer
39. Great White
40. heart

Best TV News Channels/Networks

3038 votes by 1005 people

1. CNN
2. Fox
3. NBC
4. MSNBC
5. ABC
6. CBS
7. BBC
8. C-SPAN
9. PBS
10. CNN Headline News
11. Comedy Central
12. HBO
13. ESPN
14. BBC World
15. Sky News
16. CBC
17. Fox News Network
18. Discovery Channel
19. WB
20. BBC America
21. scifi
22. Bloomberg
23. The Weather Channel
24. UPN
25. MTV
26. Bravo
27. TLC
28. VH1
29. A&E
30. Showtime
31. G4
32. Cp24
33. MSN
34. Al-Jazeera
35. History Channel
36. HLN
37. CTV (Canadian Television)
38. KTLA
39. The BBC
40. CN

Top Pizza Parlors in Minneapolis, MN
372 votes by 115 people

1. Pizza Luce
2. Punch Neapolitan Pizza
3. Fat Lorenzo's
4. Red's Savoy Inn and Pizza
5. Cossetta's Italian Market & Pizzeria
6. Leaning Tower of Pizza
7. Davanni's
8. J's Restaurant & Pizza Parlor
9. Davanni's Pizza & Hot Hoagies
10. Vescio's
11. Broadway Pizza
12. Mangia
13. Godfathers
14. Pizza Hut
15. Dominoes
16. Carbone's
17. Snap! Pizza & Ice Cream
18. Beek's
19. Galactic Pizza
20. Old Chicago
21. Andrea Pizza
22. Campus Pizza & Pasta
23. Country Pizza Parlor
24. Paradise Pizza
25. A Slice of New York
26. Mama's Pizza
27. Pizza Factory
28. Dulono's Pizza
29. Duffy's Dinkytown Pizza
30. Classic Pizza & Ice Cream
31. Green Mill
32. Detellos Pizza & Pasta
33. Gooloney's
34. Savoy's Pizza
35. Pizza Pazza
36. Paesano's Pizza
37. Casalinda's
38. Food-N-Fuel
39. A & J Pizza
40. Lake Harriet Pizza

Best Fine Dining near Harrisonburg, VA

153 votes by 37 people

1. Joshua Wilton House
2. L'Italia Restaurant
3. Hank's Smokehouse & Deli
4. Calhoun's Restaurant & Brewing Company
5. Bavarian Chef
6. The Dining Room
7. Panos Restaurant
8. Outback Steakhouse
9. Dave's Downtown Taverna
10. Dan's Steak House
11. Bennihana's
12. Tiffany's Seafood Restaurant
13. The Lists
14. Wayne's 2 Worlds – Cafe and Emporium
15. Mazamitla
16. Luigi's
17. Bluemont Bed and Breakfast
18. Asia Inn
19. Manor House Restaurant at Poplar Springs Inn
20. Antiquers Paradise
21. Roosters
22. Artful Dodger
23. IHOP
24. Oxo Restaurant
25. by the Side of the Road Bed & Breakfast
26. Jordan Hollow Farm
27. Depot Grille
28. Perseco
29. Weyers Cave Bed and Breakfast Inn
30. Ruth's Chris Steakhouse
31. Garden of Sheba
32. McCormmick's & Smidt's
33. Stonewall Jackson Inn – Bed and Breakfast
34. Anarkali
35. Basye Gourmet Ltd
36. South River Grill
37. The Guriot
38. Ocharleys
39. America on Parade
40. One Block West

Top Independent Italian Restaurants in Seattle
354 votes by 120 people

1. Mamma Melina Ristorante
2. Assaggio Ristorante
3. Serafina
4. Pink Door
5. Buca di Beppo
6. Tulio Ristorante
7. IL Terrazzo Carmine
8. Il Bistro
9. Bizzarro Italian Cafe
10. Perche'No
11. Machiavelli Ristorante
12. Salumi
13. AL Boccalino
14. Fremont Classic Pizzeria & Trattoria
15. Cucina Cucina Italian Cafe
16. La Vita E' Bella Ristorante & Pizzeria
17. Bizarro
18. Pasta Freska
19. Pasta Bella
20. La Panzanella
21. Ciao Bella
22. Tutta Bella
23. Palermo Gourmet Pizza & Pasta
24. Filiberto's Italian Restaurant & Delicatessen
25. Romio's Pizza & Pasta-Eastlake
26. La Spiga
27. Mama Stortini's
28. Pontevecchio Italian Bistro
29. Asteroid Cafe
30. Poulsbo Pasta Co
31. Cafe Lago
32. Belltown Pizza
33. La Piazza
34. Buca Di Bepo
35. Assaggio
36. Volterra
37. La Medusa
38. Assagio
39. Ab Pasta Renaissance
40. Isabella Ristorante

Top Hip Neighborhoods to Live in New York City

809 votes by 239 people

1. Soho
2. Greenwich Village
3. East Village
4. Chelsea
5. Tribeca
6. Upper East Side
7. Williamsburg
8. Lower East Side
9. Harlem
10. Park Slope
11. Meatpacking District
12. Astoria
13. Hell's Kitchen
14. Nolita
15. Chinatown
16. Central Park West
17. Marble Hill
18. Red Hook
19. Financial District
20. Cobble Hill
21. Midtown
22. Little Italy
23. Union Square
24. Midtown West (Clinton)
25. Midtown East (Murray Hill)
26. Washington Heights
27. Battery Park
28. Dumbo
29. Noho
30. Times Square
31. Bedford Stuyvesant
32. Brooklyn Heights
33. Alphabet City
34. Upper West Side
35. Bushwick
36. Gramercy Park
37. Ridgewood
38. Prospect Park
39. Hoboken
40. Corona

Top Web Sites That You Secretly Visit

1651 votes by 547 people

1. myspace.com
2. somethingawful.com
3. eBay
4. playboy.com
5. DealTaker.com
6. livejournal.com
7. fark.com
8. neopets.com
9. Google
10. porn
11. slickdeals.net
12. cnn.com
13. Amazon
14. victoriassecret.com
15. rotten.com
16. espn.com
17. literotica.com
18. Match.com
19. ebaumsworld.com
20. collegehumor.com
21. drudgereport.com
22. suicidegirls.com
23. fatwallet.com
24. Mechanical Turk
25. thehun.com
26. hustler.com
27. Luelinks
28. 89.com
29. Adult Friend Finder
30. 4chan.org
31. worldsex.com
32. woot.com
33. penthouse.com
34. GameFAQs
35. americanidol.com
36. thesuperficial.com
37. Slashdot
38. people.com
39. Cosmo
40. mtv.com

Best Places to Visit
1549 votes by 512 people

1. Paris, France
2. London, England
3. New York City, USA
4. Rome, Italy
5. Tokyo, Japan
6. Sydney, Australia
7. Las Vegas, Nevada
8. Dublin, Ireland
9. Venice, Italy
10. San Francisco, USA
11. Toronto, Canada
12. Amsterdam, Netherlands
13. Florence, Italy
14. Hong Kong
15. Chicago, USA
16. Honolulu, Hawaii
17. Beijing, China
18. Athens
19. Cairo, Egypt
20. Orlando, Florida
21. Barcelona, Spain
22. Boston, USA
23. Vancouver, Canada
24. Melbourne, Australia
25. Montreal, Canada
26. Berlin, Germany
27. Washington DC, USA
28. Seattle, USA
29. Miami USA
30. Prague, Czech Republic
31. Jerusalem, Israel
32. Madrid, Spain
33. Shanghai, China
34. Maui, Hawaii
35. Cancun, Mexico
36. Geneva, Switzerland
37. Whitsunday Islands, Australia
38. China
39. New Orleans, USA
40. Yosemite National Park

Top Baseball 1ˢᵗ Basemen
764 votes by 242 people

1. Lou Gehrig
2. Albert Pujols
3. Mark McGwire
4. Jimmie Foxx
5. Derrek Lee
6. Eddie Murray
7. Jason Giambi
8. Carlos Delgado
9. David Ortiz
10. Willie McCovey
11. Don Mattingly
12. Jim Thome
13. Mark Teixeira
14. Todd Helton
15. Keith Hernandez
16. Jeff Bagwell
17. Frank Thomas
18. Rafael Palmeiro
19. Hank Greenberg
20. Harmon Killebrew
21. Mark Grace
22. J.T. Snow
23. George Sisler
24. Sean Casey
25. Tino Martinez
26. John Olerud
27. Boog Powell
28. Cecil Fielder
29. Cap Anson
30. Paul Konerko
31. Steve Garvey
32. Stan Musial
33. Babe Ruth
34. Gil Hodges
35. Richie Sexson
36. Ernie Banks
37. Pete Rose
38. Lyle Overbay
39. Wade Boggs
40. Kent Hrbek

Sexiest Movies of All-Time
347 votes by 114 people

1. Basic Instinct
2. 9 1/2 weeks
3. Blue Lagoon
4. Fatal Attraction
5. Last Tango in Paris
6. Wild Things
7. Damage
8. Six and a Half Weeks
9. Eyes Wide Shut
10. Showgirls
11. Body Heat
12. Color of Night
13. Ghost
14. Lolita
15. Debbie Does Dallas
16. The Graduate
17. 10
18. Some Like It Hot
19. Mulholland Dr.
20. The Lover
21. Deep Throat
22. Dirty Dancing
23. Pretty Woman
24. Gone with the Wind
25. Sliver
26. Sin City
27. Indecent Proposal
28. Betty Blue
29. The English Patient
30. The Summer of '42
31. Emmanuelle
32. Mr. and Mrs. Smith
33. When Harry Met Sally
34. Secretary
35. Y Tu Mama Tambien
36. Shakespeare in Love
37. Unfaithful
38. Veronica 2030
39. Harold & Maude
40. I like the Girls Who Do

Most Overrated Football Players

886 votes by 284 people

1. Peyton Manning
2. Terrell Owens
3. Tom Brady
4. Michael Vick
5. Deion Sanders
6. Joe Namath
7. OJ Simpson
8. Dan Marino
9. Emmitt Smith
10. Brett Favre
11. Troy Aikman
12. John Elway
13. Jerry Rice
14. Donovan McNabb
15. Ryan Leaf
16. Steve Young
17. Dante Culpepper
18. Randy Moss
19. Warren Sapp
20. Joe Montana
21. Kurt Warner
22. Keyshawn Johnson
23. Brian Bosworth
24. Ricky Williams
25. Eli Manning
26. Barry Sanders
27. Ray Lewis
28. David Beckham
29. Jerome Bettis
30. Terry Bradshaw
31. Ben Rothlisberger
32. Drew Bledsoe
33. Pelé
34. Jake Plummer
35. Antonio Freeman
36. Warren Moon
37. George Best
38. Jim Kelly
39. Maurice Clarrett
40. Peter Boulware

Top Music Acts to Hang It up
2664 votes by 884 people

1. Rolling Stones
2. Britney Spears
3. Madonna
4. Aerosmith
5. Backstreet Boys
6. Ashlee Simpson
7. Michael Jackson
8. U2
9. Metallica
10. Jessica Simpson
11. Eminem
12. 50 Cent
13. Kiss
14. Cher
15. Mariah Carey
16. Paul McCartney
17. Bon Jovi
18. Black Eyed Peas
19. Lindsay Lohan
20. Justin Timberlake
21. Green Day
22. Kevin Federline
23. The Who
24. INXS
25. Limp Bizkit
26. Hillary Duff
27. Rod Stewart
28. Jennifer Lopez
29. Christina Aguilera
30. Mötley Crüe
31. Celine Dion
32. Ozzy Osbourne
33. Elton John
34. Nickelback
35. Barry Manilow
36. Linkin Park
37. Queen
38. P Diddy
39. The Eagles
40. Janet Jackson

Top Brands of Bottled Water

2241 votes by 744 people

1. Evian
2. Dasani
3. Aquafina
4. Perrier
5. Poland Spring
6. Fiji
7. Arrowhead
8. Deer Park
9. San Pellegrino
10. Crystal Geyser
11. Dannon
12. Volvic
13. Ozarka
14. Ice Mountain
15. Zephyrhills
16. Vittel
17. Nestle
18. Deja Blue
19. spa
20. Crystal Springs
21. Smart Water
22. Bislery
23. Propel
24. Naya
25. Mountain Spring
26. Calistoga
27. Voss
28. San Benedetto
29. Sparkletts
30. Trinity
31. Aberfoyle
32. Alhambra
33. Mount Franklin
34. Kirkland
35. Acqua Panna
36. Borjomi
37. Nestle Pure Life
38. Montclair
39. Polar
40. Hidden Springs

Top NFL Coaches
869 votes by 278 people

1. Vince Lombardi
2. Bill Belichick
3. Tony Dungy
4. Tom Landry
5. Bill Parcells
6. Don Shula
7. Joe Gibbs
8. Bill Walsh
9. Mike Ditka
10. Andy Reid
11. Bill Cowher
12. John Madden
13. Mike Holmgren
14. John Fox
15. Mike Shanahan
16. Paul Brown
17. Lovie Smith
18. Romeo Crennel
19. Nick Saban
20. Mike Sherman
21. Jimmy Johnson
22. Mike Nolan
23. Jon Gruden
24. George Allen
25. Steve Mariucci
26. Herman Edwards
27. Chuck Noll
28. Mike Tice
29. Marv Levy
30. Tom Coughlin
31. Dick Vermeil
32. Hank Stram
33. George Halas
34. Bud Grant
35. Jeff Fisher
36. Norv Turner
37. Dan Reeves
38. Wayne Fontes
39. Brian Billick
40. Jim Mora

Top "Artsy" Movie Theaters in Seattle, WA

482 votes by 161 people

1. Egyptian
2. Harvard Exit
3. Grand Illusion
4. The Neptune
5. The Varsity
6. Seven Gables
7. Guild 45th
8. Cinerama
9. Pacific Place
10. Crest Cinema Center
11. Uptown
12. 5th Avenue
13. Northwest Film Forum
14. Cineplex Odeon
15. A Contemporary Theater
16. Big Picture
17. Columbia City Cinema
18. Majestic Bay Theatres
19. Admiral Twin
20. Central Cinema
21. Little Theatre
22. Seattle Imax Dome Theater
23. Metro
24. Media Arts Center
25. Re-Bar
26. Regal Lakewood 15
27. The Paramount
28. Theater Schmeater
29. Seattle Repertory Theatre
30. Crossroads
31. Greenlake Outdoor Theater
32. Village Theatre
33. Avenue Films
34. Herkimer Coffee
35. Regal Cinnema
36. Blink's
37. The Blue Mouse
38. The Showbox
39. Kirkland Parkplace Cinema
40. Gap Theatre Co

Top TV Game Shows Ever
3031 votes by 1007 people

1. Jeopardy
2. The Price is Right
3. Wheel of Fortune
4. Who Wants to Be a Millionaire
5. Family Feud
6. Press Your Luck
7. Match Game
8. Let's Make a Deal
9. Pyramid
10. Weakest Link
11. Hollywood Squares
12. Double Dare
13. Newlywed Game
14. Win Ben Stein's Money
15. The Gong Show
16. Password
17. Card Sharks
18. Distraction
19. Deal or No Deal
20. Survivor
21. Lingo
22. Jokers Wild
23. Fear Factor
24. The Dating Game
25. Name That Tune
26. What's My Line
27. Tic Tac Dough
28. To Tell the Truth
29. Supermarket Sweep
30. Concentration
31. Win, Lose, or Draw
32. Greed
33. $64,000 Question
34. Shop Til You Drop
35. Cash Cab
36. Love Connection
37. Whammy
38. You Bet Your Life
39. The Mole
40. Remote Control

Top Movies Adapted from Books

1847 votes by 611 people

1. The Lord Of the Rings
2. Harry Potter
3. The Lord of the Rings: Fellowship of the Ring
4. The Lion, the Witch and the Wardrobe
5. Jurassic Park
6. The Lord of the Rings: the Return of the King
7. Gone with the Wind
8. Fight Club
9. The Godfather
10. Pride and Prejudice
11. The Shawshank Redemption
12. Harry Potter and the Sorcerer's Stone
13. Harry Potter and the Goblet of Fire
14. The Lord of the Rings: The Two Towers
15. The Shining
16. Silence of the Lambs
17. Memoirs of a Geisha
18. Hitchhiker's Guide to the Galaxy
19. The Notebook
20. The Green Mile
21. Bridget Jones's Diary
22. To Kill a Mockingbird
23. V for Vendetta
24. A Clockwork Orange
25. The Stand
26. Schindler's List
27. Doctor Zhivago
28. The Firm
29. Adaptation
30. The Princess Bride
31. The Hunt for Red October
32. Harry Potter and the Prisoner of Azkaban
33. Harry Potter and the Chamber of Secrets
34. Jaws
35. The Wizard of Oz
36. It
37. Da Vinci Code
38. The Bourne Identity
39. Interview with the Vampire
40. Blade Runner

Top NFL Players
1027 votes by 314 people

1. Joe Montana
2. Peyton Manning
3. Walter Payton
4. Tom Brady
5. Jerry Rice
6. Brett Favre
7. Barry Sanders
8. Jim Brown
9. Shaun Alexander
10. Dan Marino
11. John Elway
12. Ladanian Tomlinson
13. Terrell Owens
14. Michael Vick
15. Johnny Unitas
16. Randy Moss
17. Tiki Barber
18. Joe Namath
19. Lawrence Taylor
20. Emmitt Smith
21. Troy Aikman
22. Ben Roethlisberger
23. Donovan McNabb
24. Jerome Bettis
25. Terry Bradshaw
26. Derrick Brooks
27. Steve Young
28. Ray Lewis
29. Brian Urlacher
30. Carson Palmer
31. Gale Sayers
32. Reggie White
33. Marvin Harrison
34. O.J. Simpson
35. Drew Bledsoe
36. Deion Sanders
37. George Blanda
38. Larry Allen
39. Dick Butkus
40. Bart Starr

Top Hockey Players
1098 votes by 353 people

1. Wayne Gretzky
2. Mario Lemieux
3. Bobby Orr
4. Gordie Howe
5. Mark Messier
6. Bobby Hull
7. Joe Sakic
8. Peter Forsberg
9. Patrick Roy
10. Jaromir Jagr
11. Brett Hull
12. Maurice Richard
13. Steve Yzerman
14. Ilya Kovalchuk
15. Sidney Crosby
16. Joe Thornton
17. Jarome Iginla
18. Mike Modano
19. Sergei Fedorov
20. Dominik Hasek
21. Phil Esposito
22. Brian Leetch
23. Rick Nash
24. Brendan Shanahan
25. Martin Brodeur
26. Pavel Bure
27. Curtis Joseph
28. Alexander Ovechkin
29. John Leclair
30. Ed Belfour
31. Paul Kariya
32. Vladislav Tretiak
33. Martin Erat
34. Chris Chelios
35. Tim Horton
36. Patrice Bergeron
37. Ray Bourque
38. Guy Lafleur
39. Ron Francis
40. Todd Bertuzzi

Most Irritating Top 10 Lists

1507 votes by 515 people

1. Best Dressed
2. Top 10 Celebrities
3. movies
4. Most Irritating Top 10 Lists
5. songs
6. David Letterman
7. food
8. Best Hair
9. Sexiest Men
10. Top 10 Models
11. Best Celebrity Hair
12. Best Politician
13. Most Beautiful People
14. Gwen Stefani Songs
15. Richest People
16. Best Eminem Songs
17. Music Artists
18. Celebrity Couples
19. Top 10 Cars
20. Top 10 Bands
21. Top 10 TV Shows
22. Clutch Athletes
23. Worst Hair
24. Music
25. Sports Teams
26. Music Videos
27. Men You Would Leave Your Partner for
28. Names
29. Top 10 Inventions
30. Dog Breeds
31. Hottest Models
32. Famous People
33. Top 10 Top 10 Lists
34. books
35. Top 10 Albums of All Time
36. Favorite Color
37. Sexiest Man Alive
38. Hottest Guys
39. Reasons to Marry a Man
40. Top 10 Presidents

Top Personal Heroes
314 votes by 95 people

1. my dad
2. my mom
3. George Bush
4. Albert Einstein
5. my grandmother
6. Michael Jordan
7. Nelson Mandela
8. Bill Clinton
9. Superman
10. My Grandparents
11. Bono
12. Bill Gates
13. Martin Luther King Jr.
14. family
15. Lance Armstrong
16. Jesus Christ
17. Mother Theresa
18. my father
19. Benjamin Franklin
20. Abraham Lincoln
21. Theodore Roosevelt
22. Jesus
23. Colin Powell
24. Noam Chomsky
25. Madonna
26. Mahatma Gandhi
27. Sigmund Freud
28. Jim Cramer
29. Martin Luther King Jr
30. Donald Trump
31. Billy Graham
32. Sandra Day Oconnor
33. Sylvester Stallone
34. Eiri Yuki
35. Sir Edmund Hilary
36. John Martyn
37. Steve Jobs
38. Sally Ride
39. Howard Dean
40. Ghandi

Best US Airports

2474 votes by 826 people

1. JFK – New York City
2. Chicago O'Hare International Airport
3. LAX
4. Hartsfield-Jackson Atlanta International Airport
5. San Francisco International Airport
6. Denver
7. Minneapolis St. Paul International Airport
8. Boston Logan International Airport
9. DFW (Dallas Fort-Worth)
10. Newark Liberty International Airport
11. LaGuardia
12. Orlando
13. Miami International
14. Seatac
15. Dulles
16. Las Vegas
17. Detroit
18. Washington National
19. Pittsburgh
20. Portland International Airport
21. Baltimore/Washington International Airport
22. Houston Bush Intercontinental Airport
23. Philadelphia International Airport
24. Phoenix
25. Oakland
26. Cincinnati
27. Chicago Midway
28. Honolulu
29. Mineta San Jose International
30. Long Beach
31. Salt Lake City
32. Charlotte
33. LA/Ontario International Airport
34. Raleigh-Durham International (RDU)
35. Milwaukee
36. St. Louis
37. John Wayne Airport (SNA)
38. TF Green
39. Cleveland OH
40. West Palm Beach

Worst Things about Philadelphia, PA
435 votes by 131 people

1. Traffic
2. Crime
3. Mayor Street
4. Pollution
5. City wage tax
6. Homeless people
7. trash
8. smell
9. Septa
10. City government
11. People
12. Weather
13. Dirty Streets
14. Parking
15. Snow
16. smog
17. politics
18. poverty
19. Taxes
20. The Schukyll Expressway
21. North Philadelphia
22. Sports Fans
23. US Airways
24. High Crime
25. Lousy winter weather
26. summer heat
27. No Jobs
28. Random Violence
29. Government
30. Highway Systems
31. The Poverty
32. The Mayor
33. Rocky Balboa
34. Mayor
35. Traffic on I-95 (Getting There)
36. Trash in Streets
37. Traffic on I-95
38. Mass transit expensive & inadequate
39. Safe areas are very small and expensive to live in
40. Philadelphia Schools.

Best Cities to Live in If You Are Rich
2884 votes by 964 people

1. New York
2. Los Angeles
3. San Francisco
4. Miami
5. Beverly Hills
6. London
7. Paris
8. Las Vegas
9. Boston
10. Seattle
11. Chicago
12. Tokyo
13. Hollywood
14. San Diego
15. Washington DC
16. Aspen, CO
17. Dallas
18. Monaco
19. Dubai
20. Honolulu
21. London, England
22. Malibu, CA
23. Palm Beach
24. San Jose
25. Houston
26. Toronto
27. California
28. Rome
29. Denver
30. Austin, TX
31. Greenwich, CT
32. Barcelona
33. Tokyo, Japan
34. Santa Barbara
35. Los Angeles, California
36. Hong Kong
37. Scottsdale, AZ
38. Monte Carlo
39. Portland
40. Vancouver

Top World Vacation Destinations
1543 votes by 508 people

1. Paris, France
2. Hawaii
3. London, England
4. Italy
5. Australia
6. New York
7. Disney World, Florida
8. Bahamas
9. Rome, Italy
10. Las Vegas
11. Jamaica
12. Japan
13. Cancun
14. Orlando, Florida
15. Disneyland
16. Carribean
17. Florida
18. Venice, Italy
19. New Zealand
20. Tokyo
21. Mexico
22. Ireland
23. Egypt
24. Fiji
25. Amsterdam, The Netherlands
26. Spain
27. Tokyo, Japan
28. Hong Kong
29. Aruba
30. Alaska
31. Greece
32. Europe
33. Sydney, Australia
34. Grand Canyon
35. Brazil
36. India
37. Thailand
38. Cuba
39. Prague
40. Costa Rica

Top Small Live Music Venues in Atlanta, GA
295 votes by 85 people

1. Andrews Upstairs
2. Tabernacle
3. Smith's Olde Bar
4. Masquerade
5. The Earl
6. Variety Playhouse
7. Eddie's Attic
8. Blind Willie's
9. Fuzzy's Place
10. Roxy
11. Dark Horse Tavern & 10 High Club
12. The Cotton Club
13. Chastain Park
14. Apres Diem
15. Cowboys
16. Apache Cafe
17. Cafe 290
18. Sambuca
19. Lenny's
20. Red Light Cafe
21. Churchill Grounds
22. Star Community Bar
23. Eyedrum
24. Blues in the Alley
25. 97 Estoria
26. Northside Tavern
27. McDuff's Irish Pub
28. Surin of Thailand
29. Apache Café
30. Oar
31. Las Margaritas
32. Anis Cafe & Bistro
33. Atmosphere
34. Beluga Martini Bar
35. Carnaval Bar & Lounge
36. The Extreem
37. Echo Lounge LLC
38. Fox
39. Earthlink Live
40. Underground Atlanta

Hottest Models
1544 votes by 509 people

1. Tyra Banks
2. Heidi Klum
3. Cindy Crawford
4. Gisele Bundchen
5. Kate Moss
6. Naomi Campbell
7. Adriana Lima
8. Claudia Schiffer
9. Elle MacPherson
10. Alessandra Ambrosio
11. Paris Hilton
12. Christie Brinkley
13. Milla Jovovich
14. Kathy Ireland
15. Carmen Electra
16. Laetitia Casta
17. Iman
18. Nikki Taylor
19. Petra Nemcova
20. Christy Turlington
21. Pamela Anderson
22. Jessica Alba
23. Jessica Simpson
24. Linda Evangelista
25. Carolyn Murphy
26. Carol Alt
27. Isabeli Fontana
28. Fabio
29. Angie Everhart
30. Rachel Hunter
31. Estella Warren
32. Kaylani Lei
33. Tyson Beckford
34. Molly Sims
35. Elisha Cuthbert
36. Naomi Watts
37. Ursula Mayes
38. Marisa Miller
39. Francine Dee
40. Natasha Yi

Top National Parks
1533 votes by 506 people

1. Yellowstone National Park
2. Yosemite National Park
3. Grand Canyon National Park
4. Acadia National Park
5. Zion National Park
6. Glacier National Park
7. Rocky Mountain National Park
8. Everglades National Park
9. Great Smoky Mountains National Park
10. Sequoia & Kings Canyon National Park
11. Redwood National and State Parks
12. Grand Teton National Park
13. Denali National Park and Preserve
14. Arches National Park
15. Death Valley National Park
16. Big Bend National Park
17. Joshua Tree National Park
18. Mammoth Cave National Park
19. Bryce Canyon National Park
20. Mount Rainier National Park
21. Carlsbad Caverns National Park
22. Olympic National Park
23. Gwaii Haanas National Park Reserve and Haida Heritage Site
24. Mount Rushmore National Memorial
25. Gettysburg National Military Park
26. Lake District National Park (England)
27. Banff National Park of Canada
28. Crater Lake National Park
29. Hot Springs National Park
30. Hawai'i Volcanoes National Park
31. Niagara Falls
32. Anacostia Park (U.S. National Park Service)
33. Kruger National Park (South Africa)
34. Shenandoah National Park
35. Aztec Ruins National Monument
36. Apostle Islands National Lakeshore
37. Appalachian National Scenic Trail
38. Allegheny National Forest
39. Valley Forge National Historical Park
40. Mesa Verde National Park

Best Things about the City in Toronto, ON
521 votes by 161 people

1. CN Tower
2. Multiculturalism
3. People
4. Toronto Maple Leafs
5. Clean
6. the food
7. culture
8. shopping
9. Nightlife
10. Friendly people
11. Cultural Diversity
12. Toronto's CN Tower
13. The Toronto Raptors
14. Safe
15. Weather
16. Canadian
17. Restaurants
18. Kensington Market
19. Toronto Blue Jays
20. Diversity
21. Hockey Hall of Fame
22. Music
23. Leafs
24. Skydome
25. Location
26. Hockey Games
27. Cleanliness
28. Ontario Science Centre
29. Bata Shoe Museum
30. Ethnic Diversity
31. Multiculturalism (fifth largest city in North America! Many ethnic neighborhoods)
32. It's in Canada – a lovely country and one I very much enjoy living in.
33. The District
34. Jazz Festivals
35. Summer Is Not Too Hot
36. Cosmopolitan
37. cool
38. Big City Atmosphere
39. Not Many Crimes
40. Lots of Entertainment Options

Best Cartoons of the 1960s and 1970s

334 votes by 102 people

1. The Flintstones
2. Scooby Doo
3. Bugs Bunny
4. The Jetsons
5. Tom & Jerry
6. Rocky and Bullwinkle
7. Speed Racer
8. Roadrunner
9. Woody Woodpecker
10. Popeye
11. The Pink Panther
12. Looney Tunes
13. Mighty Mouse
14. Super Friends
15. Yogi Bear
16. Hong Kong Phooey
17. Jonny Quest
18. Wacky Races
19. peanuts
20. Herculoids
21. Top Cat
22. Underdog
23. Daffy Duck
24. The Beatles
25. Fat Albert
26. Felix the Cat
27. Mickey Mouse
28. Spider-Man
29. Deputy Dawg
30. Snoopy
31. Snagglepuss
32. Heckle & Jeckle
33. League of Super Heroes
34. Gigantor
35. Magilla Gorilla
36. Mazinger Z
37. Robotech
38. Ruff and Ready
39. Adam Ant
40. Symposium on Popular Songs

Top Debut Albums
1418 votes by 469 people

1. Led Zeppelin – Led Zeppelin
2. Are You Experienced?
3. Appetite for Destruction
4. Meet the Beatles
5. Pearl Jam – Ten
6. Please Please Me – the Beatles
7. U2 – Boy
8. The Ramones, the Ramones
9. The Who, "The Who Sings My Generation"
10. Alanis Morissette – Jagged Little Pill
11. Oasis – Definitely Maybe
12. The Doors
13. Metallica – Kill 'Em All
14. Weezer – the Blue Album
15. Nine Inch Nails – Pretty Hate Machine
16. Boston – Boston
17. Van Halen
18. Boston
19. Madonna
20. Bjork
21. Linkin Park – Hybrid Theory
22. The Doors – the Doors
23. Rage against the Machine – Rage against the Machine
24. Slim Shady LP
25. My Aim Is True – Elvis Costello
26. Stone Roses – Stone Roses
27. The Ramones
28. The College Dropout
29. Baby One More Time
30. Green Day – Dookie
31. Parachutes
32. The Smiths – The Smiths
33. Black Sabbath – Black Sabbath
34. Beck – Mellow Gold
35. Bleach
36. Kill 'Em All
37. Jagged Little Pill
38. Garbage – Garbage
39. Prodigy – Experience
40. Radiohead – Pablo Honey

Top Independent Book Stores in Silicon Valley, CA

236 votes by 67 people

1. Kepler's
2. Hicklebee's Children's Books
3. Lee's Comics
4. Willow Glen Books
5. Stacey's
6. Know Knew Books
7. Green Apple Books
8. Bell's in Palo Alto
9. Bell's Bookstore
10. Technical Book Shop
11. Cody's Books
12. Stanford Bookstore
13. Printers Inc. Bookstore and Cafe
14. Bay Book & Video Company
15. Bay Books
16. M Is for Mystery
17. Amana Christian
18. Spartan Bookstore
19. Thunderbird Bookshops Inc.
20. Bookshop Santa Cruz
21. Roberts Book Store
22. Lincoln Avenue Books
23. Aardvark
24. City Lights Books
25. Books Inc, Stanford Mall
26. Printer's Ink
27. Books Inc
28. A Clean Well-Lighted Place for Books
29. Bell's Bookstore – Palo Alto
30. Dog Eared Books
31. Cody's Book Store
32. Carter's
33. Contemporary Book Shops
34. Stacey's Bookstore, Palo Alto
35. Lion & the Lamb Bookstores Incorporated
36. Roberts Book Store (San Jose)
37. City Lights
38. Bukstore
39. Stacey's Bookstore
40. Odyssey Books

Disappointing Movies
1703 votes by 566 people

1. Star Wars Episode 1
2. King Kong
3. Matrix Reloaded
4. Matrix Revolutions
5. Titanic
6. Memoirs of a Geisha
7. Gigli
8. The Matrix
9. Brokeback Mountain
10. Fantastic 4
11. The Village
12. Elizabethtown
13. Jurassic Park 3
14. Van Helsing
15. Waterworld
16. War of the Worlds
17. Alexander
18. Terminator 3
19. The Blair Witch Project
20. Doom
21. The Hitchhiker's Guide to the Galaxy
22. Kingdom of Heaven
23. Star Wars
24. Crash
25. Ocean's Twelve
26. Hulk
27. Vanilla Sky
28. Eyes Wide Shut
29. Signs
30. The League of Extraordinary Gentlemen
31. Troy
32. Bewitched
33. Catwoman
34. Daredevil
35. Basic Instinct 2
36. Lord of the Rings
37. Godfather III
38. V for Vendetta
39. Scary Movie 3
40. Resident Evil

Top American Idol Contestants

1684 votes by 558 people

1. Kelly Clarkson
2. Clay Aiken
3. Bo Bice
4. Ruben Studdard
5. Carrie Underwood
6. William Hung
7. Fantasia Barrino
8. Constantine
9. Diana Degarmo
10. Tamyra Gray
11. Justin Guarini
12. Sarah Mather
13. Latoya London
14. Melinda Lira
15. Chris Daughtry
16. Kimberly Locke
17. Justin
18. Ryan Starr
19. George Huff
20. Mikalah Gordon
21. Frenchie
22. Jessica Sierra
23. Jennifer Hudson
24. Nadia Turner
25. Josh Gracin
26. Anthony Federov
27. Corey Clark
28. Bob Dylan
29. Mario Vasquez
30. Lindsey Cardinale
31. Anwar Robinson
32. Jasmine Trias
33. Nikki McGibbon
34. Joseph Murena
35. John Stevens
36. Kimberly Caldwell
37. Nikko Smith
38. Keith Beukelaer
39. Paris Bennett
40. Donnell Brown

Best Sports Uniforms
1647 votes by 470 people

1. New York Yankees
2. Green Bay Packers
3. Dallas Cowboys
4. Oakland Raiders
5. Los Angeles Lakers
6. Pittsburgh Steelers
7. Boston Red Sox
8. Cleveland Browns
9. Cincinnati Bengals
10. Chicago Cubs
11. basketball
12. New York Mets
13. Los Angeles Dodgers
14. Denver Broncos
15. Ohio State Buckeyes
16. Boston Celtics
17. Chicago Bears
18. San Diego Chargers
19. Houston Astros
20. Chicago White Sox
21. Detroit Pistons
22. Atlanta Braves
23. New England Patriots
24. Tennis
25. Chicago Bulls
26. Orlando Magic
27. Denver Nuggets
28. San Francisco 49ers
29. Seattle Seahawks
30. Red Sox
31. Detroit Red Wings
32. Miami Dolphins
33. Montreal Canadiens
34. Rugby
35. Carolina Panthers
36. New York Knicks
37. Bengals
38. Cleveland Indians
39. Philadelphia Eagles
40. Atlanta Falcons

Top Chinese Restaurants in Atlanta, GA

818 votes by 232 people

1. Lin's Chinese Cuisine at Windward
2. Chin Chin II Chinese Restaurant
3. Fuwah Chinese Restaurant
4. MU Lan
5. Hong Kong Harbour Restaurant
6. Mr Wang's Chinese Restaurant
7. Hsu's at Peachtree Ctr
8. Buffalo China
9. Hsu's Gourmet Chinese Restaurant
10. China Cooks
11. Little Szechuan
12. Canton Chopsticks Chinese Restaurant
13. Canton House
14. House of Chan
15. Peking Dragon Chinese Rstrnt
16. Fortune Cookie Restaurant INC
17. Chai Peking Chinese Restaurant Restaurant
18. Yen Jing
19. Lin's Chinese Cuisine
20. Lucky China
21. Mama Fu's Noodle House
22. Chinese Buddha
23. Doc Chey's Noodle House
24. Hot Wok
25. Hsu's
26. Canton Cooks
27. Phoenix Noodle Cafe
28. China Five
29. Hong LI Chinese Restaurant
30. Bamboo Luau's Chinatown
31. Hsu's Chinese Restaurant
32. Sampan
33. Pyng Ho Chinese Restaurant
34. Cafe Sampan
35. Pung Mie Chinese Restaurant
36. China Wok
37. First China Restaurant
38. China Delight
39. Harmony Vegetarian
40. China Garden

Top Things to Do or See in Seattle
286 votes by 91 people

1. Space Needle
2. Pike Place Market
3. Underground Tour
4. Seattle Aquarium
5. Experience Music Project
6. Pacific Science Center
7. Museum of Flight
8. Watch a Mariner's Game
9. Woodland Park Zoo
10. Mt. Rainier
11. Seattle Museum of Art
12. Rent a Canoe or Kayak from the UW. Waterfront Activity Center
13. Seattle Public Library
14. Safeco Field
15. Ballard Locks
16. Flightseeing Seaplane Tour
17. Science Fiction Museum and Hall of Fame
18. Catching the Mariners at Safeco Field
19. See a NFL/NBA/MLB Game
20. Go to a Mariners/Sonics/Seahawks Game
21. Ride the Ferry to All the Islands
22. Look for the Homes of Dead Rock Stars
23. Troll under the Bridge
24. Yada Yada Yada
25. Pioneer Square
26. Stroll around Capitol Hill
27. Visit Fremont
28. Marina Park at Kirkland Waterfront
29. Kerry Park at Top of Queen Anne Hill
30. Eat Seafood
31. Seward Park
32. Seattle Seahawks Game
33. The Curiosity Shop on the Pier
34. Lincoln Park
35. Shop for dinner at the Pike Place Market
36. Duck Tour
37. Take a Harbor Tour
38. Smith Tower
39. Hiking
40. drink coffee

Best Cities to Live in If You're 25 Years Old
2695 votes by 902 people

1. New York
2. Los Angeles
3. San Francisco
4. Chicago
5. Miami
6. Seattle
7. Boston
8. Las Vegas
9. Austin, TX
10. London
11. San Diego
12. Washington DC
13. Portland, OR
14. Dallas
15. Paris
16. Atlanta
17. Philadelphia
18. Denver
19. Tokyo
20. Amsterdam
21. Toronto
22. Orlando
23. Houston
24. Sydney
25. Tampa
26. New Orleans
27. Hollywood
28. Boulder, CO
29. Montreal
30. Phoenix, AZ
31. Pittsburgh
32. Vancouver
33. Nashville, TN
34. Minneapolis
35. Madison, WI
36. Baltimore, MD
37. Charlotte, NC
38. Berlin
39. St. Louis, MO
40. Cambridge, MA

Top Photography Books
390 votes by 128 people

1. The Camera – Ansel Adams
2. 100 Photographs That Changed the World
3. The Negative
4. On Photography
5. Understanding Exposure – Bryan Peterson
6. Americas Wilderness: the Photographs of Ansel Adams
7. Nature's America – David Muench
8. Treadwell
9. Through the Lens: National Geographic's Greatest Photographs
10. Teach Yourself Photography
11. The Nature of America: Images by North America's Premier Nature Photographers – David Middleton
12. Sleeping by the Mississippi
13. Sarah Moon: Coincidences
14. Earth from above
15. Above Yosemite – Robert W. Cameron
16. Hungry Planet
17. John Shaw's Closeups in Nature
18. Close up by Martin Schoeller
19. John Shaw's Nature Photography Field Guide
20. Henri Cartier-Bresson: the Man, the Image and the World
21. National Geographic: the Photos
22. Photography – Barbara London and John Upton
23. The Making of 40 Photographs by Ansel E. Adams
24. Creative Canine Photography
25. The Photographer's Guide to Light by John Freeman
26. Bowiestyle
27. Photographs: Annie Leibovitz 1970- 1990
28. Photography by Bruce Warren
29. Light: Science and Magic
30. The Camera – Ansel Adams and Robert Baker
31. Other Realities by Jerry Uelsmann
32. Coal Hollow: Photographs and Oral Histories
33. John Shaw's Nature Photography
34. World Press Photo Books
35. Life Cast: behind the Mask, Willa Shalit
36. The Book of Photography
37. Immediate Family, Sally Mann
38. On This Earth: Photographs from East Africa by Alice Sebold
39. Eye to Eye
40. Nightmares in the Sky

Best Books to Give As a Gift

739 votes by 246 people

1. The Bible
2. The DaVinci Code
3. The Ultimate Hitchhiker's Guide to the Galaxy
4. Lord of the Rings
5. Chicken Soup for the Soul
6. Harry Potter and the Sorcerer's Stone
7. Harry Potter and the Half Blood Prince
8. Ender's Game
9. Jon Stewart's Naked Pictures of Famous People
10. The Five People You Meet in Heaven
11. 1984
12. Tuesdays with Morrie
13. The Hitchhiker's Guide to the Galaxy – Douglas Adams
14. Turning 40 – Dave Barry
15. Harry Potter
16. The World Is Flat: a Brief History of the Twenty-First Century
17. Betty Crocker Cookbook
18. What We Do for Love – Ilene Beckerman
19. What to Expect When You're Expecting
20. Catch 22
21. Snow Crash
22. Angels and Demons
23. The Stand
24. To Kill a Mockingbird
25. Harry Potter and the Prisoner of Azkaban
26. War and Peace
27. The Notebook
28. The Joy of Cooking
29. The Hobbit
30. Harry Potter and the Order of the Phoenix
31. Harry Potter and the Goblet of Fire
32. Wicked
33. Game of Thrones
34. Freakonomics – Leavitt
35. The World is Flat – Thomas L. Friedman
36. Latte Trouble
37. Microserfs – Douglas Coupland
38. Freakonomics : a Rogue Economist Explores the Hidden Side of Everything – Steven D. Levitt and Stephen J. Dubner
39. East of Eden
40. Written in the West – Wim Wenders

Favorite Childhood Movies
1884 votes by 619 people

1. The Wizard of Oz
2. Star Wars
3. Bambi
4. The Lion King
5. E.T.
6. The Goonies
7. The Neverending Story
8. The Little Mermaid
9. Mary Poppins
10. Aladdin
11. The Sound of Music
12. Toy Story
13. The Princess Bride
14. Beauty and the Beast
15. Ghost Busters
16. Cinderella
17. Snow White
18. Chitty Chitty Bang Bang
19. Willy Wonka and the Chocolate Factory
20. The Land Before Time
21. Lady and the Tramp
22. Labyrinth
23. Sleeping Beauty
24. Home Alone
25. Jungle Book
26. Back to the Future
27. 101 Dalmations
28. The Dark Crystal
29. Teenage Mutant Ninja Turtles
30. Superman
31. Fantasia
32. Dumbo
33. Annie
34. Charlie and the Chocolate Factory
35. Alice in Wonderland
36. Raiders of the Lost Ark
37. The Last Unicorn
38. Short Circuit
39. Return of the Jedi
40. The Empire Strikes Back

Top Things You Do with Your Free Time

2733 votes by 911 people

1. read
2. surf the internet
3. watch tv
4. sleep
5. Play videogames
6. watch movies
7. Play computer games
8. listen to music
9. Hang Out with Friends
10. mturk
11. write
12. Play with My Kids
13. work out
14. walk
15. sex
16. play sports
17. shopping
18. masturbate
19. knit
20. gardening
21. travel
22. eat
23. cook
24. Photography
25. Hiking
26. Golf
27. Play Guitar
28. relax
29. draw
30. Chat Online
31. drink
32. Play Music
33. play
34. play tennis
35. meditate
36. blog
37. Homework
38. play soccer
39. Spend Time with Family
40. study

Most Honest American Politicians

1515 votes by 503 people

1. Abraham Lincoln
2. George Washington
3. Bill Clinton
4. Jimmy Carter
5. Abe Lincoln
6. George W. Bush
7. John McCain
8. John F. Kennedy
9. Ronald Reagan
10. Franklin Roosevelt
11. Thomas Jefferson
12. John Kerry
13. Theodore Roosevelt
14. Barack Obama
15. Al Gore
16. John Adams
17. Ralph Nader
18. Teddy Roosevelt
19. Harry Truman
20. Howard Dean
21. Benjamin Franklin
22. Colin Powell
23. Richard Nixon
24. Russ Feingold
25. FDR
26. none
27. Bob Dole
28. JFK
29. Dick Cheney
30. Dwight Eisenhower
31. Gerald Ford
32. Arnold Schwarzenegger
33. Rudy Giuliani
34. Andrew Jackson
35. Bush
36. John Edwards
37. Ross Perot
38. There
39. John Stewart
40. Donald Rumsfeld

Pleasantly Surprising Movies

1468 votes by 485 people

1. V for Vendetta
2. Serenity
3. Shrek
4. The Matrix
5. The Chronicles of Narnia
6. The Notebook
7. Garden State
8. Ice Age
9. Crash
10. Titanic
11. King Kong
12. Amelie
13. Brokeback Mountain
14. Fight Club
15. Napoleon Dynamite
16. Pirates of the Caribbean
17. Batman Begins
18. Pulp Fiction
19. The Butterfly Effect
20. The Princess Bride
21. Walk the Line
22. Spiderman
23. Sixth Sense
24. Mr. and Mrs. Smith
25. Love Actually
26. Memento
27. Finding Nemo
28. X-Men
29. Chicken Little
30. Shawshank Redemption
31. Saw
32. The Ring
33. Forrest Gump
34. The Island
35. 13 Going on 30
36. 10 Things I Hate about You
37. Vanilla Sky
38. Kill Bill
39. 50 First Dates
40. Toy Story

Top TV Shows You Secretly Watch

2046 votes by 679 people

1. American Idol
2. Desperate Housewives
3. Friends
4. The OC
5. Gilmore Girls
6. Survivor
7. Sex and the City
8. America's Next Top Model
9. Real World
10. Lost
11. Charmed
12. 24
13. Oprah
14. Project Runway
15. Buffy the Vampire Slayer
16. Smallville
17. Grey's Anatomy
18. Flavor of Love
19. Jerry Springer
20. Will and Grace
21. Veronica Mars
22. One Tree Hill
23. Deal or No Deal
24. Southpark
25. Simpsons
26. Big Brother
27. Full House
28. Law and Order
29. Wife Swap
30. Cops
31. Golden Girls
32. Surreal Life
33. General Hospital
34. ER
35. Family Guy
36. Queer Eye for the Straight Guy
37. Battlestar Galactica
38. Maury
39. Laguna Beach
40. CSI

Most Interesting Things You Can See from Where You Are Sitting

2114 votes by 700 people

1. computer
2. TV
3. my cat
4. trees
5. books
6. my dog
7. My Garden
8. my laptop
9. cell phone
10. My wife
11. Birds
12. My DVD Collection
13. My Laptop Screen
14. My iPod
15. Pictures of My Kids
16. my husband
17. monitor
18. Window
19. flowers
20. mountains
21. The Sky
22. the street
23. buildings
24. Bookshelf
25. The Sea
26. girlfriend
27. lake
28. my daughter
29. People
30. My son
31. outside
32. myself
33. Fish Tank
34. porno
35. My Guitar
36. Bong
37. My Screen
38. Mt. Rainier
39. The Horizon
40. Puget Sound

Top Overpaid Jobs

1920 votes by 647 people

1. CEO
2. athletes
3. actors
4. Lawyer
5. baseball player
6. Politician
7. Doctor
8. President
9. football player
10. Singers
11. manager
12. Dentist
13. CFO
14. accountant
15. Senator
16. Teacher
17. Model
18. Consultant
19. Airline Pilot
20. Investment Banker
21. Plumbers
22. garbage man
23. Engineers
24. Mutual-Fund Managers
25. Congressman
26. janitor
27. President of the United States
28. Real Estate Agents
29. Executives
30. Oil Company CEO
31. CIO
32. Management
33. Pharmacist
34. Construction Workers
35. Orthodontist
36. Pilot
37. Hockey Player
38. Corporate Attorneys
39. Programmers
40. Director

Top Operas
1388 votes by 454 people

1. Carmen
2. Madame Butterfly
3. La Boheme
4. Aida
5. La Traviata
6. The Magic Flute
7. Phantom of the Opera
8. The Marriage of Figaro
9. Don Giovanni
10. The Barber of Seville
11. Der Ring Des Nibelungen
12. Rigoletto
13. Tosca
14. Turandot
15. Tristan Und Isolde
16. Les Miserables
17. Otello
18. Cosi Fan Tutte
19. Carmina Burana
20. Nabucco
21. Strauss: Salome
22. Les Pecheurs de Perles
23. Wagner – Die Meistersinger Von Nurnberg
24. Cats
25. Romeo and Juliet
26. Die Fledermaus
27. Cavalleria Rusticana
28. Claudio Monteverdi – L'Orfeo
29. Capriccio
30. Pirates of Penzence
31. Tommy
32. Pagliacci
33. Fidelio
34. Porgy and Bess
35. Faust
36. Falstaff
37. Wozzeck
38. Macbeth
39. Adelia
40. The Flying Dutchman

Top Movies That Make You Laugh

1875 votes by 618 people

1. Monty Python and the Holy Grail
2. Dumb and Dumber
3. Office Space
4. American Pie
5. Old School
6. Shrek
7. Scary Movie
8. Wedding Crashers
9. Anchorman
10. Zoolander
11. Happy Gilmore
12. Super Troopers
13. Napoleon Dynamite
14. Caddyshack
15. There's Something about Mary
16. Airplane
17. Meet the Parents
18. Tommy Boy
19. Ice Age
20. The Big Lebowski
21. Spaceballs
22. Billy Madison
23. 40 Year Old Virgin
24. Animal House
25. The Jerk
26. Blazing Saddles
27. Some Like It Hot
28. Clerks
29. The Naked Gun
30. The Princess Bride
31. The Blues Brothers
32. Pink Panther
33. Liar Liar
34. Bruce Almighty
35. Harold and Kumar Go to White Castle
36. Ghost Busters
37. Austin Powers
38. Ace Ventura Pet Detective
39. Toy Story
40. Swingers

Best Wine Bar in Seattle

122 votes by 30 people

1. Portalis
2. The Sitting Room
3. Cafe Metropolitain
4. Eva Restaurant & Wine Bar
5. Smash Wine Bar & Bistro
6. Impromptu Wine Bar
7. Bricco Della Regina Anna (Queen Anne)
8. Impromptu Wine Bar Cafe
9. Volterra
10. Purple Cafe and Wine Bar
11. The Grape Choice
12. The Buckaroo Tavern
13. Tarragona Wine & Food
14. Commuter Comforts Cafe & Wine Bar
15. Starbucks
16. The Tasting Room
17. Cafe Campagne
18. Lead Gallery and Wine Bar
19. Impromptu Wine Bar Cafe
20. The White Horse Trading Co.
21. Barca
22. Canlis
23. Viceroy
24. The Herbfarm
25. World Cup Espresso & Wine
26. The Bungalow
27. Volterra
28. Ravenna Third Place Pub
29. Seattle's Historic Triangle Pub

Top US Cities for Pizza
2759 votes by 921 people

1. New York, NY
2. Chicago, IL
3. Boston, MA
4. Los Angeles, CA
5. Philadelphia, PA
6. San Francisco, CA
7. Miami, FL
8. Seattle, WA
9. Detroit, MI
10. New Haven, CT
11. St. Louis, MO
12. Houston, TX
13. Dallas, TX
14. Washington, D.C.
15. Phoenix, AZ
16. Las Vegas, NV
17. Denver, CO
18. Cleveland, OH
19. Atlanta, GA
20. San Diego, CA
21. Pittsburgh, PA
22. Buffalo, NY
23. Minneapolis
24. Kansas City
25. Austin
26. Newark
27. New Orleans
28. Rochester, NY
29. Hollywood
30. Providence, RI
31. Hoboken
32. Old Forge, PA
33. Portland, OR
34. San Antonio
35. Milwaukee
36. Cincinnati, OH
37. Orlando, FL
38. Baltimore
39. Atlantic City, NJ
40. Hartford, CT

Top Lines from Caddyshack
311 votes by 94 people

1. Last time I saw a mouth like that, it had a hook in it.
2. Hey everybody, we're all gonna get laid!
3. Be the ball
4. It's in the Hole!
5. You'll get nothing and like it
6. Remember Danny – Two wrongs don't make a right but three rights make a left.
7. Oh, this your wife, huh? a lovely lady. Hey baby, you must've been something before electricity.
8. This is good stuff. I got it from a negro. You're probably high already and you don't even know it.
9. A flute without holes isn't a flute. A donut without a hole is a danish.
10. Thank you very little.
11. Woah, somebody step on a duck?
12. So I got that goin' for me. Which is nice.
13. Do you use drugs Danny?
14. So I Jump ship in Hong Kong and make my way over to Tibet, and I get on as a looper at a course over in the Himalayas. a Looper, you know, a caddy, a looper, a jock. so, I tell them I'm a Pro Jock, and who do you think they give Me? the Dalai Lama
15. And I say, 'Hey, Lama, hey, how about a little something, you know, for the effort, you know.' and he says, 'Oh, uh, there won't be any money, but when you die, on your deathbed, you will receive total consciousness.' so i got that goin' for me
16. This crowd has gone deadly silent, a Cinderella Story outta nowhere. former greenskeeper and now about to become the masters champion.
17. It's a Cinderella Story
18. You're rather attractive for a beautiful girl with a great body.
19. You're a lot of woman, you know that? yeah, wanna make 14 dollars the hard way?
20. We have a pool and a pond...the pond would be good for you
21. We can do that. we don't even have to have a reason.
22. Don't sell yourself short judge, you're a tremendous slouch.
23. Oh Danny, this isn't Russia. Is this Russia? This isn't Russia is it?
24. I've sentenced boys younger than you to the gas chamber. Didn't want to do it. I felt I owed it to them.
25. I Smell Varmint Poontang.
26. Oh, but it looks good on you!
27. Yeah well, your Uncle molests collies.
28. Bark like a dog.
29. 100 Says He Eats It
30. Don't you people have homes?
31. I guess you'll just have to keep beating yourself.
32. Score

Top Sushi Restaurants in San Francisco, CA
842 votes by 264 people

1. Ebisu
2. Blowfish Sushi to Die for
3. Sushi Groove South
4. Tsunami
5. Anzu
6. Okoze
7. Sushi Bistro
8. Hama-Ko
9. Ozumo
10. Kabuto a&S
11. Zushi Puzzle
12. Kyo-Ya
13. Tokyo Go Go
14. Sushi Ran
15. Koo
16. Maki
17. Sanraku
18. Sushi Rock
19. Hamano Sushi
20. Niko Niko Sushi
21. Sushi Rika
22. Opera Plaza Sushi
23. Kirala
24. Kyoto Sushi
25. Yokoso Nippon
26. Sakana
27. Mifune Restaurant
28. We Be Sushi
29. Isobune
30. Osaka Japanese Restaurant
31. Minako
32. Godzila
33. Kiki
34. Kamakura Restaurant
35. Chin Sushi
36. Ace Wasabi's Rock 'N' Roll Sushi
37. Deep Sushi
38. Naked Fish
39. Ino Sushi
40. House of Sushi

Top Sports to Watch in Person

1521 votes by 502 people

1. American Football
2. Hockey
3. baseball
4. basketball
5. Soccer
6. Tennis
7. Rugby
8. Golf
9. boxing
10. Cricket
11. Volleyball
12. wrestling
13. NASCAR Racing
14. Figure Skating
15. Lacrosse
16. auto racing
17. gymnastics
18. Professional Wrestling
19. Curling
20. Handball
21. Rugby Union
22. Badminton
23. Billiards
24. ice skating
25. Mixed Martial Arts
26. horse racing
27. swimming
28. Kobe Bryant
29. Tiger Woods
30. Polo
31. Drag Racing
32. Water Polo
33. Skateboarding
34. Rugby League
35. Mud Wrestling
36. Woman's Vollyball
37. One Day Cricket
38. Equestrian Vaulting
39. Croquet
40. Professional Basketball

Most Overpaid Athletes
1519 votes by 503 people

1. Alex Rodriguez
2. Tiger Woods
3. Kobe Bryant
4. Terrell Owens
5. Michael Jordan
6. Shaquille O'Neal
7. Lebron James
8. Derek Jeter
9. Barry Bonds
10. David Beckham
11. Peyton Manning
12. Shaq
13. Sammy Sosa
14. Keyshawn Johnson
15. Johnny Damon
16. Kurt Warner
17. Michael Schumacher
18. Jason Giambi
19. Manny Ramirez
20. Dennis Rodman
21. Ken Griffey Jr
22. Kevin Brown
23. Allen Iverson
24. Michael Vick
25. Mike Tyson
26. Randy Moss
27. Brett Favre
28. Shawn Kemp
29. Mark McGwire
30. Jason Sehorn
31. Kevin Garnett
32. Grant Hill
33. Brett Farve
34. Anna Kournikova
35. Randy Johnson
36. Latrell Spreewell
37. Bryant Reeves
38. Mike Hampton
39. Ronaldo
40. Tom Brady

Most Hated Sports Teams

2053 votes by 688 people

1. New York Yankees
2. Dallas Cowboys
3. Los Angeles Lakers
4. Oakland Raiders
5. Boston Red Sox
6. Pittsburgh Steelers
7. New England Patriots
8. Green Bay Packers
9. Manchester United
10. Chicago Bulls
11. New York Mets
12. Chicago Cubs
13. Seattle Seahawks
14. Detroit Pistons
15. Philadelphia Eagles
16. Miami Dolphins
17. Detroit Red Wings
18. Denver Broncos
19. New York Giants
20. Red Sox
21. Atlanta Braves
22. NY Mets
23. Toronto Maple Leafs
24. Chicago Bears
25. New York Knicks
26. Chelsea
27. Washington Redskins
28. Minnesota Vikings
29. Duke Blue Devils
30. New York Rangers
31. Arsenal
32. Cleveland Browns
33. Miami Heat
34. New Jersey Devils
35. Tampa Bay Buccaneers
36. St. Louis Cardinals
37. White Sox
38. Chicago White Sox
39. Montreal Canadiens
40. Baltimore Ravens

Best Takeout Food in Seattle
242 votes by 74 people

1. Ezell's Famous Chicken
2. Pecos Pit BBQ
3. Pasta & Co
4. Sea-Thai
5. Dick's Drive-In
6. Pagliacci Pizza
7. Uwajimaya Inc.
8. Judy Fu's Snappy Dragon
9. Tutta Bella Neapolitan Pizzeria
10. Hana Restaurant
11. Romio's Pizza & Pasta- Eastlake
12. Philadelphia Fevre
13. Husky Deli
14. Red Mill Burgers Interbay
15. Shanghai Garden
16. New York Pizza Place
17. Salumi
18. Olympia Pizza
19. McDonald's
20. Thai Tom
21. The Cheesecake Factory
22. Porcella Urban Market
23. Mr. Gyros
24. Taco Del Mar
25. Chinese Deli Restaurant
26. Flying Pie Pizzeria
27. Buddha Ruksa
28. Phad Thai on 1st Ave.
29. Seattle Deli
30. Wendy's
31. Snap Dragon
32. Geneva
33. Ivar's Acres of Clams/Ivar's Seafood Bar
34. Golden Singha
35. Romio
36. Pasta & Co,
37. Five Point Cafe
38. Pagliacci Pizza, Any Pizza with a Salad
39. Applebees
40. Ruth's Chris Steak House

Best Things about the City in Portland, OR
310 votes by 101 people

1. People
2. Powell's Books
3. Weather
4. Parks
5. Close to Nature
6. Public Transportation
7. Scenery
8. Portland Trailblazers
9. Cleanliness
10. The Summers
11. Greenery
12. Rain
13. shopping
14. Great shopping—better than Seattle even though it's smaller
15. Downtown
16. culture
17. Forest Park
18. Diversity
19. No Sales Tax
20. beer
21. Oregon Zoo
22. 37,000 Acres of Parks
23. environment
24. Saturday Market
25. Bicycling – Awesome Trails and Support
26. Close to Mountains
27. Oregon Museum of Science & Industry
28. Size of the City
29. Liveability
30. Lack of Smog
31. Pambiche.
32. Bigger City with a Small-Town Feel
33. Brewpubs
34. The Landscapes
35. Civic Planning
36. Dynasty
37. Friendly people
38. Portland Steak & Chophouse
39. Original Nike Store Downtown
40. Community

Best Superhero Movies
272 votes by 107 people

1. Spider-man
2. Batman Begins
3. Batman
4. X2 – X-Men United
5. Superman 2
6. Batman Returns
7. Blade
8. Hellboy
9. Superman
10. The Hulk
11. Daredevil
12. Dr. Strange
13. Darkman
14. The Incredible Hulk
15. Spider-Man 2
16. Mission Impossible
17. The Punisher
18. Fantastic 4
19. James Bond Movie Series
20. X-Men Series
21. Terminator
22. Mystery Men
23. Catwoman
24. Unbreakable
25. Spawn
26. Men in Black
27. X-Men
28. The Incredibles
29. Superman Returns
30. Aeon Flux
31. The Hulk (Remake)
32. Batman Series
33. Batman Forever
34. Elektra
35. Teenage Mutant Ninja Turtles
36. V for Vendetta
37. The Crow
38. Ironman
39. The Matrix
40. Sin City

Top NFL Running Backs

708 votes by 228 people

1. Walter Payton
2. Barry Sanders
3. Jim Brown
4. Shaun Alexander
5. Emmitt Smith
6. LaDainian Tomlinson
7. Tiki Barber
8. Eric Dickerson
9. O.J. Simpson
10. Priest Holmes
11. Gale Sayers
12. Clinton Portis
13. Edgerrin James
14. Jerome Bettis
15. Marshall Faulk
16. Larry Johnson
17. Brian Westbrook
18. Corey Dillon
19. Tony Dorsett
20. Rudy Johnson
21. Curtis Martin
22. Ricky Williams
23. Tomlinson
24. Deshaun Foster
25. Earl Campbell
26. Jamal Lewis
27. Marcus Allen
28. Willis McGahee
29. Rich Alexis
30. Warrick Dunn
31. John Riggins
32. Chris Brown
33. Terrel Davis
34. Bo Jackson
35. Reggie Bush
36. Terry Metcalf
37. P. Holmes
38. Alexander, Shaun
39. Ahman Green
40. William Perry

Worst Things about Minneapolis, MN

328 votes by 107 people

1. Traffic
2. Weather
3. Cold Winters
4. Crime
5. Snow
6. Lack of Public Transportation
7. Parking
8. Bad drivers
9. Road Construction
10. Lake Street
11. Pollution
12. Violence
13. mosquitos
14. Urban Sprawl
15. Mall of America (Overrated)
16. The excess of Caribou Coffee locations
17. High Taxes
18. I35w and I94 Merge and Unmerge
19. Vandalism
20. Too Much Traffic, Hard to Commute to Work
21. nothing
22. Nicollet Mall has bad hours on weekends
23. Traffic in Rush Hour
24. litter
25. Police
26. High Population
27. Public Transit (But the Light Rail Is Helping a Lot)
28. Terrible Airport (MSP)
29. men
30. Republicans in Government
31. Crack Heads
32. Winter Driving
33. Constant Road Construction
34. The Poor Club Scene
35. Minnesota Twins
36. Smell on Block E Form Sewers
37. Sort of boring
38. Nightlife
39. Smoking Ban
40. Expensive

Top Celebrity Hair

2528 votes by 783 people

1. Jennifer Aniston
2. Jessica Simpson
3. Angelina Jolie
4. Brad Pitt
5. Tom Cruise
6. Nicole Kidman
7. Eva Longoria
8. Paris Hilton
9. Jessica Alba
10. George Clooney
11. Julia Roberts
12. Jennifer Lopez
13. Catherine Zeta-Jones
14. Johnny Depp
15. Halle Berry
16. Gwen Stefani
17. Lindsay Lohan
18. Charlize Theron
19. Reese Witherspoon
20. Katie Holmes
21. Britney Spears
22. Marcia Cross
23. Madonna
24. Donald Trump
25. Cameron Diaz
26. Pamela Anderson
27. Cher
28. Heather Locklear
29. Debra Messing
30. Meg Ryan
31. Scarlett Johansson
32. Nicole Richie
33. Beyonce
34. Gwyneth Paltrow
35. Natalie Portman
36. Ashlee Simpson
37. Hilary Duff
38. Conan O'Brien
39. Demi Moore
40. Orlando Bloom

Top Musical Instruments
2871 *votes by 963 people*

1. Guitar
2. Piano
3. Drums
4. Electric Guitar
5. Violin
6. Saxophone
7. Bass guitar
8. Trumpet
9. Cello
10. Flute
11. Synthesizer
12. Keyboard
13. Trombone
14. Clarinet
15. Harp
16. Organ
17. Banjo
18. Harpsichord
19. Voice
20. French Horn
21. Fender Stratocaster
22. Tuba
23. Sitar
24. Viola
25. Theremin
26. Harmonica
27. Bagpipes
28. Mandolin
29. Accordion
30. Bassoon
31. Electric Bass
32. Cowbell
33. Grand Piano
34. Oboe
35. Hammond Organ
36. Timpani
37. Kazoo
38. Triangle
39. 12 String Guitar
40. Upright Bass

Top US Cities for Mexican Food
2337 votes by 777 people

1. Los Angeles
2. San Antonio
3. San Diego
4. Houston
5. Dallas
6. New York
7. Austin
8. El Paso
9. Phoenix
10. Santa Fe
11. San Francisco
12. Miami
13. Albuquerque
14. Chicago
15. Tucson, AZ
16. San Jose
17. Las Vegas
18. Denver
19. LA
20. San Diego, California
21. Boston
22. New Mexico
23. Texas
24. Los Angeles, California
25. Mexico City
26. El Paso, Texas
27. Fort Worth
28. Tuscon
29. Seattle
30. Phoenix
31. Detroit
32. Santa Barbara
33. Washington, DC
34. Brownsville, TX
35. Tampa
36. NYC
37. Baja, CA
38. Sacramento
39. Phoenix, Arizona
40. Portland, OR

Top after Work Bars in San Francisco, CA
609 votes by 190 people

1. The Cellar
2. Tony Niks
3. Royal Exchange
4. Vertigo
5. Wish
6. Elixir
7. Zeitgeist
8. Lush Piano Bar
9. Irish Bank
10. Catalyst Cocktails
11. Mars Bar & Restaurant
12. Arrow Bar
13. Lion Pub
14. Beale Street Bar & Grill
15. Beach Chalet
16. Club Six
17. Le Colonial
18. Martuni's
19. DNA Lounge
20. Top of the Mark
21. Metreon
22. Marriott San Francisco
23. Trader Vic's
24. Blondie's Bar and No-Grill
25. Nova
26. First Crush Restaurant Wine Bar & Lounge
27. Cav
28. Ruth's Chris Steak House
29. Madrone Lounge
30. San Francisco Brewing Company
31. Edinburgh Castle
32. Bix
33. Tunnel Top
34. Biscuits and Blues
35. London Wine Bar
36. Schroeder's
37. Beale Street Bar
38. Magnet
39. Lingba Lounge
40. Asiasf

Best Memories of Your Childhood

1774 votes by 587 people

1. Going to Disney World
2. Family Vacations
3. Christmas
4. first kiss
5. birthdays
6. camping
7. school
8. Friends
9. going to the beach
10. Family Trips
11. Christmas Mornings
12. Playing with Friends
13. Riding My Bike
14. Birthday Parties
15. Summer camp
16. playing
17. sports
18. My Grandparents
19. baseball
20. swimming
21. Hiking
22. reading
23. Climbing Trees
24. Learning to Ride a Bike
25. traveling
26. sex
27. My First Dog
28. my dog
29. horseback riding
30. Easter
31. Kindergarten
32. Playing with My Brother
33. Going to School
34. Fishing
35. My First Girlfriend
36. Holidays
37. First Puppy
38. Staying at My Grandparents' House
39. First Bike
40. Hanging Out with My Cousins

Top Small Live Music Venues in Minneapolis, MN
252 votes by 77 people

1. Fine Line Music Cafe
2. First Avenue
3. The Quest
4. First Avenue & 7th Street Entry
5. Cabooze
6. 7th Street Entry
7. Fine Line
8. Turf Club
9. The Liffey Irish Pub
10. Rossi's Blue Star Room
11. Triple Rock Social Club
12. Four Hundred Bar
13. Venue Night Club & Live Music
14. Triple Rock
15. Minnesota Music Cafe
16. Quest Club
17. Big V's
18. First Avenune
19. The Fine Line
20. Varsity Theater
21. Dinkytowner Cafe
22. Kieran's Irish Pub
23. Myth
24. The Nomad
25. 331 Club
26. The Varsity Theatre
27. 7 St Entry
28. The Quest Club
29. Martini's
30. The Times
31. Shout House Dueling Pianos
32. The Gay 90's
33. Famous Dave's
34. Gluek's Bar & Restaurant
35. Weisman Art Museum Theatre
36. The Steak Knife
37. TC (Twin Cities) Underground
38. Glass J

Most Adventurous Things You Have Done

2037 votes by 674 people

1. Skydiving
2. rock climbing
3. bungee jumping
4. mountain climbing
5. white water rafting
6. Scuba diving
7. got married
8. parasailing
9. Parachuting
10. Cliff Diving
11. Skiing
12. snowboarding
13. Hiking
14. River Rafting
15. skinny dipped
16. travel
17. Public Sex
18. Surfing
19. Jumped Out of a Plane
20. Cliff Jumping
21. Rapelling
22. camping
23. flying
24. Kayaking
25. Jumped off a Cliff
26. downhill skiing
27. Climbed Mount Everest
28. Climbing MT. Rainier
29. threesome
30. Started My Own Business
31. Rollercoaster
32. Drag Racing
33. Run Away from Home
34. Caving
35. Joined the Army
36. Free Climbing
37. Sex Outdoors
38. BASE Jumping
39. Abseiling
40. Swam with Dolphins

Best Pubs in Washington, DC
140 votes by 40 people

1. Kelly's Irish Times
2. The Dubliner
3. Brickskeller Saloon
4. Finn MacCool's
5. Duffy's Irish Restaurant and Pub
6. Fado Irish Pub
7. Nanny O'Briens
8. MacKey's Public House
9. Lucky Bar
10. Fox and Hound
11. Townhouse Tavern
12. Irish Channel
13. Atomic Billiards
14. Georgetown Station
15. Madam's Organ
16. fireplace
17. Tombs
18. Mr. Smith's
19. Legends
20. Ye Olde Curiosity Shoppe
21. Ireland's Four Courts
22. O'Toole's Restaurant Pub
23. Post Pub Inc
24. K Street Whores
25. Maggie Moos
26. 51st State
27. Ireland's Four Provinces
28. The Ugly Mug
29. Capitol City Brewing Co.
30. Pike's Place Market
31. Watergate Hole
32. Ireland's Four Green Fields
33. The Post Pub
34. Blue Gin
35. Kirkpatrick's Irish Pub, Sports Bar & Family Grille
36. Froggy Bottom Pub
37. 930 Club
38. Fireplace
39. McKeevers Pub
40. Tequila Beach

Top Jobs You Wanted When You Were a Child

2192 votes by 730 people

1. Fireman
2. Doctor
3. Astronaut
4. Teacher
5. Policeman
6. Veterinarian
7. Lawyer
8. Nurse
9. Scientist
10. Pilot
11. Baseball Player
12. Writer
13. Artist
14. Actress
15. Marine Biologist
16. Ballerina
17. Singer
18. Computer Programmer
19. Actor
20. Rock Star
21. Architect
22. Engineer
23. Paleontologist
24. Dancer
25. President
26. Football Player
27. Soldier
28. Musician
29. Archeologist
30. Garbage Man
31. Mommy
32. Chef
33. Astronomer
34. Florist
35. Race Car Driver
36. Fighter Pilot
37. Farmer
38. Zoo Keeper
39. Truck Driver
40. Librarian

Top Diet Drinks
1644 votes by 550 people

1. Diet Coke
2. Diet Pepsi
3. Diet Dr. Pepper
4. Diet Sprite
5. water
6. Tab
7. Slim Fast
8. Diet Mountain Dew
9. Fresca
10. Coke Zero
11. Diet 7-Up
12. Crystal Light
13. Diet Cherry Vanilla Dr. Pepper
14. Ensure
15. Diet Coke with Lime
16. Diet Vanilla Coke
17. Diet Cherry Coke
18. Diet Root Beer
19. tea
20. green tea
21. milk
22. iced tea
23. diet soda
24. Diet Snapple
25. Celebrity Diet
26. bottled water
27. Atkins Advantage
28. grapefruit juice
29. Diet Coke with Splenda
30. Diet Gingerale
31. lemonade
32. Diet Coke with Lemon
33. Orange Juice
34. hot tea
35. Boost
36. Coke Light
37. juice
38. Carb Solutions
39. Diet Fanta
40. Diet Cream Soda

Top Steak Houses in New York, NY

679 votes by 210 people

1. Peter Luger
2. The Strip House
3. Sparks
4. Ruth's Chris Steak House
5. Old Homestead
6. Frankie & Johnnie's Steakhouse
7. Del Frisco's Double Eagle Steak House
8. Uncle Jack's Steakhouse
9. Gallagher's Steak House
10. BLT Prime
11. Les Halles
12. Blt Steak
13. Mark Joseph Steakhouse
14. Morton's
15. Joe Broadway Steak House
16. Dylan Prime
17. Ben Benson's
18. Delmonico's
19. Keens Steakhouse
20. Smith and Wollensky
21. Churrascaria Plataforma
22. Bobby Van's Steakhouse
23. Outback Steakhouse
24. Manhattan Grille
25. MacElleria
26. Shula's Steak House
27. Michael Jordan's Steak House
28. The Steakhouse at Monkey Bar
29. Soho Steak
30. Palm
31. Angelo & Maxie's
32. Wogies Restaurant
33. Peter Lugers
34. Ruth Chris
35. Ruth's Chris
36. Uncle Jacks
37. Maloney and Porcelli
38. Keens Steak House
39. Heartland Brewery Chop House
40. Ruth Chris Steakhouse

Top NFL Quarterbacks

987 votes by 321 people

1. Joe Montana
2. Peyton Manning
3. Tom Brady
4. Dan Marino
5. John Elway
6. Brett Favre
7. Johnny Unitas
8. Joe Namath
9. Steve Young
10. Brett Farve
11. Carson Palmer
12. Donovan McNabb
13. Terry Bradshaw
14. Michael Vick
15. Troy Aikman
16. Ben Roethlisberger
17. Bart Starr
18. Roger Staubach
19. Matt Hasselbeck
20. Eli Manning
21. Otto Graham
22. Daunte Culpepper
23. Drew Bledsoe
24. Vince Young
25. Jim McMahon
26. Sammy Baugh
27. Kerry Collins
28. Phil Simms
29. Bob Griese
30. Bernie Kosar
31. Jake Delhomme
32. Rex Grossman
33. Joey Harrington
34. Joe Theisman
35. Drew Brees
36. Mark Brunell
37. Kurt Warner
38. Jim Kelly
39. Micheal Vick
40. Brad Johnson

Most Beautiful View Spots in Boston, MA

461 votes by 140 people

1. Top of the Hub
2. Boston Common
3. Boston Harbor
4. Fenway Park
5. Boston Public Garden
6. Charles River
7. Freedom Trail
8. Charles River Esplanade
9. Bunker Hill Monument
10. Meritage
11. Waterfront
12. Bunker Hill
13. Prudential Center
14. Harvard Square
15. Jamaica Pond
16. Christian Science Center
17. Long Wharf
18. Harvard Yard
19. The Roof of the Tisch Library, Tufts University
20. Longfellow Bridge
21. Back Bay
22. Old North Church
23. Castle Island
24. The Zakim Bunker Hill Bridge
25. Quincy Market
26. Bay View
27. Beacon Hill
28. U.S.S. Constitution
29. Decordova Museum and Sculpture Park
30. Walden Pond
31. Nickerson
32. The Cheers Bar
33. North End
34. Boston Harbor Islands – looking back towards Boston
35. The Radisson Hotel
36. Bay Tower Room
37. Boston Harbor Island National Park
38. Downtown
39. Esplanade
40. Castle Island Pier

Top Guilty Pleasure Movies
1399 votes by 463 people

1. Titanic
2. American Pie
3. Dirty Dancing
4. Mean Girls
5. Showgirls
6. Bring it On
7. The Notebook
8. Clueless
9. 10 Things I Hate about You
10. Pretty Woman
11. Police Academy
12. The Princess Bride
13. Basic Instinct
14. Pulp Fiction
15. Beaches
16. Harry Potter
17. Star Wars
18. Steel Magnolias
19. Weekend at Bernies
20. Super Troopers
21. Legally Blonde
22. Dumb and Dumber
23. Zoolander
24. The Secretary
25. Armageddon
26. Just One of the Guys
27. Notting Hill
28. Kill Bill
29. Ice Age
30. Sleepless in Seattle
31. The Little Mermaid
32. Toy Story
33. Forrest Gump
34. Pretty in Pink
35. Revenge of the Nerds
36. When Harry Met Sally
37. Eyes Wide Shut
38. Bill & Ted's Excellent Adventure
39. 40 Year Old Virgin
40. Better Off Dead

Worst Things about Atlanta, GA

357 votes by 111 people

1. Traffic
2. Crime
3. Pollution
4. smog
5. Weather
6. Humidity
7. traffic congestion
8. Not enough walking areas
9. Terrible Traffic
10. Bums
11. Bad drivers
12. Conservative People
13. City Politics
14. Weather-hot and humid spring/summers
15. Rush Hour
16. MARTA doesn't go enough places
17. Traffic on All Major Roads and Highways
18. Diversity
19. Rednecks
20. Michael Vick
21. Public Transportation
22. Abundant Bad Drivers
23. Taxes
24. Gas Prices
25. cost of living
26. Rain
27. Panhandlers & crackheads all over downtown
28. Traffic on I75/85
29. Religious Zealots
30. Education
31. Extreme climate, if hot very hot if cold very cold
32. Ton of People
33. too many people
34. Weather = Humidity
35. Bulloch Hall
36. Bonadochie
37. Atlanta Hawks
38. Homeless
39. Crowed
40. radio

Best Breakfast Places in Bellevue, WA

183 votes by 52 people

1. Pancake Corral
2. 12th Avenue Cafe
3. Eques
4. My Favorite Piroshky
5. IHOP
6. Maltby Cafe the
7. Bellevue Bed and Breakfast
8. Lil Jon's
9. Five Point Cafe
10. Denny's
11. El Greco
12. Tully's Coffee – Bellevue
13. Marsee's Bakery
14. Wild Mountain Cafe
15. The Dumpster
16. The Fremont Dock
17. Thai Ginger Restaurants
18. Belle Pastry
19. Dunkin Donuts
20. Organic to Go
21. Vera's Restaurant
22. Sweet Addition
23. Dish
24. Original Pancake House
25. Gilbert's Main Street Bagel
26. Cinnabon
27. Cafe Aura
28. Costal Kitchen
29. McCormmick's & Smidt's
30. Big Apple Bagels
31. Cafe Soleil
32. Friendly's
33. Bellevue Breakfast Rotary Club
34. Firenze Ristorante Italiano
35. Bouchee Creperie and Cafe
36. Ramada Inn
37. Uwajimaya
38. Tulio Ristorante
39. Salish Lodge Dining Room
40. Cafe Flora

Top Sports Quotes

897 votes by 299 people

1. It ain't over till it's over. – Yogi Berra
2. If practice makes perfect, and no one is perfect, why practice?
3. Show me a guy whos afraid to look bad, and I'll show you a guy you can beat every time. -Lou Brock
4. Winners don't wait for chances, they take them
5. Float like a butterfly, sting like a bee.
6. Baseball is 90% mental—the other half is physical.
7. Winning means you're willing to go longer, work harder, and give more than anyone else. – Vince Lombardi
8. Win One for the Gipper
9. Champions aren't made in the gyms. Champions are made from something they have deep inside them—a Desire, a Dream, a Vision.
10. If at first you don't succeed, you are running about average.
11. You don't win the silver, you lose the gold
12. Pain is only temporary but victory is forever
13. It's déja vu all over again.
14. Do you believe in miracles?
15. Don't look back. something might be gaining on you
16. Sweat plus sacrifice equals success.
17. There is no I in team
18. It is a rough road that leads to the heights of greatness.
19. I'm going to Disney World
20. There's no substitute for guts.
21. When I Step onto the court, I don't have to think about anything. If I have a problem off the court, I find that after I play, my mind is clearer and I can come up with a better solution. It's like therapy. It relaxes me and allows me to solve problems.
22. He shoots, He scores
23. "Boom"- John Madden
24. Players win games, teams win championships
25. No one knows what to say in the loser's locker room.
26. You have to expect things of yourself before you can do them.
27. Doctors and scientists said that breaking the four-minute mile was impossible, that one would die in the attempt. Thus, when I got up from the track after collapsing at the finish line, I figured I was dead.
28. I am the greatest
29. Whoever said, 'It's not whether you win or lose that counts,' probably lost. – Martina Navratilova
30. Impossible is nothing. Impossible is just a big word thrown around by small men who find it easier to live in a world that they have been given than to explore the power they have to change it. Impossible is not a fact. It's an opinion. Impossible is not a declaration. It's a dare. Impossible is potential. Impossible is temporary. Impossible is nothing

31. Sure, luck means a lot in football. not having a good quarterback is bad luck.

32. The only way to overcome is to hang in. even I'm starting to believe that.

33. Love is playing every game as if it's your last. – Michael Jordan

34. The will to win is important, but the will to prepare is vital.

35. It ain't over till the fat lady sings

36. Bench warming isn't a position

37. Have Another Donut, You Fat Pig! – Jim Schoenfeld

38. Don't give up. don't ever give up.

39. Just win baby

Best Mothers Day Gifts

317 votes by 103 people

1. flowers
2. chocolate
3. Jewelry
4. card
5. breakfast in bed
6. gift certificate
7. candy
8. Dinner at a nice restaurant
9. iPod Nano
10. perfume
11. Spa Products
12. Airplane Tickets
13. money
14. A Poem
15. Nice Dinner Out
16. a book
17. massage
18. Orchids
19. Beautiful flowers for her garden
20. Framed Print
21. A Vibrator
22. A hug
23. Any Kind of Crystal
24. coffee mug
25. Home Made Salmon Dinner
26. Spend Time with Her
27. travel
28. A trip to somewhere she's never been before
29. scented candles
30. Custom CD burned with pictures of all her kids and grandkids
31. Jewelry – maybe involving diamonds
32. Anything Homemade
33. Wash Her Car
34. Trip to the Spa
35. Sarah Jessica Parker's lovely perfume
36. Framed Photos
37. Visit in Person
38. iPod or mp3 Player
39. Take her to her favorite restaurant with all her children.
40. cake

Worst Superheroes of All Time

327 votes by 108 people

1. Aquaman
2. Robin
3. Captain Planet
4. Superman
5. Wonder Woman
6. Batman
7. Spiderman
8. Green Lantern
9. Captain America
10. The Flash
11. Wonder Twins
12. Hulk
13. Daredevil
14. Shazam
15. Birdman
16. Bat Girl
17. Mighty Mouse
18. Bouncing Boy
19. Flash Gordon
20. Plastic Man
21. Radioactive Man
22. Thing
23. the Shmoo
24. Iceman
25. Superted
26. All X-Men
27. Cyclops (X-Men)
28. Jubilee
29. Supergirl
30. Nighthawk
31. The Incredible Hulk
32. Superdog
33. Diaper Boy
34. The Fantastic Four
35. Buttman
36. Superball
37. Spawn
38. Mister Fantastic
39. Hitler
40. Tighty Whitey Man

Best Things about the City in Atlanta, GA

481 votes by 157 people

1. Weather
2. The Braves
3. Georgia Aquarium
4. food
5. Georgia Tech
6. People
7. Underground Atlanta
8. Good Restaurants
9. Hospitality
10. shopping
11. The Varsity
12. Friendly people
13. Parks
14. Turner Field
15. Little Five Points
16. Zoo Atlanta
17. Entertainment
18. Diversity
19. Affordable Living
20. Atlanta Falcons
21. Climate
22. trees
23. culture
24. Atlanta Botanical Garden
25. Midtown
26. Six Flags
27. sports
28. Beautiful City
29. Buckhead
30. Soul Food
31. International Airport Hub
32. Stone Mountain
33. Music scene
34. You're just minutes away from the airport!
35. Excellent Restaurants
36. Its in the South
37. B.O.H
38. The Spirit of the People
39. Jumping off point to southern day-trips
40. Coca-Cola Pavilion

Least Romantic US Cities
2447 votes by 817 people

1. Detroit
2. Los Angeles
3. Cleveland
4. Pittsburgh
5. Chicago
6. Dallas
7. Houston
8. New York
9. Atlanta
10. Las Vegas
11. Washington DC
12. Newark
13. Miami
14. Salt Lake City
15. Boston
16. Orlando
17. Buffalo, NY
18. Denver
19. New Orleans
20. Seattle
21. Philadelphia
22. Boise
23. Gary, IN
24. Omaha
25. Baltimore
26. Phoenix
27. Gary, Indiana
28. Fargo, ND
29. New Jersey
30. Tulsa
31. Austin
32. Kansas City
33. Little Rock
34. Indianapolis
35. Oklahoma City
36. San Francisco
37. El Paso, TX
38. Portland, OR
39. Milwaukee
40. Cincinnati

Top After-work Bars in Los Angeles, CA

502 votes by 153 people

1. Cabo Cantina
2. Bungalow Club
3. Cat & Fiddle
4. Red Lion Tavern
5. Crown City Brewery
6. Red Rock
7. Cat N' Fiddle Pub & Restaurant
8. Backstage
9. Colorado Bar
10. Abbey
11. Señor Fred
12. Boardner's
13. Akbar
14. Lowenbrau Keller
15. The Well
16. El Coyote
17. Boardwalk 11
18. Positive
19. Barney's Beanery
20. Bigfoot Lodge
21. Beauty Bar
22. Malo
23. Vault 350
24. Fox & Hounds
25. Bodega de Cordova
26. Trader Vics
27. Liquid Kitty
28. Derby
29. White Lotus
30. Maloney's
31. The Abbey
32. The Mint
33. The Bowery
34. Father's Office
35. Grand Avenue Sports Bar
36. El Carmen Restaurant
37. Burgundy Room
38. Bar Marmont
39. Aloha Sharkeez, Hermosa Beach
40. Balboa Saloon

Best Things about the City in Houston, TX

237 votes by 72 people

1. Restaurants
2. People
3. Weather
4. shopping
5. Diverse Culture
6. Houston Rockets/Yao Ming
7. Houston Astros
8. Space Center Houston
9. NASA
10. Entertainment
11. Music Venues
12. Nightlife
13. Cheaper Living
14. Museums
15. Major Sports Teams—Astros, Rockets, Texans, Aeros
16. sports
17. beach
18. Low cost of living (for big city)
19. Booming Economy
20. Houston Dynamo
21. Home buying
22. Rice University
23. It's Not Florida
24. Downtown
25. Great Atmosphere
26. Cheap Housing
27. Metro
28. The Hyatt
29. Sports Support
30. One of the fastest growing cities in the US.
31. Friendly Residents
32. Hospitals
33. The Women
34. size
35. The Medical Center
36. Punk Scene
37. Bill White
38. Things to Do
39. Medical Center
40. Stores

Your Favorite UTF-8 Character

444 votes by 139 people

1. 簡
2. ₪
3. ö
4. ⛄
5. $
6. ♪
7. ♠
8. !
9. ©
10. @
11. ~
12. æ
13. Ÿ
14. &
15. ∞
16. ¥
17. ☙
18. £
19. ℧
20. ð
21. #
22. ç
23. §
24. ⌘
25. °
26. é
27. ™
28. ʔ
29. ☞
30. Й
31. Ц
32. à
33. ▨
34. ☺
35. Non-Breaking Space (160)
36. ﷽
37. ㅋ
38. 𝑚
39. €
40. ₲

Our Lists

Members of the UnSpun team created many lists. Many of these reflect personal interests and hobbies. Others were spurred by a desire to see what the community would enter or to learn something new about a topic. Note: The creator of a list has no control over the content of a list, and may not agree with the inclusion or ordering of the items presented here.

Best Classic Rock Instrumental

Jonathan

1. Little Wing – Stevie Ray Vaughan
2. Black Mountain Side – Led Zeppelin
3. Interstellar Overdrive – Pink Floyd
4. Glad – Traffic
5. In Memory of Elizabeth Reed – the Allman Brothers
6. Peaches En Regalia-Mothers of Invention
7. Any Colour You like
8. Soul Sacrifice – Santana
9. Fire on High – ELO
10. Jessica
11. Green Onions
12. Lazy-Deep Purple
13. Lark's Tongue in Aspic – King Crimson
14. Beck's Bolero – Jeff Beck
15. Hocus Pocus – Focus
16. Steamer Lane Breakdown – Doobie Brothers
17. Moby Dick – Led Zeppelin
18. Frankenstein – Edgar Winter Group
19. Funeral for a Friend – Elton John

Best Paul McCartney Song (Solo Career)

Jonathan

1. Band on the Run
2. Live and Let Die
3. my love
4. No More Lonely Nights
5. Say Say Say (With Michael Jackson)
6. Let Me Roll It
7. Maybe I'm Amazed
8. Jet
9. Here Today (Song For John Lennon)
10. Hi Hi Hi
11. Silly Love Song
12. Ebony and Ivory
13. Listen to What the Man Said
14. Let 'Em in
15. Helen Wheels
16. Ram on
17. Nobody Knows
18. Mull of Kintyre
19. Back on My Feet
20. Coming up
21. Another Day
22. Press
23. Distractions
24. The Girl Is Mine
25. Peace in the Neighborhood
26. Uncle Albert /Admiral Halsey
27. Too Many People
28. With a Little Luck
29. Ever Present past
30. Tug of War
31. Waterfalls
32. We All Stand Together
33. Temporary Secretary
34. Junior's Farm
35. Getting Closer
36. Daytime Nighttime Suffering
37. Take It Away
38. Warm and Beautiful
39. Beautiful Night
40. Dance Tonight

Funniest Saturday Night Live Comedian
Jonathan

1. John Belushi
2. Will Ferrell
3. Adam Sandler
4. Chris Farley
5. Chevy Chase
6. Jimmy Fallon
7. Phil Hartman
8. Mike Meyers
9. Gilda Radner
10. Bill Murray
11. Dan Aykroyd
12. Dana Carvey
13. Eddie Murphy
14. Tina Fey
15. Chris Rock
16. Dennis Miller
17. Darrell Hammond
18. Martin Short
19. Molly Shannon
20. Norm MacDonald
21. Seth Meyers
22. Al Franken
23. Kristen Wiig
24. Kevin Nealon
25. Amy Poehler
26. Billy Crystal
27. Maya Rudolph
28. Garrett Morris
29. David Spade
30. Jon Lovitz
31. Cheri Oteri
32. Chris Kattan
33. Fred Pyror
34. Sarah Silverman

Favorite Sesame Street Muppet
Jonathan

1. Oscar the Grouch
2. Big Bird
3. Elmo
4. Kermit the Frog
5. Ernie
6. Cookie Monster
7. Grover
8. Bert
9. The Count
10. Snuffleupagus
11. Prairie Dawn
12. Two Headed Monster
13. Herry Monster
14. Barkley
15. The Honkers
16. Rosita
17. Guy Smiley
18. Telly
19. Bert and Ernie
20. Alice
21. The Martians
22. Don Music
23. Slimey
24. Zoe
25. Baby Bear
26. Natasha
27. Betty Lou

Best Alternate History Books

Jonathan

1. The Man in the High Castle by Philip K. Dick
2. America the Book
3. The Intuitionist
4. HG Wells – Men like Gods
5. The Guns of the South
6. For the Glory of God by Rodney Stark
7. Holy Blood, Holy Grail by Michael Baigent
8. Gunpowder Empire – Harry Turtledove
9. The Eyre Affair
10. Lost in a Good Book
11. A People's History of the US
12. Hitler Victorious by Benford
13. Anything Written by Howard Zinn
14. Annals of the World by James Ussher
15. Fingerprints of the Gods by Graham Hancock
16. Alternate Generals
17. Two Georges
18. Pavane
19. Alternate Generals by Harry Turtledove
20. Terry Pratchett – Night Watch
21. The Probability Broach – L. Neil Smith
22. The Great War in England in 1897
23. Night Watch
24. The Guns of the South by Harry Turtledove
25. Anything Written by Noam Chomsky
26. Vladimir Nabokov – Ada or Ardor
27. The Ultimate Solution
28. The 12th Planet by Zecharia Sitchin
29. And Having Writ – D.R. Benson
30. World War (Harry Turtledove Series)
31. The 12th Planet
32. What If?
33. Fatherland
34. A Connecticut Yankee in King Arthur's Court

Most Important Things to Do before You Die
Jeff

1. Have a lot of Sex
2. Have children
3. Write a Will
4. Tell your family how much you love them
5. Make sure not to die as a virgin
6. Fall in love
7. Travel around the world
8. get married
9. Visit New Zealand
10. Make sure you are right with God
11. Raise happy and healthy children
12. Enjoy life
13. Let others know how you feel about them
14. Climb the Great Pyramid.
15. Pay off all debts
16. Respect other people
17. Reconcile with your parents
18. Leave money to loved ones
19. Take a lazy train trip across Europe
20. Plant a Tree
21. Visit Paris France
22. Visit at least half of the United States
23. Find true love
24. Make the world a better place then when you where born.
25. Love deeply
26. Experience life as much as is possible
27. Making as many people as possible feel beloved
28. Read all the books in my collection
29. Learn as many languages & visit as many countries as you're able to
30. Write a novel
31. Let everyone you love know that you love them.
32. Accept Jesus as your saviour
33. Skydive
34. Build a "Generations House"
35. Love others selfishly
36. Visit New York City
37. Admit sin, repent, and receive Jesus Christ as your lord and savior.
38. Write a book
39. Tell people you love them
40. Spend all of your money

Best Places to Buy Robotics Components
Jeff

1. Lego Catalog
2. Radio Shack
3. Digikey
4. Future-Bot Components.
5. Amazon.com
6. Jameco Electronics
7. Home Depot
8. banebots.com
9. Parallax Inc.
10. Arrick Robotics
11. Quanser Inc.
12. Fry's
13. usedrobot.com
14. active-robots.com
15. Junk Yard
16. Acroname
17. Fanuc World
18. Phidgets
19. Circuit City
20. Wal-Mart
21. robotmarketplace.com
22. Hobby Shack
23. National Instruments
24. budgetrobotics.com
25. speechchip.com
26. poweronline.com
27. Mondo-Tronics Robot Store
28. Denso
29. Best Buy
30. buy.com
31. lynxmotion.com
32. New Micros, Inc
33. ATI Industrial Automation
34. Electronic Goldmine
35. robotic.directory.alibaba.com
36. Milford Instruments
37. Automatrics.
38. dajin.en.ec21.com
39. Technobots

Best Pubs in Charlottesville, VA

Andy H.

1. O'Neill's Pub
2. Court Square Tavern
3. South Street Brewery
4. Biltmore Grill
5. Buddhist Biker Bar and Grill
6. Club 216
7. Durty Nelly's Pub
8. Starr Hill Restaurant, Brewery & Music Hall
9. Firehouse Bar and Grill
10. Down under
11. The Ups
12. Charlottes Publishers
13. Mudhouse
14. Halloway's
15. Starbucks
16. O'Neill's Irish Pub
17. Outback Lodge
18. Sharkey'S Bar and Grill
19. Treior
20. Burger King
21. Tavern
22. TJ's Sports Pub & Club Office
23. Club
24. Frank's Pub
25. Hilton Publishers
26. Harvey Publishers
27. Cagué
28. Shebeen Pub & Braai
29. Lovingstons Cafe
30. TJ's Sports Pub
31. Wendy's
32. Prism Coffeehouse
33. Northern Exposure
34. South Street Brewery
35. Irish JO's Tavern

Best Pubs in Harrisonburg, VA

Andy H.

1. Alston's Pub
2. Cally's Restaurant & Brewing Co.
3. Dave's Taverna
4. Mainstreet Bar & Grill
5. BW3's
6. Donegans Inn & Pub
7. Artful Dodger
8. Time-Out Sports Lounge
9. Key West Beach Bar & Grill
10. Hank's Smokehouse and Deli
11. Boston Beanery Restaurant and Tavern
12. Mulligan's Pub & Eatery (Staunton)
13. Legend Brewing Co
14. O'Neill's Irish Pub
15. South Street Brewery
16. Finnegan's Cove
17. Chili's Grill & Bar
18. Chisholm's Lounge
19. Sheep 'N Wellies Pub
20. Highlawn Pavilion
21. Valley Cigar Pub (Waynesboro)

Best Practical Jokes Ever
Andy H.

1. Fake Vomit
2. Salt in the Sugar Container.
3. Covering Cubical in Aluminum Foil
4. Stapler in Jello
5. Short Sheeting a Bed
6. Having everybody in the office call Dwight, Dwayne all day
7. Kick Me Signs
8. Fake Doggie Doo
9. Lift car up onto bricks
10. The Chinese Fire Drill
11. Itching powder in the shampoo.
12. Clear plastic wrap over toilet bowl
13. Apple's Iloo
14. Rubber Snake
15. Student Removal
16. Holes in a Straw
17. Cover Desk in Tin Foil
18. Waiting for your friend to pass out, spray shaving cream on his hands, and tickle his face.
19. Request VD Info. in Someone Else's Name
20. Jello in Toilet
21. Farting Poop
22. Human Parts Coming Out of Closed Pots Served
23. Office Cube Full of Packing Foam
24. Tissue Paper over Teacher's House
25. Car Parked Upside down on Front Lawn
26. April 1, 1987 – the TP to End All TP's
27. MIT Balloon Inflated during Harvard Yale Game
28. Cherry Bomb in Toilet
29. Paris Hilton's Career
30. Cream Pie
31. Strap Victim to Chair with Packing Tape
32. "Is Your Refrigerator Running?"
33. Plastic Fake Vomit
34. Bush's Inauguration
35. Knock Knocks
36. Order Pizza Sent to Another House
37. Chain Letters
38. Itching Powder in a Jockstrap
39. Superglue Everything to Ceiling
40. Anything Whoopie-Cushion Related

Best Dr. Seuss Books
Michael

1. Green Eggs and Ham
2. The Cat in the Hat
3. One Fish, Two Fish, Red Fish, Blue Fish
4. The Lorax
5. How The Grinch Stole Christmas
6. Hop on Pop
7. Oh, the Places You'll Go!
8. Horton Hears a Who!
9. The Butter Battle Book
10. Fox in Socks
11. The Seven Lady Godivas
12. There's a Wocket in My Pocket!
13. Horton Hatches the Egg
14. Gerald McBoing Boing
15. Oh Say Can You Say
16. Dr. Seuss's Sleep Book
17. The Sneetches and Other Stories
18. The Foot Book
19. Yurtle the Turtle
20. Thidwick the Big Hearted Moose
21. Go Dog Go
22. Hunches in Bunches
23. Brown Cow
24. The B Book
25. The 500 Hats of Bartholomew Cubbins
26. Mr. Brown Can Moo! Can You?
27. The Cat in the Hat Comes Back
28. Dr. Seuss's ABC: an Amazing Alphabet Book!
29. The King's Stilts
30. On Beyond Zebra!
31. If I Ran the Circus
32. Happy Birthday to You!
33. The Foot Book: Dr. Seuss's Wacky Book of Opposites

Best Exotic Vacation Destinations
Michael

1. Bahamas
2. Hawaii, US
3. Tahiti
4. Vietnam
5. Fiji
6. Aruba
7. Jamaica
8. Thailand
9. Cancun
10. Australia
11. The Caribbean
12. Costa Rica
13. Bali
14. Mauritius
15. Japan
16. India
17. Antarctica
18. Beetown, WI
19. Ushuaia
20. English Castle
21. Sri Lanka
22. Boracay Island, Philippines
23. Honduras
24. Galapagos
25. St. Martin
26. Bermuda
27. Key West
28. Nepal
29. Mediterranean
30. Cozumel
31. Bahrain
32. Goa
33. Las Vegas
34. Rajasthan
35. Cabo San Lucas
36. China
37. Amsterdam
38. New Zealand
39. Burma
40. turkey

Best Cheese for a Cheeseburger
Michael

1. American
2. cheddar
3. Swiss
4. Provolone
5. Monterey Jack
6. pepper jack
7. Mozzarella
8. Blue Cheese
9. Gorgonzola
10. muenster
11. Extra Sharp Cheddar
12. Jack
13. bleu
14. Colby
15. Dana Blue
16. Gouda Cheese (Old)
17. blue
18. Jalapeno Jack
19. Wisconsin Cheese
20. none
21. Muenster
22. Cheesesteak

Must Have Items for a Camping/Backpacking Trip
Michael

1. Tent
2. sleeping bag
3. first aid kit
4. flashlight
5. water
6. matches
7. Canteen
8. knife
9. food
10. backpack
11. Bug Repellant
12. Pocket Knife
13. Coleman Lantern
14. Good Boots
15. toilet paper
16. swiss army knife
17. Multi Tool
18. Matches or Lighter
19. Head Lamp
20. Ingredients to Make S'Mores
21. Lantern
22. Water Purification
23. Air Mattress
24. Quick-Drying Towel
25. Water/Water Filter
26. bug spray
27. 8 1/2
28. Can Opener!
29. Hiking Poles
30. 2 Way Radio
31. cell phone
32. Torch
33. Compass
34. insect repellant
35. Zip-Lock Bags
36. Portapotty
37. Mosquito Repellent.
38. Canned Goods (Food)
39. Protective Tarp for under Tent
40. Non-Battery Lantern

Funniest Movies of All Time

Mark

1. Airplane!
2. Monty Python and the Holy Grail
3. Office Space
4. Blazing Saddles
5. Space Balls
6. Caddyshack
7. Dumb and Dumber
8. Spinal Tap
9. Old School
10. Napoleon Dynamite
11. Animal House
12. Anchorman
13. History of the World: Part I
14. The Jerk
15. It's a Mad Mad Mad Mad World
16. Some Like It Hot
17. Monty Python's "The Meaning of Life"
18. Dr. Strangelove
19. Monty Python's Life of Brian
20. Super Troopers
21. Christmas Vacation
22. Harold and Kumar Go to White Castle
23. Austin Powers: International Man of Mystery
24. The Producers
25. Ace Ventura: Pet Detective
26. The Big Lebowski
27. 40 Year-Old Virgin
28. Trading Places
29. Ghostbusters
30. Top Secret!
31. Pink Panther (1963)
32. Zoolander
33. Scary Movie 1
34. The Naked Gun
35. Tootsie
36. O Brother Where Art Thou?
37. MASH
38. Duck Soup
39. Groundhog Day
40. Coming to America

Best Ways to Celebrate a Wedding Anniversary
Mark

1. go out to dinner
2. Cruise
3. Vacation
4. Go on a Second Honeymoon
5. Romantic Day
6. sex
7. Play the 'You Haven't Changed A Bit' board game at the party
8. Go to Paris
9. Renew Vows
10. movie
11. Weekend Getaway
12. Quiet night at home
13. Dancing
14. Exchange Gifts
15. Dinner out at favorite memorable restaurant
16. Vacation Trip to Hawaii
17. Renew wedding vows
18. Revisit site of proposal
19. Go back to the place you got married
20. Windjammer Cruise
21. Going to Europe, just the two of you
22. Picnic for Two
23. Theater Show
24. Bed & Breakfast Get Away
25. Hot Air Balloon Ride
26. Going on a trip to the place you first met. For me and my husband, it would be revisiting our college. Very romantic
27. Mini Vacation
28. Revisit location where proposal took place
29. Go back to the spot where you went on your honeymoon
30. Take the day off from work and go to lunch and dinner.
31. At home
32. Stay at johnny seesaw in vermont
33. Just a quiet dinner with only the anniversary couple
34. Dinner cruise on a river
35. Dinner with members of wedding party
36. Cook a romantic meal at home
37. With family
38. Intimacy
39. Romantic dinner at a favorite restaurant
40. Spend the weekend together in a romantic hotel

Best Uses of RFID
Mark

1. Inventory Tracking
2. Cattle Tracking Ear Tags
3. Race Chips
4. Banking
5. Heating Clothes
6. Cards at Casinos
7. Cooking
8. Nike + iPod Sport Kit
9. Citizen Identification Chips
10. Work Badges
11. Passports
12. Finding Lost Pets
13. flu
14. Open Road Tolling
15. RFID Number License Plates
16. Tracking the Terror
17. Track Payments
18. Mass transit fare payment
19. Business resource labeling
20. Chips in Soccer Balls:
21. Car tracking in rental lots
22. UPC Codes
23. Painting
24. Sorting Garbage
25. Finding Golf Balls
26. Intelligent Refrigerators
27. Washing Machines
28. Robots that organize clutter
29. Preventing Water Wastage
30. Dynamic Pricing
31. Smart Shelves
32. Quarantining in Hospitals
33. Self-Scan checkout carts
34. Monitoring critically ill patients
35. Electronic Car Security
36. The Road Beacon System
37. Prevent doctors from performing the wrong surgery on you
38. Smart Medicine Cabinet
39. Monitoring Geriatrics
40. Replacement for the Postage Stamp

Top Things a Father Should Teach His Son
Mark

1. Honesty
2. Be respectful to women
3. Respect for other people
4. How to Treat a Woman
5. How to Shave
6. Good Manners
7. How to Drive
8. How to Treat a woman with respect & courtesy
9. Responsibility
10. Respect for Himself
11. How to Save Money
12. How to Play Baseball
13. About Sex
14. Tie a Tie
15. How to throw a baseball and football
16. How to Be a Good Father.
17. How to Fish
18. How to throw and catch a baseball
19. To Keep Your Word.
20. Golf Swing
21. Birds and Bees
22. Car Repair/Maintenance
23. How to Ride a Bicycle
24. The Bible
25. To Go to the Bathroom Correctly
26. The Value of Education
27. About God
28. play ball
29. Always respect women, they are your equal and they should be treated as such
30. Love Your Mother
31. How to treat a woman lovingly, gently, and with respect
32. hunting
33. A Good Work Ethic
34. Love
35. sports
36. How to Invest
37. How to change the oil in his car.
38. hard working
39. How to manage money and debt wisely
40. How to fix a car

Best Lunch Spots in Palo Alto
Vidal

1. Creamery
2. Pizza My Heart
3. Zao Noodle House
4. Thaiphoon
5. Darbar Indian
6. Whole Foods Market
7. Blue Chalk Cafe
8. Tamarine
9. Andale
10. Gordon Biersch
11. Mint Leaf Asian Noodle House
12. Max's Opera Cafe
13. Plutos
14. Homma's Brown Rice Sushi
15. Hobee's
16. Fraiche
17. Cheesecake Factory
18. California Pizza Kitchen
19. Patxi's Chicago Pizza
20. Siam Royal Authentic Thai Cuisine
21. Taxi's Hamburgers
22. Quiznos
23. Nolas

Most Romantic Honeymoon Destinations
Peter

1. Paris
2. Bahamas
3. Tahiti
4. Italy
5. Jamaica
6. Fiji
7. Hawaii
8. Venice, Italy
9. Niagara Falls
10. Rome
11. New York
12. Honolulu, Hawaii
13. Bermuda
14. Alaska
15. Barcelona, Spain
16. Florence, Italy
17. Las Vegas
18. Key West, FL
19. Bali
20. San Francisco
21. Cancun
22. London
23. Malta
24. Kauai
25. New Zealand
26. Maui
27. Positano, Italy
28. Ocho Rios, Jamaica
29. Seychelles
30. Cayo Espanto, Belize
31. Hawii
32. bed
33. Puerto Vallarta, Mexico
34. Lanai, Hawaii
35. Gatlinburg, Tennessee
36. Loire Valley, France
37. Montego Bay, Jamaica
38. Turks and Caicos
39. St. Lucia
40. Sandals St. Lucia

Sexiest Movies of All-Time
Andy J.

1. Basic Instinct
2. 9 1/2 weeks
3. Blue Lagoon
4. Fatal Attraction
5. Last Tango in Paris
6. Wild Things
7. Damage
8. Six and a Half Weeks
9. Eyes Wide Shut
10. Showgirls
11. Body Heat
12. Color of Night
13. Ghost
14. Lolita
15. The Graduate
16. Debbie Does Dallas
17. 10
18. Mulholland Dr.
19. Some Like It Hot
20. The Lover
21. Dirty Dancing
22. Deep Throat
23. Pretty Woman
24. Gone with the Wind
25. Sliver
26. Sin City
27. Indecent Proposal
28. Betty Blue
29. The English Patient
30. The Summer of '42
31. Emmanuelle
32. Mr. and Mrs. Smith
33. When Harry Met Sally
34. Secretary
35. Y Tu Mama Tambien
36. Shakespeare in Love
37. Unfaithful
38. Veronica 2030
39. Trystan and Isolde
40. I like the Girls Who Do

Favorite Athletes of All-Time

Andy J.

1. Michael Jordan
2. Babe Ruth
3. Tiger Woods
4. Magic Johnson
5. Mohammed Ali
6. Lance Armstrong
7. Michael Johnson
8. Joe Montana
9. Carl Lewis
10. Mickey Mantle
11. Bo Jackson
12. Kobe Bryant
13. Lebron James
14. Mark Messier
15. Pelé
16. Larry Bird
17. Charles Barkley
18. Lawrence Taylor
19. Wayne Gretzky
20. Linford Christie
21. Kelly Holmes
22. Roberto Clemente
23. David Beckham
24. Michelle Kwan
25. Kareem Abdul Jabbar
26. Sammey Sosa
27. Tony Dorsett
28. Krisit Yamaguchi
29. Johnny Unitas
30. Mary Rand
31. Jackie Robinson
32. Jonty Rhodes
33. David Ortiz – Boston Red Sox
34. Joe DiMaggio
35. Dale Murphy
36. Franco Harris
37. Hideki Matsui
38. Scottie Pippen
39. Bruce Jenner – Track & Field
40. Peter Foresberg

Top Controversial Movies of All-Time
Andy J.

1. Fahrenheit 9/11
2. The Last Temptation of Christ
3. Da Vinci Code
4. A Clockwork Orange
5. The Passion of the Christ
6. Caligula
7. Brokeback Mountain
8. Last Tango in Paris
9. JFK
10. Irreversible
11. United 93
12. Schindlers List
13. Exorcist
14. American History X
15. Deep Throat
16. The Passion
17. Monty Python's Life of Brian
18. Super Size Me
19. Cider House Rules
20. M*A*S*H
21. Pulp Fiction
22. Apocalypse Now
23. The Graduate
24. Mississippi Burning
25. South Park: Bigger, Longer, and Uncut
26. Taxi Driver
27. Pink Flamingos
28. Natural Born Killers
29. I Spit on Your Grave
30. Boondock Saints
31. kids
32. The Birth of a Nation, or the Clansmen
33. Cannibal Holocaust
34. Lolita
35. Fahrenheit 451
36. Strip Tease
37. The Godfather
38. Romeo and Juliet
39. All the Presidents Men
40. The Passion

Top Songs You'd Want Played at Your Funeral
Andy J.

1. Amazing Grace
2. Wind Beneath My Wings
3. Dust in the Wind – Kansas
4. Angels – Robbie Williams
5. Freebird
6. Paradise City
7. Ave Maria
8. Always Look on the Bright Side of Life
9. Who Let the Dogs Out? by Baha Men
10. Go Rest High on That Mountain
11. Yesterday
12. Pink Floyd – Wish You Were Here
13. Dancing Queen
14. Stairway to Heaven by Led Zeppelin
15. Star Spangled Banner
16. I Did It My Way
17. How Great Thou Art
18. We Are Sailing – Rod Stewart
19. Oh Danny Boy
20. Crowded House – Don't Dream It's over
21. Morning Has Broken
22. Evanescence – Bring Me to Life
23. Tubeway Army – Basic J.
24. Josh Groban – Remember Me (Troy Soundtrack)
25. Goodbye to Romance
26. You Remind Me (Nickleback)
27. Joy Division: Atmosphere
28. Someone Saved My Life Tonight – Elton John
29. Pink Floyd – Shine on You Crazy Diamond (Part 1)
30. Jerusalem – Edward Elgar/William Blake
31. Macarena
32. Book of Days by Enya
33. Nobody Does It Better by Carly Simon
34. Paint It Black
35. Finnegan's Wake
36. Orange Mocha Frappucino!
37. Tears in Heaven – Eric Clapton
38. The Imperial March (From Star Wars)
39. Unchained by Johnny Cash
40. Going Home

Cool Science Words
Matt

1. Quantum
2. Quark
3. Bunsen Burner
4. Plasma
5. Osmosis
6. Beaker
7. Subcutaneous
8. Pi
9. Thermodynamics
10. Photosynthesis
11. Deoxyribonucleic
12. Igneous
13. Neutrino
14. Mutation
15. Astronomical
16. Mitochondria
17. Eukaryote
18. Endoplasmic Reticulum
19. Phytoplankton
20. Nanotechnology
21. Singularity
22. Supernova
23. Apoptosis
24. Isotopes
25. Neutron
26. String Theory
27. Condensation
28. fusion
29. Pahoehoe and Aa
30. Sublimate
31. Sphingomyelin
32. Quasar
33. Medulla Oblongata
34. Avogadro's Constant
35. Mitochondrion
36. Metamorphosis
37. Viscosity
38. Effervescent
39. Phenotype
40. Half-Life

Biggest Dot Com Busts
Matt

1. pets.com
2. Webvan (1997-2001)
3. E-Toys (1997 - 2001)
4. kozmo.com (1998-2001)
5. flooz.com
6. boo.com
7. excite.com
8. furniture.com
9. Egghead
10. freeinternet.com
11. napster.com
12. mylackey.com
13. beenz.com
14. Peapod
15. Go.Com
16. govworks.com
17. groceries.com
18. Cmgi
19. Pointcast
20. geocities.com
21. Webcrawler
22. Urban Fetch
23. Date.Com
24. Pixelon
25. Northpoint Communications
26. 12dailypro.com
27. Value America
28. backflip.com
29. purchasepro.com
30. Riffage
31. altavista.com
32. Cuecat
33. alladvantage.com
34. liveugli.com
35. Free-PC
36. Devine Ventures
37. powerdime.com
38. Cdnow
39. pipesforyou.com
40. happypuppy.com

Best Cover Song
Matt

1. Jimi Hendrix—All along the Watchtower
2. Norah Jones – Are You Lonesome Tonight (Elvis Cover)
3. Smells like Teen Spirit by Tori Amos
4. Personal Jesus by Johnny Cash (A Depeche Mode Cover)
5. Fools Rush in (Ub40)
6. Nirvana – Lake of Fire
7. Love
8. I Will Always Love You, Whitney Houston
9. Let It Be
10. Sweet Home Alabama
11. I Got You
12. Mandy Moore – Have a Little Faith in Me
13. DHT – Listen to Your Heart
14. Lay Lady Lay – Ministry
15. Hotel California
16. After Midnight- Eric Clapton
17. Run-D.M.C.'s 1986 Cover of Aerosmith's Walk This Way
18. Angie- Tori Amos/Orig. Rolling Stones
19. Oooh Child by Beth Orton (A Five Stairsteps Cover)
20. Big Yellow Taxi (Counting Crows)
21. Wanted Dead or Alive (Chris Daughtry)
22. Renegades of Funk – Rage against the Machine
23. Moonshiner by Uncle Tupelo
24. Stolen Car
25. China Girl (David Bowie)
26. Dreams
27. Boys of Summer by the Ataris
28. Welcome to the Jungle
29. Hurt – Johnny Cash
30. Life
31. Crazy Mary – Pearl Jam
32. Gin and Juice – the Gourds
33. Norah Jones – I'll Be Your Baby Tonight (Bob Dylan Cover)
34. Turn the Page, Metallica
35. Freebird
36. Your Song
37. Peace Train by 10,000 Maniacs
38. The Number of the Beast
39. This Might Be the Place
40. Holly Cole – Que Sera, Sera

Favorite Cereal
Matt

1. Cheerios
2. Honey Nut Cheerios
3. Raisin Bran
4. Lucky Charms
5. frosted flakes
6. Frosted Mini Wheats
7. Grape Nuts
8. Cocoa Puffs
9. Kellogg's Corn Flakes
10. Honey Bunches of Oats
11. Red Berry Special K
12. fruit loops
13. Quaker Oatmeal
14. shredded wheat
15. Fruity Pebbles
16. Cap'n Crunch
17. Blueberry Morning
18. Apple Jacks
19. Peanut Butter Captain Crunch
20. Life
21. Cocoa Pebbles
22. Cookie Crisp
23. Weetabix
24. Booberry
25. sesame
26. Cracklin' Oat Bran
27. Nabisco Shredded Mini Wheats
28. Count Chocula
29. Zimties
30. Granola
31. Sugar Smacks
32. Kellogg's All Bran
33. Porridge
34. Kellogg's Special K Chocolatey Delights
35. Kellogg's Rice Krispies
36. Honeycomb
37. Kellogg's Frosties
38. Cinnamon Toast Crunch
39. Trix
40. Kellogg's Special K

The UnSpun Blog

In 2008 we started a blog to help promote the site. We used our widget to embed the relevant list and discuss it.

Home Appliances it Cannot be Home Without

Have you ever sat there, looked around your house, and noticed the myriad of small appliances you have? It's incredible. Look in your kitchen – microwave, toaster oven, coffee maker, coffee grinder, mixer. All small appliances, all important. What about a fan or a window air conditioner? Small appliances and almost crucial on certain days of the year.

Small appliances are the little (and sometimes not so little) things that make our worlds just that much easier. They're not necessarily essentials, but they can be hard to live without.

If you get ton of credit card applications, or other junk mail that could destroy your credit rating if not disposed of properly, you want a paper shredder. You don't need one. You could sit there with scissors and make all the paper into confetti by hand, but a paper shredder would save you valuable time. I take out my George Foreman Grill almost every single week, if I had to cook for my family without it, I could do it, but it would be far more difficult. Apparently a lot of you feel similarly about your George Foremans, because it's sitting at number six on UnSpun's list of "Can't-Do-Without Small Home Appliances":

Can't-Do-Without Small Home Appliances
Based on 153 votes by 52 people

VOTE		
▲ ✔	1. toaster oven	🛒 Buy
▲ ✔	2. coffee maker	🛒 Buy $16.99
▲ ✔	3. microwave	🛒 Buy $94.00
▲ ✔	4. can opener	🛒 Buy $16.95
▲ ✔	5. Blender	🛒 Buy $69.89
▲ ✔	6. George Foreman Grill	🛒 Buy $51.99
▲ ✔	7. Food Processor	🛒 Buy Too low to display
▲ ✔	8. iron	🛒 Buy $53.58
▲ ✔	9. Humidifier	🛒 Buy $34.99
▲ ✔	10. Waffle Iron	🛒 Buy $46.99
▲ ✔	11. Electric Can Opener	🛒 Buy $24.99

I have to say, I'm moderately surprised that toaster oven is currently beating out coffee maker for the top spot. I can go without a toasted bagel on a daily basis, but not without a cup of coffee. Do you really feel differently?

Trying to Reason with Football Season

We're heading into the fourth week of the NFL season, and I think we're starting to separate the wheat from the chaff. We're really starting to see which football teams have it this year and which can't even pretend like they can hang with the big boys. That makes this the perfect time to visit the "Best NFL Team in 2008" list on UnSpun.

Looking at it, I'm actually moderately surprised, as of my writing this, the New England Patriots are still sitting on top of the list. Oh, don't get me wrong, they're a great team, but without Tom Brady I'm pretty convinced that they're not the best in the NFL. Indianapolis, currently with a record of 1-2 is sitting in the second position. Do we actually believe that they have just been unlucky thus far? Now, the Giants and the Cowboys, both at 3-0, are in positions 3 and 4. I might put them higher, but it certainly doesn't seem like they ought to be much lower.

Take a look at the whole kit and caboodle:

Best NFL Team in 2008
Based on 188 votes by 52 people
VOTE
⬆ⱽ   1. New England Patriots
⬆ⱽ   2. Indianapolis Colts
⬆ⱽ   3. New York Giants
⬆ⱽ   4. Dallas Cowboys
⬆ⱽ   5. San Diego Chargers
⬆ⱽ   6. Green Bay Packers
⬆ⱽ   7. New York Jets
⬆ⱽ   8. Denver Broncos
⬆ⱽ   9. Chicago Bears
⬆ⱽ   10. Baltimore Ravens
⬆ⱽ   11. Washington Redskins

This is really one of those fun lists. It's one of those lists that you need to come back to so you can update your rankings as the season progresses (the Pats might have deserved the top spot prior to their opening week's game, but they don't now). Just you watch this list change as the season progresses, you see who slides to where and what happens. Maybe we'll even talk about it again in the future.

Be it Saltwater or Freshwater, I Love Eel

I don't know, maybe it's the fact that it's mid-afternoon (that disquieting time between lunch and dinner), or maybe it's the fact that I've gone without for so long, or maybe it's the fact that it's just plain good, but I could totally go for a rainbow roll right about now. No, no, not a rainbow roll, some spicy tuna. Wait, not tuna, unagi... no! Anagi! Yup, that would do it, some delicious anagi.

Anagi, if you haven't had it, is like unagi, except that the eel is a saltwater eel instead of a freshwater one. If you like unagi, you need to try anagi. I've actually not seen it in that many restaurants, but it's totally worth going to Hawaii for (the only U.S. state where I have seen it on a menu).

I was actually really surprised looking over the UnSpun list "Favorite Kind of Sushi" that anagi wasn't there. Naturally, I took a second and a half and added it in. Literally, that was all it took, a second and a half and now the best kind of sushi is on the list. I don't want to harp on it or anything, but the ease with which UnSpun allows any and all users to correct such omissions is one of the great things about the site.

Here, take a look at the now complete with anagi list:

Favorite Kind of Sushi
Based on 133 votes by 44 people
VOTE
1. California Roll
2. Spicy Tuna Roll
3. Toro
4. Unagi
5. Ahi Tuna
6. Unagi Sashimi
7. Tamago
8. Nigiri-Zushi
9. eel
10. Maguro
11. Inari

So, go forth, eat anagi till your heart's content, and if somehow your favorite type of sushi isn't on the list take the second and a half and add it in.

Farewell, We Hardly Knew Ye

Today is the "official" start of the new television season. It is a day that makes me, quite literally, jump for joy (and not in the way Catalina did on My Name is Earl). At this moment there are a plethora of new shows and returning favorites just itching to make their way onto your television screen. I say you should let them, goodness knows that I do.

You see, if you don't watch all your favorite shows and convince everyone you know to watch them, they're going to end up on an UnSpun list you don't want them to be on. They're going to end up on the Best TV Show Cancelled Too Early list, and that is not a happy place to be. Good old Firefly currently sits in the top spot on the list, and is followed by Arrested Development and Veronica Mars. Take a look, you're sure to find other favorites there:

Best TV Show Cancelled Too Early

Based on 294 votes by 71 people

VOTE

1. Firefly **Buy $21.90**
2. Arrested Development **Buy $44.99**
3. Veronica Mars **Buy $76.72**
4. Dark Angel **Buy $41.80**
5. Freaks and Geeks **Buy $38.46**
6. My So-Called Life **Buy $38.46**
7. Studio 60 on the Sunset Strip **Buy $39.00**
8. Sports Night **Buy $45.70**
9. Futurama
10. Homicide: Life on the Streets
11. Carnivale

Be honest, is there something on that list that you wish you'd followed a little more closely at the time and miss desperately now? It's okay, let it out, let it all out. Don't keep that upset bottled up inside, it's not healthy.

There, there, isn't that better?

Why don't you go, check out something like the Best Reality Show on Television Today list or Best Quality Television Shows list and choose a couple of shows that you, personally, will watch and try to save this year (if they're not gone already). Doesn't it feel good to try and make a difference?

Into the Great Wide Open

I come to you today not with foolish talk and banter (oh there will be that too, but that's not why I come), but rather to discuss one of my favorite artists and to show you one of the recent updates we've made here at UnSpun.

Have you ever looked at one of our lists of songs and just weren't sure when you saw a title if it was the song you were thinking of? Or, perhaps you saw a title and couldn't quite place the song itself. Frustrating, very frustrating. I know, I've been there. Well, check out the way things work now:

Top Tom Petty Songs
Based on 140 votes by 43 people

VOTE

1. American Girl [LISTEN▶] [Buy $0.99]
2. Free Fallin [LISTEN▶] [Buy $0.99]
3. Mary Jane's Last Dance [LISTEN▶] [Buy $0.99]
4. Refugee [LISTEN▶] [Buy $0.99]
5. I Won't Back Down [LISTEN▶] [Buy $0.99]
6. It's Good to Be King [LISTEN▶] [Buy $0.89]
7. You Don't Know How It Feels [LISTEN▶] [Buy $0.81]
8. Breakdown [LISTEN▶] [Buy $0.99]
9. Don't Do Me like That [LISTEN▶] [Buy $0.99]
10. Runnin' Down a Dream [LISTEN▶] [Buy $0.99]

Just above, as you see, we have the "Top Tom Petty Songs" list and next to the vast majority of the songs there's a cute little "listen" button. That's right, you click the "listen" button and you can listen to a sample of the song. Easy as pie, less caloric, and just as satisfying. Plus, these are Tom Petty (some with the Heartbreakers and some not so much) songs I've shown you, and he has to be one of the greatest artists around. Just seeing the list of songs gives me the warm fuzzies. Not only do his melodies stick with you, but the songs are awfully fun to sing yourself.

As an example of how much fun it is to sing Tom Petty, I actually figured out how to upload an mp3 of me singing "Mary Jane's Last Dance" to this piece. I was going to insert it right here, but it struck me at the last minute that I like you guys and want you to return to the blog, me singing would ensure against that. So, while I won't make you suffer listening to my singing, I will encourage you to click that little "listen" button and to hear Tom Petty perform yourself.

The Trees for the Forest

A far wiser, wittier, worldlier (and wordier), mind than mine once wrote "Why are there trees I never walk under but large and melodious thoughts descend upon me?" Has a more true thing ever been written?

Well... the answer that is "almost certainly," but to answer in such a way negates the point. To answer in such a way takes all that might be magical and wondrous in the quote and tears it apart. I'll tell you what, let me just take back the question entirely so we don't get too caught up in destroying Whitman's brilliance.

Trees.

Trees do so much for us. They help make the air breathable, they provide shade on hot days, backrests for those of use who wouldn't be able to survive a picnic without a backrest, and make for some pretty swell climbing material. Have you ever thought though about just what kind of tree is the best kind of tree? Could it be a Spruce? A Redwood? Maybe it's a Pine or a Maple or an Elm. I just don't know what the right answer is for you, and what's worse, I think you've probably never actually considered the question. Consider it now. UnSpun has a list of people's Favorite Type of Tree:

Favorite Type of Tree
Based on 153 votes by 53 people
VOTE
⬆ ⬇   1. Oak
⬆ ⬇   2. Apple
⬆ ⬇   3. Pine
⬆ ⬇   4. Weeping Willow
⬆ ⬇   5. Elm
⬆ ⬇   6. Dogwood
⬆ ⬇   7. Willow
⬆ ⬇   8. Maple
⬆ ⬇   9. Redwood
⬆ ⬇ 10. Hickory
⬆ ⬇ 11. Spruce

One of the risks of making sure you aren't caught missing the forest for the trees is that you end up missing the trees for the forest. We at UnSpun don't want that to happen to you. So take a moment, consider which tree in the forest is your tree in the forest and don't let that tree fall (in the standings) without making a sound.

You are Standing in an Open Field West of a White House...

It takes a special person to instantly recognize the title Temple of Apshai and the brilliance which it represents. The same can be said of Skate or Die, Spy Hunter, Populous, Wolfenstein 3D and the myriad of other fantastic old-school games that populate UnSpun's Best Computer Games of All Time list.

If you're anything like me, you spent hours sitting there with Apshai and Zork and Adventure (where else could you kill a dragon with your bare hands?). If you're really like me, after playing the original Prince of Persia for the 8 millionth time, you opted to turn your monitor upside down after drinking the potion that flips the graphics upside down rather than drinking the right side-up potion (the strategy really didn't work as well as it ought to have, my brain recognized the monitor was upside and tried to compensate for it despite the fact that the image on the screen was right side-up).

Go ahead, take a gander, remember all the glory of those computer games past:

Best Computer Games of All Time

Based on 282 votes by 61 people

VOTE

1. Doom [Buy]
2. World of Warcraft [Buy $10.00]
3. Pac Man [Buy $9.99]
4. Sims [Buy $27.09]
5. Starcraft [Buy $14.93]
6. Age of Empires 2 [Buy $22.00]
7. Half-Life 2 [Buy $44.45]
8. Quake [Buy $44.45]
9. Pong [Buy $1.24]
10. Tetris [Buy]
11. Diablo 2 [Buy $30.20]

There it is, and what really amazes me about the list is not just that something like Apshai is there, but that a game as old as Apshai sits right next to far newer fare. The list actually really is looking at the best computer games ever. So, as you contemplate the incredible amount of fun that some of those games were, I'm going to see if I can't save Sandy Pantz and stop the Purple Meteor once and for all.

Walking a Mile in Someone Else's Shoes

Have you ever stopped, looked around, and thought to yourself, "I like my life, but if I could be someone else, just for a single day, I'd love it." Oh sure you have. Who hasn't? Imagine it, just for one day you're Oprah or Angelina Jolie or Bill Gates or your boss. Wouldn't that just be swell?

As for me, I wouldn't want to be Oprah (too many responsibilities) or Angelina Jolie (too many kids) or Bill Gates (too semi-retired) or your boss (I don't even know your boss), but there are a few people out whose shoes I would spend some time in. I wouldn't mind be Tiger Woods for a day. I think it could be fun to be Queen Elizabeth (either the first or the second). Maybe even a day as Bill Clinton could be amusing. The point is, I think about it and you do too. Lots of people do and that's why there's a list at UnSpun focusing on people's choices. Take a look at the results thus far:

If You Could Be Someone Else for a Day Who Would You Be?
Based on 160 votes by 53 people

VOTE		
⏶ ⏷	1.	the president
⏶ ⏷	2.	George Bush
⏶ ⏷	3.	Oprah Winfrey
⏶ ⏷	4.	Angelina Jolie
⏶ ⏷	5.	Jesus
⏶ ⏷	6.	Queen Elizabeth
⏶ ⏷	7.	my boss
⏶ ⏷	8.	Bill Gates
⏶ ⏷	9.	Hugh Heffner
⏶ ⏷	10.	Tom Cruise
⏶ ⏷	11.	Warren Buffet

There are certainly a few curious choices in the list above and lots of folks I'd never want to be, but the point is not to focus only on my choices, the point is that we all get a say. So, stand up and vote, it's your civic duty.

Nobody Does it Better

We all have our heroes. You might like George Washington. Someone else might like Abraham Lincoln. A third person might really admire Bea Arthur. I too have a hero. My hero is tall, handsome, and speaks with a suave British accent. He likes a nice martini – shaken, not stirred – and carries a license to kill. He started his life in books, and has since moved to movies (though the occasional new novel still does appear).

He's returning to the big screen on November 14 in a feature entitled Quantum of Solace. I'm convinced that it's going to be truly outstanding and I can hardly wait to see it. I've been trying to console myself though with some of his other big screen adventures. My favorite, unquestionably, is From Russia With Love, but most UnSpun voters seem to prefer Goldfinger. Here's how the Best James Bond Film of All Time list currently looks:

```
            Best James Bond Film of All Time
                Based on 155 votes by 42 people

VOTE
  ▲ ∀    1. Goldfinger  [Buy $4.99]
  ▲ ∀    2. Casino Royale [Buy $15.95]
  ▲ ∀    3. Dr No  [Buy $6.22]
  ▲ ∀    4. Live and Let Die [Buy $6.04]
  ▲ ∀    5. The Spy Who Loved Me [Buy $3.98]
  ▲ ∀    6. Octopussy [Buy $7.26]
  ▲ ∀    7. From Russia with Love [Buy $8.04]
  ▲ ∀    8. Moonraker [Buy $6.48]
  ▲ ∀    9. Thunderball [Buy $6.58]
  ▲ ∀   10. The Living Daylights [Buy $3.95]
  ▲ ∀   11. For Your Eyes Only [Buy $5.96]
```

So, what do you think… Casino Royale? Thunderball? Live and Let Die? Goldeneye?

The Top Way to Top Your Pizza

A good pizza is a thing of beauty. Too few people understand that. Getting that right mixture of cheese and sauce, the right dough, and the right oven make all the difference in the world. I don't know if it's true or not, but I've been told by many a New York pizza man that the reason New York pizza is head and shoulders better than the rest of the pizza in the country is the water in the New York area.

Of course, while cheese, sauce, and dough are important (and quite possibly water too), toppings can be crucial as well. I like sardines, I think they make for a good pizza, others probably think me insane. It's Hawaiian pizza I can't stand, but some swear by it. In the end though, I'm a sausage, peppers, and onions person. I like pepperoni and tons of other toppings too, but it's sausage, peppers, and onions that I'll always return to in the end.

It may be that I'm the only one who feels this way. Here is UnSpun's list of the Top Pizza Toppings and sausage, peppers, and onions is not highly ranked:

Top Pizza Toppings

Based on 1491 votes by 505 people

VOTE

▲ ▼	1. Pepperoni
▲ ▼	2. cheese
▲ ▼	3. mushrooms
▲ ▼	4. sausage
▲ ▼	5. pineapple
▲ ▼	6. olives
▲ ▼	7. onions
▲ ▼	8. bacon
▲ ▼	9. ham
▲ ▼	10. Canadian Bacon
▲ ▼	11. chicken

So, what's your favorite? If you could put any topping in the world on a pizza, what would it be?

How Hardy are the Hardy Boys?

Who remembers the Hardy Boys? There were Frank and Joe following in their father's footsteps, tracking down the bad guys, beating them up, and getting home in time for dinner. When did they ever go to school? How did they get a car, and a boat, and their own crime lab? How I wished (when I was 7) that I was as old as those 2 boys and could have such adventures. Now I'm 44, and I'm still wondering when I'll be old enough to have those kinds of adventures.

And when you found out that Franklin W. Dixon was just a pseudonym for a multitude of writers cranking out the stories for the Stratemeyer Syndicate, did it bother you? For me, not at all. I still learned about radio transmission (The Short Wave Mystery), golf ball scavenging (The Masked Monkey), and nerve gas (The Bombay Boomerang).

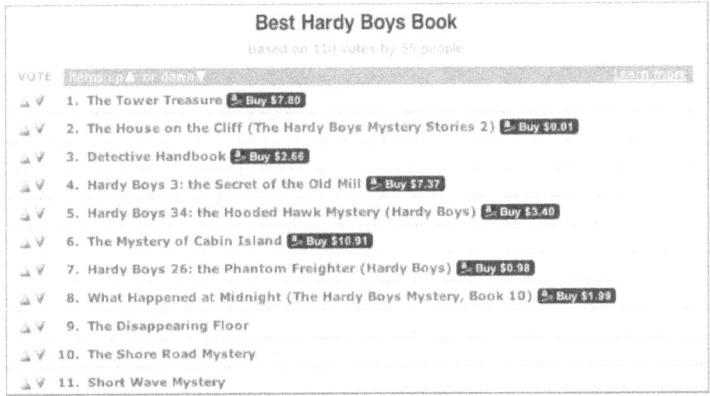

And no matter how dated some of the stories have become (what exactly is a "Roadster"?), I still look forward to sharing my complete collection with my own two boys.

Got a License to Chill?

For the record, I took off for a weekend last month just to try and recall the whole year – there were all of those faces and all of those places, I was wondering where they all disappeared. As you can probably surmise, I didn't ponder the question too long, I was hungry and went out for a bite. I ran into a chum with a bottle of rum, and we wound up listening to Buffett all night.

You truly can listen to Buffett all night. The man has put out well over 30 albums and is consistently a huge draw on tour (I myself will be seeing him in October). I think we're all beyond arguing whether or not Jimmy Buffett is great – that is well established – we're now onto which of his albums is his greatest.

That, my friends, is where UnSpun comes in. One of our newest lists asks you to vote on just that question. Here's a look at where things currently stand:

Best Jimmy Buffett Album
Based on 102 votes by 25 people

VOTE

1. Changes in Latitudes Changes in Attitudes Buy $4.23
2. Songs You Know by Heart Buy $4.26
3. License to Chill Buy $2.94
4. Meet Me in Margaritaville Buy $11.99
5. Boats, Beaches, Bars & Ballads Buy $34.95
6. Son of a Son of a Sailor Buy $4.18
7. Barometer Soup Buy $9.99
8. Off to See the Lizard Buy $4.95
9. Volcano Buy $5.69
10. A White Sport Coat and a Pink Crustacean Buy $4.34
11. Meet Me in Margaritaville: the Ultimate Collection

Well, I just blew out my flip-flop (stepped on a pop-top), my heel's bleeding so I'm going to cruise on back home. You take a minute, rank your favorite album and go and eat a cheeseburger for me (and if you're in paradise while you're doing it, so much the better).

Moving from One Universe to Another

I wanted to venture away from Sci-Fi after yesterday's discussion of all things Arthur Dent related, but find myself unable to. Looking into various lists that dealt with The Hitchhiker's Guide to the Galaxy yesterday led me to, as you might expect, a bunch of Sci-Fi themed lists, and those quickly led me to the Doctor. The new season (or "series" if you're British) of Doctor Who ended in the States back in August, but I'm already looking forward to next year's specials.

And, if you're a fan of the show (in any incarnation), you've entered into the perennial debate about which actor's portrayal of the Doctor is the best. Right now, I'm thinking either Christopher Eccleston or Tom Baker. It's not that I dislike David Tennant (I think he's fantastic), I just like the other two more. Of course, as of this moment, most people who have voted at UnSpun think I'm wrong. Most people seem to like Tennant best. Here's the current list:

Favorite Actor to Portray "Doctor Who"
Based on 51 votes by 15 people
VOTE
⬆ ✔   1. David Tennant
⬆ ✔   2. Tom Baker
⬆ ✔   3. Christopher Eccleston
⬆ ✔   4. Peter Davison
⬆ ✔   5. Colin Baker
⬆ ✔   6. Jon Pertwee
⬆ ✔   7. Paul McGann
⬆ ✔   8. William Hartnell
⬆ ✔   9. Patrick Troughton
⬆ ✔   10. Sylvester McCoy
Add an item to this list

But, my movement from Dent to the Doctor really highlights two of the best things about UnSpun – the ease, and multiple paths, with which one can move from one area of interest to another. One moment I'm on the Heart of Gold and the next, I'm in the TARDIS. You can travel a straight Sci-Fi path or (in one of many possible routes) you can go from the book version of Hitchhiker's to the BBC series and the Best British Comedy Series list which also features Doctor Who. Where will I be tomorrow? Who knows, but as long as it's not Skaro I think I'll be just fine.

It's Okay, We're Mostly Harmless

Pop quiz time – What is 6 times 9 in base 13? What is a Pan Galactic Gargle Blaster? What is an acceptable logic proof that shows that God does not exist?

Unsure? Don't know the answer?

Don't panic.

You're not alone. The answers to these, and other terribly important questions (i.e., what was the final message that the dolphins left us as they fled the Earth prior to its destruction) can all be found in one very handy-dandy volume. And, if you read the first book, you're sure to want to read the rest of the trilogy (which does, despite being a trilogy, number more than three books in total).

The first volume also appears in plenty an UnSpun list. It is currently number one on the Top Science Fiction Book list and is number five on the Best Infocom Game list. (That's probably fine, some of those old-school games were truly fantastic, and I always had trouble making it past the bulldozer at the very beginning of the game anyway.)

What concerns me though is that The Hitchhiker's Guide to the Galaxy is only number four on the Best Books You Ever Read list. Look:

Best Book You Ever Read
Based on 200 votes by 61 people

VOTE

▲ ∀   1. The Holy Bible Buy $14.19
▲ ∀   2. Catch 22 by Joseph Heller Buy $16.09
▲ ∀   3. Gone with the Wind Buy $10.58
▲ ∀   4. The Hitchhiker's Guide to the Galaxy Buy $6.69
▲ ∀   5. My Sister's Keeper Buy $6.02
▲ ∀   6. The Da Vinci Code Buy $0.70
▲ ∀   7. HP and the Half Blood Prince by Rowling Buy $5.97
▲ ∀   8. Lord of the Rings Trilogy by Tolkien Buy $53.04
▲ ∀   9. Harry Potter Buy $34.94
▲ ∀   10. Where the Sidewalk Ends Buy $9.99
▲ ∀   11. To Kill a Mockingbird Buy $4.78

See? It's a travesty. I know that I shouldn't influence your vote, but I think that if we work hard, we can see Hitchhiker's get all the way up to the top spot without too much trouble.

And, isn't that what Zaphod would want?

The Best Thing Since Sliced Bread

I don't know about you, but there are certain things I just can't live without. As I look around me right now I notice a myriad of them, everything from my HD TiVo to my James Bond collection to my family. Oddly, two of those three things don't appear on the UnSpun list I want to bring to your attention to day. Today, it's all about the Best Inventions ever created.

This list is a monster one, upwards of 600 items, and they range from the computer to the Rubik's Cube to Tibetan singing bowls. Heck, even sliced bread is on the list (currently sitting, impressively, at number 17). Take a gander...

Best Inventions
Based on 3151 votes by 985 people

VOTE

1. computer
2. Internet
3. Lightbulb
4. Wheel
5. Automobile
6. Telephone
7. Electricity
8. Television
9. Printing Press
10. Cell Phone
11. Toilet

Isn't that just fantastic? The incredible diversity of responses to a single question astounds me. Paper. The steam engine. The concept of time. All valid responses, all completely different, and all have led us to where we are today.

What I want to know now is if "family" should in fact appear somewhere on the list. Invention or nature? If the concept of time is on the list, family would seem to fit, but it still just feels different to me somehow. Any thoughts? Come on now, vote and make your voice heard.

Images of the UnSpun Site

Some memories of the UnSpun site, and the accompanying Facebook Application.

UnSpun Homepage

UnSpun is community opinions... *ranked!*

1. **FIND** A LIST ABOUT ANYTHING.
2. **CREATE** A LIST OR **ADD** TO EXISTING LISTS.
3. **VOTE** YOUR OPINION, AND **COMPARE** TO OTHERS.

FIND: the best, worst, funniest, cheapest...

Most Popular Lists | Recently Created Lists | Palo Alto Lists
All Time | Last 30 Days | Last 7 Days

1. Best Original Score for a Feature Film
2. Most Missed Xbox 360 Back Compat Titles
3. Most Wanted Artists to Be DLC in Rock Band
4. What iPhone Applications Are You Waiting for?
5. Worst Leopard Quirks
6. Name Mac OS 10.6
7. Best MMA Radio Shows
8. What Would You Do for an iPhone?
9. Best Disney DVD Movie
10. What Should Be Redstate's Top Platform Issue for the GOP...
11. Best Leopard Features
12. Best 80's Songs
13. fantasyliterature.net Reader Poll -- Favorite Fantasy Epics
14. Gamer Vote - Top Video Games of 2007
15. Who Won E3 2007?
16. gamerdeals.net - Best Game at E3 2007
17. I Migliori Album Italiani
18. The Hottest Actresses in Movies
19. Best Stock Market Blogs
20. The Compusa Closings from an Apple Point of View

Share and Subscribe
<> Widget for your blog or site
📶 RSS feeds

Most popular recent tags

2008 album **book** books
brand character college
eat film **food game** games
movie movies **music** name
online **place places** player
restaurant seattle **song**
team television **thing** what

Try UnSpun on **facebook**

UnSpun Homepage - Search Results

COMMUNITY | YOUR SPIN | FAQS | BLOG | Search UnSpun   GO

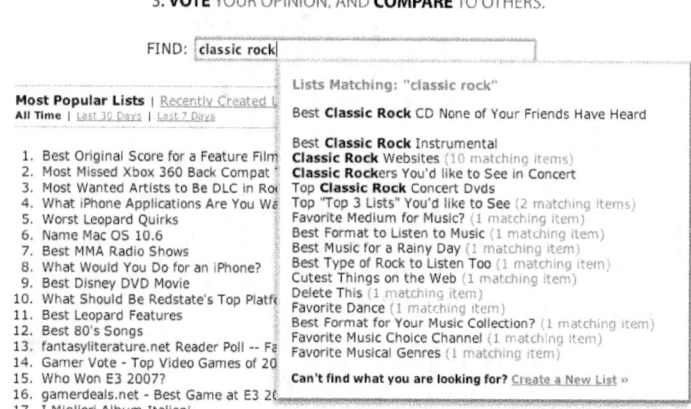

UnSpun is community opinions... *ranked!*

1. **FIND** A LIST ABOUT ANYTHING.
2. **CREATE** A LIST OR **ADD** TO EXISTING LISTS.
3. **VOTE** YOUR OPINION, AND **COMPARE** TO OTHERS.

FIND: classic rock

Most Popular Lists | Recently Created L
All Time | Last 30 Days | Last 7 Days

1. Best Original Score for a Feature Film
2. Most Missed Xbox 360 Back Compat
3. Most Wanted Artists to Be DLC in Ro
4. What iPhone Applications Are You Wa
5. Worst Leopard Quirks
6. Name Mac OS 10.6
7. Best MMA Radio Shows
8. What Would You Do for an iPhone?
9. Best Disney DVD Movie
10. What Should Be Redstate's Top Platf
11. Best Leopard Features
12. Best 80's Songs
13. fantasyliterature.net Reader Poll -- Fa
14. Gamer Vote - Top Video Games of 20
15. Who Won E3 2007?
16. gamerdeals.net - Best Game at E3 20
17. I Migliori Album Italiani
18. The Hottest Actresses in Movies
19. Best Stock Market Blogs
20. The Compusa Closings from an Apple Point of View

Lists Matching: "classic rock"

Best **Classic Rock** CD None of Your Friends Have Heard

Best **Classic Rock** Instrumental
Classic Rock Websites (10 matching items)
Classic Rockers You'd like to See in Concert
Top **Classic Rock** Concert Dvds
Top "Top 3 Lists" You'd like to See (2 matching items)
Favorite Medium for Music? (1 matching item)
Best Format to Listen to Music (1 matching item)
Best Music for a Rainy Day (1 matching item)
Best Type of Rock to Listen Too (1 matching item)
Cutest Things on the Web (1 matching item)
Delete This (1 matching item)
Favorite Dance (1 matching item)
Best Format for Your Music Collection? (1 matching item)
Favorite Music Choice Channel (1 matching item)
Favorite Musical Genres (1 matching item)

Can't find what you are looking for? Create a New List »

UnSpun List – Community Ranking

Best Classic Rock Instrumental
Looking for songs with no lyrics. Enter in the form: Song Name - Artist/Band Name

Community Ranking | Your Ranking

1. Little Wing - Stevie Ray Vaughan (2069)
Stevie Ray Vaughan, bluesman, guitarist and legend, was only 35 at the time of his death, but in his lifetime he managed to revitalize the blues, influence a... read more

   http://www.amazon.com - http://www.amazon.com/dp/B0013bLL6C?tag=uns-20

   http://www.amazon.com - The Essential Stevie Ray Vaughan and Double Trouble:

   http://www.amazon.com - Amazon.com: Stevie Ray Vaughan - Greatest Hits: Musi...

▼ edit this item | all links (4) | comments (1)

2. Glad - Traffic (1336)
   http://www.amazon.com - http://www.amazon.com/dp/B000W02RT0?tag=uns-20

▼ edit this item | add a link | comments (1)

3. Black Mountain Side - Led Zeppelin (1000)
As it turned out, Led Zeppelin's infamous 1969 debut album was indicative of the decade to come--one that, fittingly, this band helped define with its decadently exaggerated, bowdlerized... read more

   http://www.amazon.com - Amazon.com: Led Zeppelin 1: Music: Led Zeppelin

   http://www.amazon.com - Amazon.com: Black Mountain Side (Album Version): MP3...

▼ edit this item | add a link | add a comment

4. Interstellar Overdrive - Pink Floyd (850)
While they took their name from blues musicians Pink Anderson and Floyd Council when they started out as an R&B combo in the mid-60s, Pink Floyd's leader, guitarist... read more

   http://www.amazon.com - Amazon.com: The Piper at the Gates of Dawn: Music: P...

   http://www.amazon.com - Amazon.com: Interstellar Overdrive: Music: Pink Floyd

▼ edit this item | add a link | add a comment

5. Fire on High - ELO (690)
   http://www.amazon.com - Amazon.com: Face the Music: Music: Electric Light Or...

   http://www.amazon.com - http://www.amazon.com/dp/B0013bFP28?tag=uns-20

▼ edit this item | add a link | add a comment

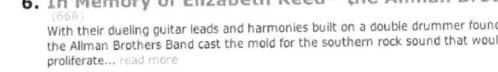

6. In Memory of Elizabeth Reed - the Allman Brothers (666)
With their dueling guitar leads and harmonies built on a double drummer foundation, the Allman Brothers Band cast the mold for the southern rock sound that would proliferate... read more

UnSpun List – Expanded Details

Best Classic Rock Instrumental
Looking for songs with no lyrics. Enter in the form: Song Name - Artist/Band Name

Community Ranking | Your Ranking

1. Little Wing - Stevie Ray Vaughan (2069)

Stevie Ray Vaughan, bluesman, guitarist and legend, was only 35 at the time of his death, but in his lifetime he managed to revitalize the blues, influence a generation of guitarists and produce a phenomenal body of work. His story is told in detail here in Guitar World Presents Stevie Ray Vaughan, a collection of articles about the great guitarist from the pages of Guitar World magazine. This deluxe volume features probing interviews held over the years with Stevie Ray, instructional material, a complete discography of his recorded works, and living reminiscences by his fellow musicians. This is essential reading for every fan of SRV! (hide)

http://www.amazon.com - http://www.amazon.com/dp/B00136LLSC?tag=uns-20

http://www.amazon.com - The Essential Stevie Ray Vaughan and Double Trouble:...

http://www.amazon.com - Amazon.com: Stevie Ray Vaughan - Greatest Hits: Musi...

▼ edit this item | all links (4) | comments (1)

2. Glad - Traffic (1336)

http://www.amazon.com - http://www.amazon.com/dp/B000W02RT0?tag=uns-20

▼ edit this item | add a link | comments (1)

3. Black Mountain Side - Led Zeppelin (1000)

As it turned out, Led Zeppelin's infamous 1969 debut album was indicative of the decade to come—one that, fittingly, this band helped define with its decadently exaggerated, bowdlerized blues-rock. In shrieker Robert Plant, ex-Yardbird Jimmy Page found a vocalist who could match his guitar pyrotechnics, and the band pounded out its music with swaggering ferocity and Richter-scale-worthy volume. Pumping up blues classics such as Otis Rush's "I Can't Quit You Baby" and Howlin' Wolf's "How Many More Times" into near-cartoon parodies, the band also hinted at things to come with the manic "Communication Breakdown" and the lumbering set stopper "Dazed and Confused." --Billy Altman (hide)

http://www.amazon.com - Amazon.com: Led Zeppelin 1: Music: Led Zeppelin

http://www.amazon.com - Amazon.com: Black Mountain Side (Album Version): MP3...

▼ edit this item | add a link | add a comment

4. Interstellar Overdrive - Pink Floyd (850)

While they took their name from blues musicians Pink Anderson and Floyd Council when they started out as an R&B combo in the mid-60s, Pink Floyd's leader, guitarist... read more

http://www.amazon.com - Amazon.com: The Piper at the Gates of Dawn: Music: P...

http://www.amazon.com - Amazon.com: Interstellar Overdrive: Music: Pink Floyd

▼ edit this item | add a link | add a comment

UnSpun List – Your Ranking

Best Classic Rock Instrumental

Looking for songs with no lyrics. Enter in the form: Song Name - Artist/Band Name

Community Ranking | **Your Ranking**

RANKING

To add an item to your list you can type it in the text box below or click the arrow next to the item on the right. If you'd like to change the order of your ranking drag the item up or down the list by its number.

Your Ranking (public view)

1. Glad - Traffic (x)

2. Fire on High - ELO (x)

3. Beck's Bolero - Jeff Beck (x)

4. Hocus Pocus - Focus (x)

5. Frankenstein - Edgar Winter Group (x)

6. green onions (x)

7. Interstellar Overdrive - Pink Floyd (x)

8. In Memory of Elizabeth Reed - the Allman Brothers (x)

9. Jessica - the Allman Brothers (x)

10. Black Mountain Side - Led Zeppelin (x)

11. Funeral for a Friend - Elton John (x)

12. Green Onions - Booker T & the M.G.'s (x)

13. [   ] Add

Community Ranking

1. Little Wing - Stevie Ray Vaughan (2069)

2. Glad - Traffic (1336)

3. Black Mountain Side - Led Zeppelin (1000)

4. Interstellar Overdrive - Pink Floyd (850)

5. Fire on High - ELO (890)

6. In Memory of Elizabeth Reed - the Allman Brothers (668)

7. Any Colour You like (517)

8. Peaches En Regalia-Mothers of Invention (517)

9. Soul Sacrifice - Santana (485)

10. Beck's Bolero - Jeff Beck (386)

11. Hocus Pocus - Focus (345)

12. Jessica (316)

13. green onions (302)

14. Lark's Tongue in Aspic - King Crimson (259)

15. Lazy-Deep Purple (259)

16. Moby Dick - Led Zeppelin (172)

17. Steamer Lane Breakdown - Doobie Brothers (172)

18. Frankenstein - Edgar Winter Group (103)

19. Funeral for a Friend - Elton John (43)

UnSpun – Item Details

Little Wing - Stevie Ray Vaughan
Back to list: Best Classic Rock Instrumental

TOP LINKS   Login to add link

Login to vote for the best links or to add your own.

http://www.amazon.com/dp/B00006L3J4?tag=uns-20
The Essential Stevie Ray Vaughan and Double Trouble: Music: Stevie Ray Vaughan and Double Trouble

http://www.amazon.com/dp/B000002AOU?tag=uns-20
Amazon.com: Stevie Ray Vaughan - Greatest Hits: Music: Stevie Ray Vaughan

More Links

ITEM IMAGES

GIVE US YOUR SPIN   Login to add comment

" SRV's cover of Jimi Hendrix classic "
Posted on 11 Sep 17:57

THIS ITEM APPEARS IN THE FOLLOWING LIST

Best Classic Rock Instrumental (rank: 1)

UnSpun – Community Spin

Community Spin
Snapshot | Popular | California Lists | Recent | All | Your Spin

MOST POPULAR LISTS
All Time | **Last 30 days** | Last 7 days

1. Most Trustworthy Dog Food Company
2. My Favorite Websites
3. Best Halloween Costume for Kids
4. Most Essential Computer Accessory
5. Best TV Shows Available on Hulu
6. Favorite Musicians
7. Favorite Programs on NPR
8. The World's Greatest Living Hero
9. My Stuff and Other Things
10. Top Tennis Player of All Time
11. Essential Cook Books
12. Greenest Companies
13. Best Peter Sellers Movie
14. Best Halloween Costumes for Dogs
15. Top Reasons Not to Eat at the Dining Hall.
16. What Do You Hate Most about Bill Gates?
17. Wedding Gifts
18. Best Laptops You Have Used so Far
19. Best Place to Purchase Raw Dog Food Online
20. Friends I Want by My Side in the Event...
21. Favorite NCIS Character
22. Funniest Dog Breeds
23. Best Horatio Hornblower Book
24. What's the Best Name for Our Economic C...
25. Best Salma Hayek Movie

More >>

CALIFORNIA LISTS change

1. What's Your Favorite Tourist Attraction...
2. What's Your Favorite Theme Park in Cali...
3. Best California Sports Team
4. Best Chinese Food in Orange County, Cal...
5. Favorite Sixties California Band
6. Favorite City in California's Central V...
7. Favorite University of California Campus
8. Favorite College in California
9. Favorite Mountain Range in California
10. Favorite National Park in California
11. Most Scenic River in California
12. Favorite Wilderness Area in California
13. Favorite Southern California County
14. Best City in California
15. Best Sports Arena in Southern California.
16. Favorite Carmel California Hotel/Motel
17. Favorite Governor of California
18. Favorite University or College in Calif...
19. Favorite Song with California in the Title
20. Favorite All Time California Angels Player
21. Best Irish Pubs in Southern California
22. Worst California City
23. Favorite Cities in California
24. Best Cheesecake in California
25. Least Favorite Professional Sports Fran...

More >>

UnSpun Widget

UnSpun Lists for Your Site or Blog

Choose from any of our thousands of lists, or create your own list with just a few clicks (create one now)

Let your visitors vote without leaving your site.

It's Easy to Embed an UnSpun List Widget:

1. Find or create the list you want to add to your site

2. Go to the list page, look in the right hand column (see example below), and copy the HTML code

3. Paste the HTML into your site or blog

4. The UnSpun List Widget will look just like the one to the right (go ahead and try it)

That's All!

Do you want the widget displayed on the right?

Copy and paste the HTML below to include this widget on your webpage.

```
<script type="text/javascript" src="http:/
```

Preview and Learn More   Customize

No? Search for a different List:

| Search UnSpun | GO |

Example UnSpun List Widget

Best Classic Rock Instrumental

Based on 49 votes by 14 people

VOTE

1. Little Wing - Stevie Ray Vaughan LISTEN! Buy $0.99
2. Glad - Traffic LISTEN! Buy $0.99
3. Black Mountain Side - Led Zeppelin LISTEN! Buy $0.99
4. Interstellar Overdrive - Pink Floyd Buy $16.30
5. Fire on High - ELO LISTEN! Buy $0.99
6. In Memory of Elizabeth Reed - the Allman Brothers Buy $0.89
7. Any Colour You like LISTEN! Buy $0.99
8. Peaches En Regalia-Mothers of Invention Buy $11.01
9. Soul Sacrifice - Santana Buy $5.79
10. Beck's Bolero - Jeff Beck Buy $0.62

UnSpun Blog

The UnSpun Blog
Our own spin on the lists of the day. Hot lists, cool lists, fun lists, and strange lists.

« Be it Saltwater or Freshwater, I Love Eel | Main | Home Appliances it Cannot be Home Without »

September 20, 2008

Trying to Reason with Football Season

We're heading into the fourth week of the NFL season, and I think we're starting to separate the wheat from the chaff. We're really starting to see which football teams have it this year and which can't even pretend like they can hang with the big boys. That makes this the perfect time to visit the "Best NFL Team in 2008" list on UnSpun.

Looking at it, I'm actually moderately surprised, as of my writing this, the New England Patriots are still sitting on top of the list. Oh, don't get me wrong, they're a great team, but without Tom Brady I'm pretty convinced that they're not the best in the NFL. Indianapolis, currently with a record of 1-2 is sitting in the second position. Do we actually believe that they have just been unlucky thus far? Now, the Giants and the Cowboys, both at 3-0, are in positions 3 and 4. I might put them higher, but it certainly doesn't seem like they ought to be much lower.

Take a look at the whole kit and caboodle (and click here if you don't see it below):

This is really one of those fun lists. It's one of those lists that you need to come back to so you can update your rankings as the season progresses (the Pats might have deserved the top spot prior to their opening week's game, but they don't now). Just you watch this list change as the season progresses, you see who slides to where and what happens. Maybe we'll even talk about it again in the future.

Posted by John Larson at 03:43 PM in Sports, Time Wasters | Permalink

Facebook Application - Info

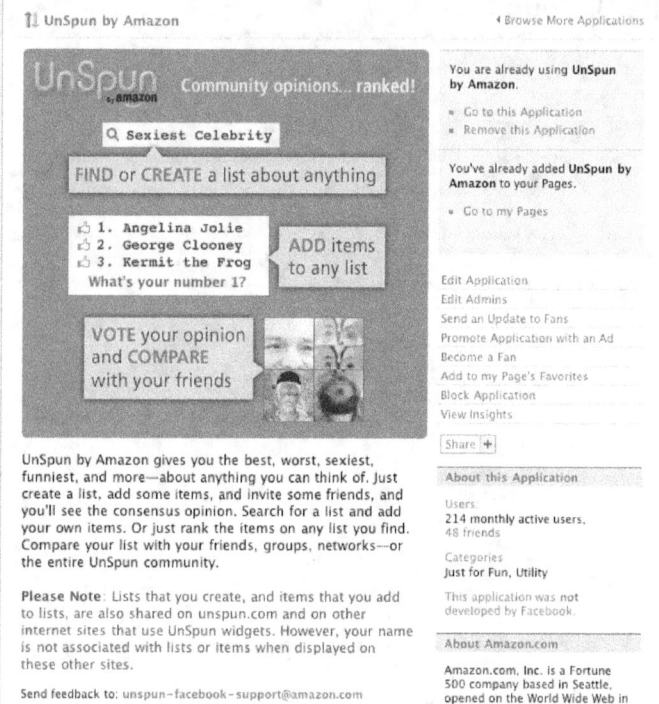

UnSpun by Amazon gives you the best, worst, sexiest, funniest, and more—about anything you can think of. Just create a list, add some items, and invite some friends, and you'll see the consensus opinion. Search for a list and add your own items. Or just rank the items on any list you find. Compare your list with your friends, groups, networks—or the entire UnSpun community.

Please Note: Lists that you create, and items that you add to lists, are also shared on unspun.com and on other internet sites that use UnSpun widgets. However, your name is not associated with lists or items when displayed on these other sites.

Send feedback to: unspun-facebook-support@amazon.com

By adding this application to your account and using it, you agree to the UnSpun Conditions of Use and Privacy Notice.

You are already using **UnSpun by Amazon**.

- Go to this Application
- Remove this Application

You've already added **UnSpun by Amazon** to your Pages.

- Go to my Pages

Edit Application
Edit Admins
Send an Update to Fans
Promote Application with an Ad
Become a Fan
Add to my Page's Favorites
Block Application
View Insights

Share +

About this Application

Users:
214 monthly active users.
48 friends

Categories
Just for Fun, Utility

This application was not developed by Facebook.

About Amazon.com

Amazon.com, Inc. is a Fortune 500 company based in Seattle, opened on the World Wide Web in July 1995 and today offers Earth's Biggest Selection. Amazon.com, Inc. seeks to be Earth's most customer-centric company,

Facebook Application – Homepage

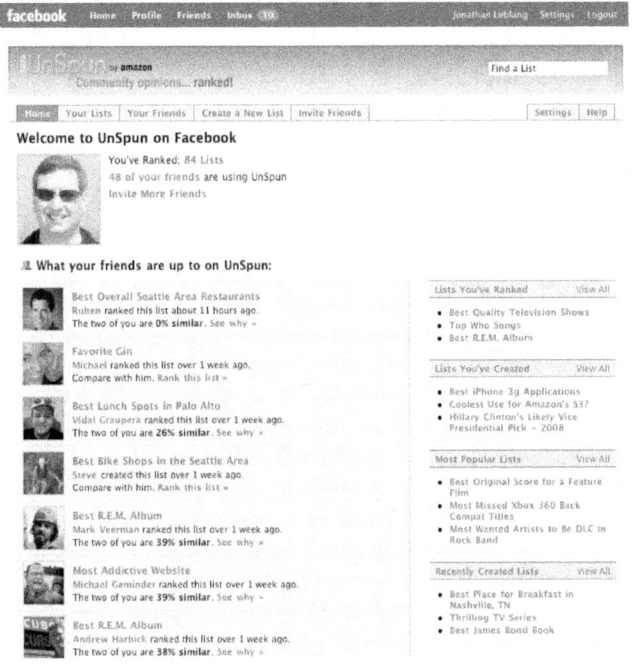

Facebook Application – Your Lists

Facebook Application – List Page

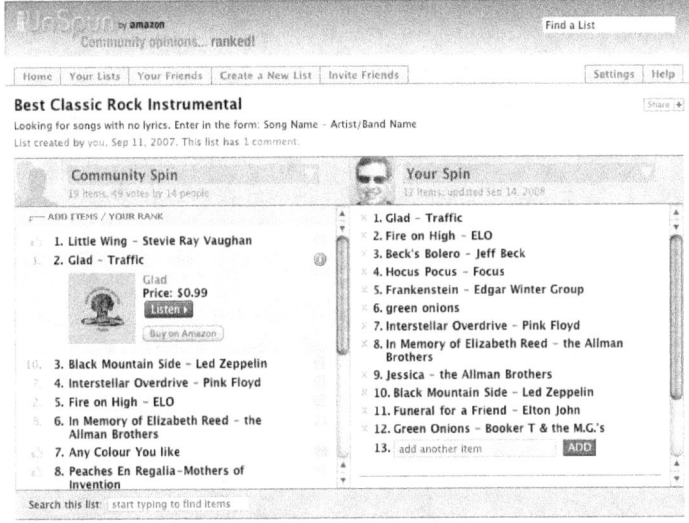

1 friend has ranked this list. Click a friend to see how you compare.

Michael
Geminder
3 items

39% SIMILAR

Facebook Application – Compare Lists

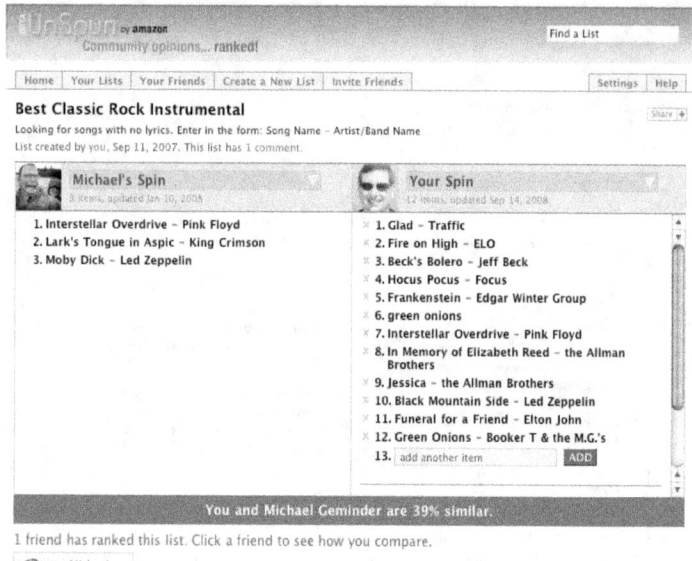

1 friend has ranked this list. Click a friend to see how you compare.

Facebook Application - Lists Page

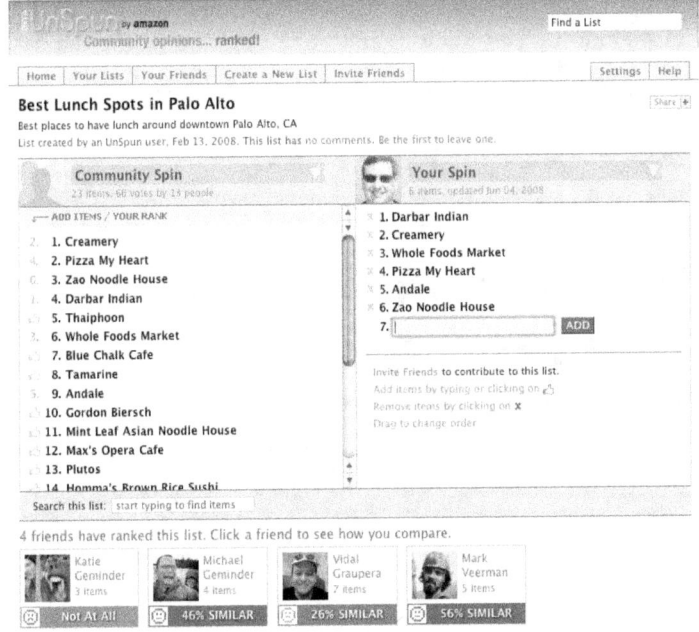

Facebook Application – Friends

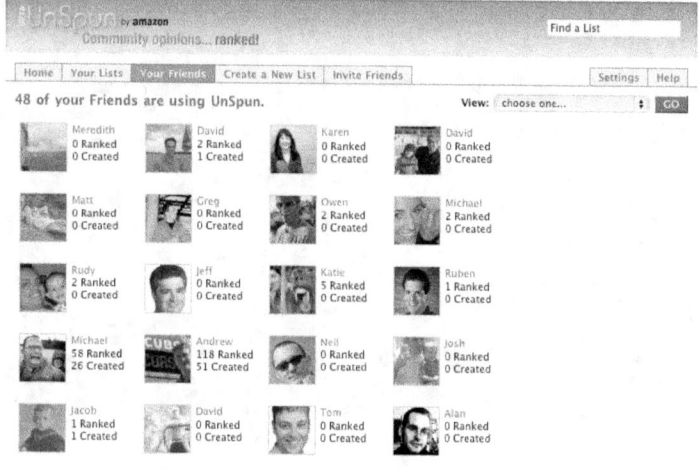

Colophon

Designed and produced on a Macintosh using Apple Pages '08.
Cover designed in Adobe Illustrator. Body and list text is set
in Garamond Premier Pro. Headings are Futura Medium.
Published and printed by CreateSpace.

The UnSpun website was built with Ruby on Rails.